Contents at a Glance

Contents

Appendixes

Introduction

Military benefits do not follow an end-to-end master plan. They are actually a hodge-podge of projects, initiatives, and traditions that have emerged over time. These programs were created to support the different needs of the military community (active duty, reserve, retired, veterans, and military dependents). This is not intended as an insult, but rather recognition of how it has become what it is today. You need to know this when trying to make sense of the many benefits.

Military benefits originated in many ways. Some were the result of congressional actions—a good idea that was funded as a part of some year's military budget law. Others evolved from informal arrangements. For example, space-available travel in military transport aircraft came about when informal local arrangements were formalized to ensure that the highest-priority passengers were assigned the first seats.

Some of the laws supporting veterans were initiated by the states during the Civil War. Eventually, many (but not all) of these hospitals, cemeteries, pensions, and military retirement homes were absorbed into the federal veteran support system. Individual states continue to provide military benefits to their citizens on top of anything the federal government provides.

Some military benefits carry on traditions from before the birth of our nation. The Navy still provides burial at sea for veterans who request it. However, without a book like this, how would you ever know what is available for you to chose from and how to apply for it?

How to Use This Book

This book has six parts. It is not designed to be read from front to back. Instead, it is intended as a reference so that you can explore the many variations of a particular topic of interest (such as the different types of active duty retirement plans).

Many of the benefits have qualifiers on them, restricting them to specific categories. The first eligibility category is for active duty, Guard/Reserve, or retired military personnel. Often the same benefit—or some portion of it—that is available to a service member depends if they are active duty, or Guard/Reserve. Other benefits, such as inexpensive vacation lodging, charge fees based on your rank. Another complication arises between active service and veterans—those who have left all types of military service.

Each of the armed forces has a "reserve" to supplement its forces during national emergencies. These are "federal" units raised by the government in Washington. Each state also raises the Army and Air National Guard. All of the benefits of the Reserves also apply to the National Guard. In those cases, the term *Guard/Reserve* is used. However, the individual states often provide additional benefits to their respective National Guard units; in those cases, eligibility will not mention "Reserve."

Finally, military benefits change frequently, maybe to tighten eligibility, to expand a benefit, or to increase the cost of whoever uses it. For example, every year Congress passes a new military budget law and uses it to change annual pay and any benefits that suit them. Use this book to find out what benefits are available, and then refer to their websites to obtain the latest information.

Part 1, "Who Gets What?", begins by identifying the seven uniformed services. Then it explores identity cards, which is the key for proving benefit eligibility.

Part 2, "Show Me the Money," describes the military pay system, with its many special pays, and explains who qualifies for what. It also details the many housing programs that apply to single and married personnel.

Part 3, "Noncash Benefits," details the many benefits the government provides, beyond pay and allowances. This includes legal services, low-cost vacation resorts, and medical insurance choices for you and your family.

Part 4, "Go to School," explains the many different military benefits to help pay for your college education, both while you are on active duty and after your release from service.

Part 5, "Guard and Reserve," explores the transition that many make from active duty to participation in one of the National Guard or Reserve components. This part also explains the benefits and pay system for Guard/Reserve, which is very different from that of active duty.

Part 6, "Leaving the Service," systematically steps you through the many benefits provided to all veterans. This might be lifetime medical treatment of injuries sustained during your military service. It includes how to apply for admission to a military retirement home and, finally, the services the government provides for your dignified burial.

Extras

To complement the material, a series of boxes throughout the book highlight key points in the material. This is to help you to understand the terms, nuances, and the most important points of each benefit.

For Your Benefits

These boxes point out important information that makes sense of the benefit or how to apply for it.

Attention!

These are things to watch for, such as something to avoid or something to be sure to do.

def•i•ni•tion

These are explanations of the many, many obscure but essential military terms you should understand to make sense of a benefit or how to apply for it.

Hot Scoop

Read these for where to find the latest information about a specific benefit.

Acknowledgments

Katrina and I would like to thank all of the people at Alpha Books for their advice, professionalism, and patience, especially Tom Stevens and Nancy Lewis. We would like to especially thank our agent, Marilyn Allen, who matched this opportunity to our background. Finally, thanks to Tom Applegate whose recent military experience provided up to date information throughout the book.

Katrina would also like to thanks her father, Larry Webber, for giving her this opportunity and her mother Nancy and brothers Fred and Joseph for their support when the going got rough during the summer and fall. Also, to her friends who advised her when it was time to get down to business.

Special Thanks from the Publisher to the Technical Editor

The Complete Idiot's Guide to Veterans Benefits was reviewed by an expert who not only checked the technical accuracy of what you will learn in this book, but also provided invaluable insight and suggestions. Our special thanks are extended to Tom Applegate.

Tom Applegate served 25½ years and retired from the U.S. Army in 1995 at the rank of First Sergeant. He received an appointment that same year as the Huntington County, Indiana Veterans' Service Officer and served in that position for 10 years. In 2005, he was selected by Indiana Governor Mitch Daniels to be the Director of the

Indiana Department of Veterans Affairs. He is responsible for the training and certification of Indiana's 91 county veterans' service officers. He oversees the operation of the Indiana Veterans' Memorial Cemetery in Madison, Indiana, and is a member of the boards of the Indiana Veterans' Home in Lafayette, Indiana and the Soldiers' and Sailors' Children's Home in Knightstown, Indiana. He is the Governor's primary advisor on veterans affairs, is the main contact for Hoosier legislators on legislative matters concerning veterans, and he is the Governor's liaison to State veterans' groups and organizations. He resides with his with, Louise, in Indianapolis.

Trademarks

All terms mentioned in this book that are known to be or are suspected of being trademarks or service marks have been appropriately capitalized. Alpha Books and Penguin Group (USA) Inc. cannot attest to the accuracy of this information. Use of a term in this book should not be regarded as affecting the validity of any trademark or service mark.

Part 1

Who Gets What?

If you ask the bureaucrats in Washington, they'll tell you that your military benefits are a part of your overall compensation. The problem is they don't tell you much else. What are these many benefits, and how do you reach out to use one? An 18-year-old recruit has no idea what to ask or where to go for these things. The same holds true for most people in the military community.

This first part provides an overview of your benefits and how you qualify for them. Military benefits are a significant expense to the government, so it needs some way to identify who deserves the benefit (so it can keep the other people away). This part also explains how you can demonstrate that you are eligible for specific benefits; not all veterans are entitled to all benefits. Discharges other than honorable conditions mean you qualify for little, no matter how sad your story.

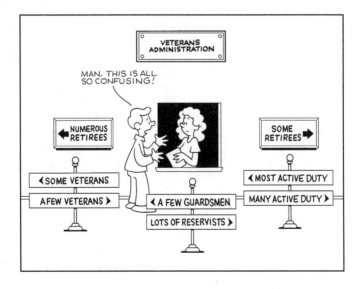

A Benefit Ain't a Benefit If You Don't Use It

In This Chapter

◆ Benefits and your military compensation

◆ Each benefit has its own eligibility

◆ How to find the latest benefit information

◆ Who gets the most benefits?

Generous benefits for U.S. military personnel and veterans are a long-standing national tradition, dating all the way back to the early colonial period. The early settlers in Massachusetts encouraged participation in a battle by promising pensions to those who were disabled defending the colony. As a reward for volunteer service, veterans of the American Revolutionary War were awarded land on the frontier. Years later, the elderly survivors were awarded small pensions. This long tradition of military benefits carries on today in many ways.

A benefit is a form of noncash compensation for services. For example, active duty personnel have a benefit of free medical service. No cash changes hands. Services are provided for free as needed. It's a good thing, too. Imagine fishing for a medical insurance card in the middle of a battle!

You may never use many of your military benefits. Unfortunately, most people never use them because they don't know that they exist. That's the job of this book. For everyone from the new recruits to the saltiest old sailor, this book identifies what is available and explains how to request it.

Over time, the number of military benefits has significantly grown. Some are extensions of basic benefits, and others have emerged due to the unique military work environment. Military benefits have also been a big driver for providing financial opportunity. You can get free money to attend college. You can get money to reduce the cost of your home loans. You can get low-cost life insurance to protect your family in case of your death, whether from a war or from an accident. If you fulfill the service requirements, you can even get a pension. No matter how poor your background or deficient your education, Uncle Sam will provide these things in exchange for your honorable service.

The key to military benefits is knowing that they exist. Pick the ones that apply to what you want to do and verify your eligibility. Finally, follow the directions in this book (or the benefit's website) to request that benefit. Just remember that benefits may change over time. Use this book to understand what is available, to check the current eligibility requirements, and to understand how to apply or use that benefit.

Some Benefits Are for Everyone

Some of the many benefits are well planned, such as the military pay system and the insurance system. Others have emerged over time; they were created by some circumstance and then lingered. For example, the Coast Guard has a few lighthouse keeper homes available for seaside recreational rental. In this case, the original need has been fulfilled, and they now provide a recreational benefit to the military community.

Benefits are created to assist some specific group. This is known as their "eligibility." Eligibility is broken down by military status, such as active duty, Reserve, National Guard, retired, or veteran. Each group has its own unique needs and benefits that were crafted to support its members. In some cases, eligibility or usage fees are broken down according to rank.

In this book, all services are considered to have essentially the same benefits unless something is specifically called out as an exception. For example, all active duty, Reserve, Guard, retirees, and dependents can use the Base Exchange. However, Army infantry does not qualify for submarine duty pay, just as medical personnel in all services qualify for medical service bonus pay. Usually, Federal Reserve and National Guard are grouped together as Guard/Reserve for situations in which they are treated the same, and they are listed individually when they vary. This is usually the case when the National Guard receives additional benefits from the states.

Active Duty

When people think about military benefits, they think first of the active duty forces, such as young people marching off to war or up the gangway of a fighting ship. However, active duty forces are much more diverse than that. They include single personnel, married couples, married couples who both serve in the military, single parents, spouses, children, young, old, and all points in between. They also include all seven of the uniformed services. Each of these groups has its own particular needs.

The United States fields one of the best-paid military forces on the planet. Of course, the term "best paid" is relative, and in this country, the military is considered to be modestly compensated for a dangerous job. Consequently, active duty personnel enjoy the greatest number of benefits. These benefits are aimed at easing their financial burdens, relieving boredom, and encouraging their physical activity during off hours.

Financial benefits include all the cash or near-cash benefits they receive. A cash benefit is monthly pay and bonuses for reenlisting, for example. Near-cash benefits include exemption from paying income taxes in a war zone, no sales tax charged on Post Exchange purchases, and low-cost life insurance.

Boredom comes from being far from home, running a bit short of cash, and having excess free time. To put this time to good use, a wide range of base recreational activities are offered for free or essentially at cost. These range from low-cost movies at the base theater, to auto-repair workshops, to woodworking classes. Civilian charities that support the military, such as the USO, also supply recreation.

Physical activity benefits abound. Swimming pools, gymnasiums, racquetball courts, and team sports are all available for free. In addition, many activities are offered at essentially cost. These include scuba classes, martial arts instruction, Rod and Gun Clubs, archery, hunting, recreational resorts, and more. With so much to do, you can be only as bored as you want to be.

For Your Benefits _____

A popular use of free time is to work on military correspondence courses or pick up some college credits.

Retirees

In the civilian sense, military retirees are relatively young. Whereas civilian workers think 55 years old is an early retirement age, military personnel retire as young as 37 years old. A 30-year veteran officer who is 52 years old is considered quite elderly. Younger retirees can more actively take advantage of the benefits available to them, such as camping trailer rentals, vacation lodgings, use of the commissary, or use of space-available air travel.

Retirement pay is based on your number of years of service and your final rank held. Beyond that, active duty and Guard/Reserve can fall into several different retirement pay programs, based on when they joined the military. Understanding these programs and how pensions are calculated may affect the timing of your retirement.

Most civilian retirement plans have eliminated medical benefits for retirees. Military retirees are provided health-care benefits through the TRICARE health insurance program and later through a combination of Medicare and TRICARE For Life. When combined with the TRICARE pharmaceutical and dental programs, this is a valuable benefit for someone living on a pension.

Retirees are eligible for most of the recreational benefits of the active forces. This is one reason they retire near military bases. From base golf courses to indoor swimming pools, retirees can still enjoy the wide range of recreation offered on a military base.

Reservists

Reservists supplement active duty forces in a crisis. They are federally controlled, and only the President can call them out. To be ready for this call-up, they train one weekend every month and typically two weeks per year.

Reservists are paid differently than active duty forces. When they are training on a weekend, they are paid four days of base pay, but no housing or subsistence allowance. Pay for two weeks of annual training or for a short-term deployment is slightly different than pay for active duty personnel. However, if Reservists are activated for a contingency operation lasting more than 30 days, pay is the same. Just as active duty personnel must understand the nuances of their pay system, so must the Reserve forces of all services.

Sometimes your civilian career is in a deep rut. One benefit of Reserve duty is that you have the potential to attend free military training to learn a new skilled Military Occupational Specialty (MOS), if you transfer into that position. This technical school can be worth a lot of money in terms of both tuition discount and how it will increase your civilian earning power. As with other benefits, you need to look around, find the open position, and apply for it.

A unique thing about the Reserves is that you can earn a tidy retirement from a part-time job. Every day of service earns credit toward retirement. No other part-time job offers such a retirement package. The key is to understand how Reserve retirement pay is calculated. Then you will know what to expect and can plan the best time to retire.

National Guard

National Guard personnel receive all the benefits that the federal government grants Reservists. States may provide supplemental pensions, annual bonuses, and state tax breaks. Another popular benefit is free college tuition to any state university—in addition to the federal GI Bill. Each state offers its own Air and Army National Guard whatever it wants. Before signing up, investigate the deals surrounding states offer.

Veterans

Veterans benefits are for people who have left their military service behind. They may include medical benefits, elderly care, and, at the end of the road, funeral benefits.

As soon as they leave military service, many veterans head straight to college. Various programs are available for active duty, for Guard, and for Reserves, all based on when you enlisted or reenlisted. GI Bill college benefits expire 10 years after discharge. The sooner you use them, the more likely you are to get all of them.

We tend to think of veterans as aging men passing time in rocking chairs at the old soldier's home. However, veterans can be anyone of adult age. Many are young and need assistance from the Veterans' Administration. Over the past 30 years, there have been an increasing number of women veterans. The Veterans Administration has adjusted its services to support the unique needs of women veterans.

For Your Benefits

A valuable veterans benefit is preferential hiring for government jobs. Federal, state, and local governments have good-paying jobs and value your military experience. They are also among the few employers still offering a pension.

Some service members are injured while on duty. A range of Veterans' Administration medical services are available, from hospital stays to regular outpatient doctor visits. The key is to have the Veterans Administration certify the injury as service related. Destitute veterans may also have medical services available.

At some point, elderly veterans may need to enter a nursing home or require assistance to continue living in their own home. The Veterans Administration has long supported old soldier's homes for all services. These services are provided to aging veterans based on their financial assets and income.

Finally, when a member of the military community dies, the Veterans Administration can assist with a range of services, from the funeral ceremony to a final resting place. Special veteran grave markers are also available. If requested, the Navy can provide a veteran's burial at sea.

Eligibility

Each benefit has its own twist on who is eligible to use it and when. At the top of the list are active duty personnel serving in the seven uniformed services (Army, Navy, Marines, Air Force, Coast Guard, Commissioned Corps of the National Oceanic and Atmospheric Administration, and Commissioned Corps of the Public Health Service. Next come the retirees, followed closely by Guard/Reserve. In some cases, Department of Defense civilians and contractors can also use a particular benefit.

The priority order for eligibility is used for allocating seats on space-available flights and for reserving rooms in one of the military resorts. Eligibility for a benefit may change from time to time based on its demand. For example, the military resorts may assign top priority for reservations to service members on Rest and Recuperation leave from war zones.

Morale, Welfare, and Recreation (MWR)

A base or ship's recreations programs are operated by its Morale, Welfare, and Recreation (MWR) organization. MWR provides a wide range of services, from escorted vacation tours, to golf courses, to riding stable, to aero clubs. MWR activities provide the facilities, skilled staff, tools, and materials for a wide range of hobby and sport activities.

One example of this is the base Rod and Gun club. This organization uses a combination of paid staff and volunteers to manage and maintain a base's recreational firing and archery ranges. Often it provides the mandatory safety classes for obtaining a base hunting permit. Another popular MWR benefit is loaned or rented recreational equipment. This might be a box of baseball equipment for starting a team or a full-size camping trailer with all the necessary camping equipment.

MWR offers a range of hobby shops equipped with tools and skilled instructors. Each base has its own offering but typically includes auto repair, woodworking, and ceramics. Participants pay for their own materials and optional training classes. MWR activities are open to all service members, their dependents, and usually retirees.

Funding

MWR programs are dual-funded by both appropriated and nonappropriated funds. The government provides appropriated funds to build new facilities, such as a new swimming pool or gymnasium. Nonappropriated funds come from a share of the Base Exchange or Ship's Store's profits, and from use fees at popular activities such as the club system, bowling alleys, and movie theaters.

Exchanges provide a wide range of services, from vending machines, to barber shops, to the main Exchange buildings. Profits from these operations fund the MWR activities. For example, the Army and Air Force Exchange system routinely contributes two-thirds of its profits to MWR funds and retains the rest to remodel Exchange facilities or to build new ones.

MWR pays to build a basic recreational facility and then charges a usage fee. This money pays for the facility's ongoing operation and maintenance, such as for the archery range and rifle range of a Rod and Gun Club. Fees are used to ensure that the foliage is trimmed, the grass is cut, and range trash is picked up, as well as to organize contests. In this way, those who use the benefit pay for its ongoing support.

For Your Benefits

Both the Commissaries and Exchanges offer a hiring preference for military spouses. They are major employers of military spouses. As military families relocate, these spouses are trained and ready to continue their employment at their next duty assignment.

Military Recreation Resort

Your basic training instructor may have referred to your barracks as a resort, but perhaps you thought it was something else. However, the military resort system is no joke. MWR owns world-class hotels in Hawaii (on Waikiki Beach), Florida (in the Disney World park), Germany, Japan, and Korea, all available to you at low-cost rates. Other vacation ideas include beach houses, mountain cabins, and on and on. The complete list would fill this book.

Each of these vacation spots has its own eligibility rules and rate structures. Rates are usually based on rank, and active duty personnel (including Guard and Reserve on extended active duty) are normally accommodated first. All of these facilities are designed and furnished to be "family friendly."

Benefits Can Change ...

The information in a book is a snapshot in time. It contains the latest information available at the point that it is written. However, benefits, their eligibility, and the application process change over time. Some benefits are created by laws Congress passes, so only Congress can change them. Beware of attention-grabbing headlines promising a certain benefit: the only proposals that matter are the ones signed into law. Also, states occasionally create new military benefits, such as a bonus paid to all veterans of a particular conflict.

Other benefits are self-funded and pay their own way through user fees. As their expenses increase (such as a significant increase in the cost of fuel), so will their fees. Still, they are much less expensive than through a for-profit commercial enterprise.

Military Supporting Charities

Civilian supporters of the military have an extensive history of service to armed forces. The charity work of these organizations depends heavily on volunteers and donations. Young service members begin the cycle by using these charities while in the military and then later contribute to their ongoing programs.

The charities that service people hear the most about are the "Reliefs" (Army Emergency Relief, Navy–Marine Corps Relief Society, Air Force Aid Society, and Coast Guard Mutual Assistance). They offer counseling, interest-free loans, and, in some cases, grants to help in difficult personal times. In times of trouble, contact the nearest relief organization.

Ever since World War II, military personnel have counted on the United Services Organization (USO) to provide first-class entertainment by the most popular performers. These shows are provided to military bases around the world. Even in war zones, the USO finds the troops and delivers the shows.

The USO also provides recreational support centers. Some USO centers are in airports, to provide a safe place to sit, nap, or snack. USO volunteers can also provide directions to local facilities. Other centers are near military installations around the world, providing recreational and counseling services.

The Armed Services YMCA is an extension of the U.S. YMCA that is dedicated to supporting the armed forces. Open to all military, but focusing on single and married junior enlisted, the Armed Services YMCA provides recreation, counseling, and, in some cases, temporary quarters.

Fisher Houses were created to provide a place for families to stay while visiting relatives in nearby military hospitals or veterans' hospitals. At a time when everyone's emotions are running high, Fisher Houses provide a quiet place for families to regroup between hospital visits. Fisher House services are provided for free. The expenses are borne by the Fisher Foundation.

Family Support

Each of the military services has developed outreach programs to include families in its military readiness programs. This reduces the number of unit deployment problems and assists the family back home until the service member returns. This includes summer activities for dependent children, stress and separation counseling, and advice on navigating the maze of military benefits. Several national veterans groups organize volunteers who also provide this assistance.

A formal support program is important for all military families, but especially for Guard and Reserve dependents who live far from a military base and who may be dispersed across several states. It includes a "welcome aboard" briefing to new unit members and their families. This is followed by a volunteer family support group that provides information about unit activities and deployments.

An important family support activity is reunion planning. After service members have been separated from their families for an extended period, each has adjusted to the separation and needs some time to readjust when reunited. Reunion planning also includes information on dealing with stress from the deployment.

The Least You Need to Know

- ◆ Learn what benefits you are eligible for.

- ◆ Prepare for your military retirement by understanding which program you qualify for.

- ◆ Morale, Welfare, and Recreation (MWR) funds are financed by the profits from the Exchange system.

- ◆ Family support programs have reduced some of the friction of Guard/Reserve deployments.

Your Ticket to the Game

In This Chapter

◆ Who is entitled to some of the many military benefits

◆ How to prove your entitlement

◆ What veterans use to prove benefit eligibility

◆ Types of discharges

So many benefits … so little time! Military benefits are everywhere if you know where to look. But before you can use one of them, you must prove you are entitled to it. This chapter identifies the many groups eligible for some piece of the military benefit pie and how you can prove you are entitled to some of them. Likely many more people are eligible to stand in line in front of you at the commissary than you think.

The Uniformed Services

Let's begin with what we mean by "military." It will help if we use the term *uniformed services* instead because some folks do not carry weapons.

Army, Navy, Air Force, Marines

When most people think about uniformed services, they think of the active duty branches of the Department of Defense: the Army, Navy, Air Force, and Marines. Together these full-time organizations have over 1.5 million members on military bases and ships at sea all around the globe. In addition to the active duty forces, each of these is supplemented by a "Reserve" force organized into different categories, depending on how much they actively participate in training. Reserves account for another 640,000.

Guardsmen

Unlike Reserve units, the Army and Air National Guard units have a dual allegiance to the federal government and their state. They can be called to duty by either the president or their state's governor. In appreciation for their service, they receive the same federal benefits as the Reserve components. State governments also provide their Guard members with additional benefits. Some of the state benefits overlap with federal benefits, such as free tuition to any state-owned college, or something unique, like free license plates for their cars.

> **For Your Benefits**
>
> Guardsmen on active duty get the most benefits! They receive both federal and state benefits.

You do not need to be a resident of a state to join its National Guard. You only need to be consistently present at the unit assemblies. So if the National Guard seems to be for you, check out nearby states to see if they offer a better deal.

Coast Guard

Can this be more complex? Yes! Add in the Coast Guard and the Coast Guard Reserve, who work for the Department of Homeland Security. When deployed for combat operations, the Coast Guard is assigned to the Navy. There's never a quiet time in the Coast Guard. This branch is always chasing down either bad guys off Iraq or drug smugglers off Florida. In between, it polices fishing regulations, tows in stranded pleasure boaters, and rescues crews off sinking ships.

NOAA

The smallest of the uniformed services is a component of the National Oceanic and Atmospheric Administration (NOAA). The NOAA is a scientific agency of the

Department of Commerce that focuses on the conditions of the oceans and the atmosphere. Its Commissioned Corps is a holdover from when the U.S. Coast and Geodetic Survey (CGS) became a part of the NOAA in 1970. The CGS began commissioning its surveyors during World War I in case they were captured. That way they would not be shot as spies while surveying.

The members of the 300-strong NOAA Commissioned Corps wear uniforms and ranks modeled after those of the Navy. They operate ships, fly aircraft, conduct diving operations, manage research projects, and serve in positions throughout the NOAA. Sea duty is a common responsibility of the men and women of the NOAA Commissioned Corps. They have a two-year sea service obligation after successfully completing the Basic Officer Training Class.

For Your Benefits

Many of the members of these uniformed services groups have qualified dependents who are entitled to most of the benefits as their sponsors. Typically this includes the spouse, children, and dependent parents.

The Commissioned Corps of the U.S. Public Health Service

Similar to the NOAA, the Department of Health and Human Services has a 6,000-strong all-officer, commissioned corps. It is led by a political appointee called the Surgeon General of the United States, with the rank of vice admiral. (You may have seen this person on TV in a Navy-like uniform telling you to quit smoking or to lose weight.) Members of the Public Health Service Commissioned Corps receive direct commissions.

The NOAA Commissioned Corps consists of skilled officers in the areas of medicine, dentistry, veterinary medicine, engineering, environmental health, and more. All are volunteers and can be called to military service by the president.

The Commissioned Corps personnel wear uniforms and rank similar to the Navy, with unique Public Health Service insignia. This group also provides medical services to the Coast Guard. While working in this capacity, personnel wear Coast Guard uniforms with Public Health Service insignia.

Retirees

After some years of service, each of these groups can apply for retirement. They typically receive a retirement check as well as military benefits. No, that is too simple.

Where active duty personnel become full-fledged military retirees after 20 or more years, Guard and Reserve become "grey area" retirees who receive benefits but no retirement pay until they turn 60. At that time, they receive the same benefits (but not the same pay) as retired active duty personnel.

Military retirement is officially considered to be reduced pay for reduced services. If the services want you back, they call you. However, unless you have unique skills, they figure that older retirees may not be able to meet the physical requirements of active service. So if you are retired for more than five years, it would likely take a big war to call you back.

Military Disabled Retirees

Military personnel (of all uniformed services) can become disabled for many reasons. Disabilities may be the result of combat injuries, an auto accident, a parachute failure, or even a chronic disease. Different types of military disability retirements exist, as determined by a medical board. Some of these retirements include money and benefits; others include only benefits.

Uniformed Services Privilege and Identification Card

With so many benefits available for all of the many classifications of service (active, Reserve, National Guard, retired), how can anyone know who is entitled to what? To prove who they are—and, therefore, what they are entitled to —the military has created a standard set of identification cards that all of the services use. A Uniformed Services Privilege and Identification Card (or military ID) is a document issued by the Department of Defense to identify a person as a member of the uniformed services or a member's dependent. This is your ticket to the many benefits of uniformed service.

For Your Benefits

The uniformed services provide temporary benefits as a transition for individuals moving from military benefits back to civilian benefit programs. While they are receiving these benefits, they are provided a dependent's ID card.

ID cards have your picture printed on them. On the front is basic information such as name, rank, expiration date, and Social Security number (which is your service number). On the back is information about some of your benefit entitlements, such as TRICARE eligibility.

Remember to update the entire family's ID cards when you reenlist or retire. Dependent ID cards expire in four years or at the end of the sponsor's enlistment (except for officers, whose expiration date is indefinite). The same holds true for Guard/Reserve members returning to Reserve status after an extended period of active duty. Time for new ID cards all around!

Who Is Eligible for an ID Card?

Several general categories of people are entitled to a Uniformed Services Privilege and Identification Card. ID cards come in different types and colors. These variations provide a quick indication of the benefit (and other) privileges of the bearer:

- Active duty uniformed services members—Green—DD Form 2

- Members of the National Guard or Reserve components—Red —DD Form 2RES

- Retirees or veterans with benefit privileges—Blue—DD Form 2RET

Anyone in one of these categories can also obtain an ID card for qualified dependents. Dependents of active duty personnel receive a brown DD Form 1173, while dependents of Guard/Reserve personnel receive a red card DD Form 1173-1. A qualified dependent is someone who depends on the sponsor for financial support. Qualified dependents must meet any of these criteria:

- Spouse of the sponsor.

- Children or stepchildren of the sponsor who are under 21 years of age. This can be extended to their twenty-third birthday if they are in school. Dependents under 10 years of age do not require their own card.

- Parents or parents-in-law, if the sponsor provides 50 percent of their support.

Who Loses Eligibility?

Life changes often alter the eligibility for military benefits. Of course, when you are discharged from the service (hopefully honorably), you lose your military benefits, unless you are retiring. Birth, death, divorce, adoption, and children passing beyond eligibility age can all bring an end to an ID card. Examples include …

- A single parent of a deceased military member who remarries after the sponsor's death.

- A student no longer enrolled full time in an accredited institution of higher learning.

Attention!

A former spouse who acquires an employer-sponsored health plan after issue of an ID card is no longer eligible for medical care through the uniformed services.

◆ A dependent child who marries. However, if that marriage ends by final divorce decree or annulment, the child may be reinstated as a dependent if he or she meets the eligibility requirements for a dependent child.

◆ A spouse when a final divorce, dissolution, or annulment occurs, unless the divorce court awards some of the military benefits in the divorce decree. In this case, the benefits end if the spouse remarries.

Common Access Card (CAC)

The "old" ID cards caused many problems. First, there was only so much room for information. Some of the information was required under international agreement (such as the Geneva Conventions). Since everyone had to carry an ID card, couldn't more be added to it, to keep everything in one place?

Second, soldiers and DoD civilians were becoming walking card decks with authentication tokens and access card for this and that. Issuing, keeping track of, recovering, and updating so many devices was a big job—not to mention the exercise of carrying them around all day.

The solution to this was the Common Access Card (CAC). A CAC card is a credit card–size device that contains one or more integrated circuit chips. It may also have a magnetic strip, bar code, radio frequency transmitter, and photo identification. CACs have a wide range of uses, such as identifying people for building entry, computer network access, and communications encryption.

CAC cards have replaced the old uniformed services ID cards for active duty military personnel, National Guard personnel, selected Reserve members, DoD civilian employees, and eligible contractor personnel. Retirees and military dependents will continue using the current identification card.

With a card that has the potential to hold so much of your personal information, what happens if you lose it? The answer is, not much. When a CAC card is issued, the person receiving the card enters an eight-digit personal identification number (PIN). Anyone trying to use the card to access something gets three chances to enter the correct PIN. After that, the card's access capabilities are disabled until it is reset by an office that can issue CAC cards.

CAC cards have been out for a few years. Technology can move a long way in a few years, so now the new, next-generation CAC cards are being issued as replacements for the original-format cards. You will receive one of the new cards when your old CAC card expires and if your card-issuing office has the equipment to issue the new card. If the card-issuing site has the old equipment, you'll still receive an old-format card when yours expires!

An important feature of both types of CAC cards is that they contain PKI credentials. PKI (public key infrastructure) allows computer users who have never seen each other to exchange encrypted messages when using a computer with a CAC card reader. This reduces the likelihood of an intercepted document or message being read by someone other than the intended recipient.

Defense Enrollment Eligibility System (DEERS)

Imagine gathering and trying to keep all the information straight for the millions of uniformed services members. To do this, the Defense Enrollment Eligibility System (DEERS) was created. DEERS contains information on all active, retired, and Reserve uniformed service personnel and their dependents. It also includes DoD civil service personnel. So far, DEERS contains over 23 million records in two redundant data centers.

Like all successful projects, DEERS has been tapped to provide information to a wide range of DoD applications. For example, it is used as a source of benefit verification for …

- ◆ TRICARE when reviewing claims. If someone's DEERS record is incorrect, claims may be rejected. TRICARE pharmacy also verifies eligibility through DEERS.

- ◆ Issue of new identification cards.

- ◆ Access to online Army and Air Force Exchange System (AAFES) shopping.

Service members are automatically registered in DEERS. Dependents must be registered in DEERS by their sponsor. Sponsors are responsible for detecting and correcting data errors. A mistake in DEERS can affect medical coverage and other benefits.

Verify DEERS information by visiting your nearest RAPIDS (Real-time Automated Personnel Identification System—discussed in the next section) site. Sponsors or registered family members may make address changes, but only the sponsor can add or delete a family member from DEERS. Legal documentation supporting the change, such as a marriage certificate, divorce decree, or birth certificate, is required. These changes may start or stop certain benefits.

Service members must update their residential address within 30 days of a move, whether a Reservist moves his household or a sailor changes ships. Every move requires an update. Also each person's record must be updated individually. So if you move your family to another place, you must update records for each family member separately, not just your own.

You can update DEERS information in several ways:

◆ You can add to or change DEERS information through your unit's personnel office. If you are in the Guard/Reserve, you can do this through a local unit.

◆ You can call the DEERS Support Office between 0600 and 1500 PST at:

1-800-527-5602   Alaska/Hawaii
1-800-334-4162   California
1-800-538-9552   All other states

◆ Mail changes to:

DEERS Support Office
ATTN: COA, 400 Gigling Road
Seaside, CA 93955-6771

For Your Benefits

The data in DEERS is also used to allocate resources like hospitals and commissaries so they are built close to where the people are.

◆ Get online access through www.tricare.osd. mil/deers.

◆ Fax address changes to DEERS at 831-655-8317.

◆ E-mail DEERS updates to addrinfo@osd. pentagon.mil. Include the sponsor's name and Social Security number, the address change, names of other family members to be changed, and the date the address change takes place.

Real-time Automated Personnel Identification System (RAPIDS)

To improve the security of identity cards, the Real-time Automated Personnel Identification System (RAPIDS) was created. RAPIDS created identity cards with a digitized photo printed on them, along with a two-dimensional bar code. RAPIDS pulls information out of DEERS to fill in the ID card.

RAPIDS are generally found in uniformed services personnel offices, on ships, and in other locations worldwide. A RAPIDS terminal can create ID cards for retirees, dependents, Guard/Reserve, and active duty personnel. It can also create CAC cards for those groups who should have them, as well as DoD civilians. You can locate the nearest RAPIDS Site at www.dmdc.osd.mil/rsl, or contact a Defense Manpower Data Center Support Office.

To obtain an ID card, bring with you two forms of ID in original form. At least one of these ID cards must be a valid state or federal government-issued picture identification. This might be a driver's license or a passport, for example. (Of course, this could be a bit tough if you lost everything in your wallet at once.) You also need to know your government e-mail account. Before the card is issued, you must select an eight-digit number as your PIN. Pick something easy to remember but hard to guess.

If you should have a CAC card, you will be issued one. If the station is capable of creating the next-generation CAC cards, you will get one of those instead.

This is required RAPIDS documentation and information for active duty military personnel, selected Reserve, DoD civilian employees, eligible contractor personnel, eligible federal personnel, and other DoD-sponsored eligible populations:

◆ Two forms of ID in original form. At least one form of ID must be a valid state or federal government-issued picture identification (passport, driver's license, or current CAC).

◆ A government ("dot" mil or gov) e-mail address. Personal e-mail addresses, such as Gmail accounts, are not accepted for issuance of an e-mail certificate.

◆ A six- to eight-digit number to use as a PIN. Your PIN should not be a number derived from something easily known about you, such as part of your Social Security number, birthday, anniversary date, telephone number, or address.

DD214—The Veteran's Ticket

The DoD issues to each person leaving the armed forces a Department of Defense Form 214, "Certificate of Release or Discharge from Active Duty" (commonly known as a DD214). This important document is a summary record of your military service, combat or overseas service, final rank, and awards. It also identifies the veteran's condition of discharge—honorable, general, other than honorable, dishonorable, or bad conduct.

Enlisted members of the armed forces are relieved of active or Reserve service by a separation or discharge. Most of the people who leave military service after completing an initial enlistment are separated rather than discharged. A discharge completely relieves the veteran of any unfulfilled military service obligation, whereas a separation may leave an unfulfilled military service obligation to complete by service in the Individual Ready Reserve. Approximately one in three recruits is released before the end of the first enlistment.

All enlistments are currently for eight years, even though the enlistment contract cannot exceed six years. The rest of that time is served in a follow-on enlistment or as an inactive (nondrilling) Reservist in the Individual Ready Reserve (IRR).

What's in the DD214?

The DD214 contains historical and identification information used to determine eligibility for specific veteran benefits. The most important part of the form contains information on the type of separation. This indicates the authority and reason for separation and reenlistment eligibility codes. These codes are used to determine whether the armed forces will ever let you back in and which veteran benefits you qualify for. On the older forms, this information was near the top. In 1979, this was moved to the bottom of the form. This allows for copies to be issued with or without the potentially negative information on why you were let go.

Other useful items on the DD214 include …

- Military education. This can be used to qualify for college credit.
- Decorations, medals, and citations. If you lose your awards, you can request free replacements.
- Total creditable service. Many government jobs credit military toward retirement and seniority standings.
- Amount of Serviceman's Group Life Insurance (SGLI) in force at separation. This is used to set the maximum amount of coverage under Veterans Groups Life Insurance (VGLI) that you are eligible for.
- Date and place of entry into active duty.
- Home address at time of entry.
- Date and place of release from active duty.

◆ Home address after separation.

◆ Last duty assignment and rank.

◆ Military job specialty.

◆ Foreign service credited.

For Your Benefits

After a DD214 is issued, corrections are issued on a DD Form 215, "Correction to DD Form 214, Certificate of Release or Discharge from Active Duty."

Not Everyone Gets a DD214

If your entire military career has been in the National Guard, but never on active duty except for training, you will receive an NGB Form 22. This is essentially the same information as a DD214 and can be used as one. However, if you were called to active service for 90 days or more, you will be issued a DD214 for that service.

If your entire military career has been in the Reserves, but never on active duty except for training, there is no form specifically for you. In general, for VA benefits, you must produce documents that show you were a drilling Reservist (not in the Individual Ready Reserve, also known as the Control Group) for at least six years. This can be done with pay slips and retirement points reports (which typically list the points earned for each year of service); about any military documentation will work.

Honorable Discharge Is the Goal

To receive an honorable discharge, you must have received a rating from good to excellent from your service branch. An honorable discharge is your best ticket to veteran benefits. Service members who meet or exceed the required standards of duty performance and personal conduct, and who complete their tours of duty, normally receive honorable discharges. However, completing a term of service is not necessary to receive an honorable discharge, provided that the reason for early discharge is not due to misconduct. For instance, someone might incur a disability in the line of duty or might be separated due to family hardship.

Rarely, an honorable discharge can be granted to a former service member (whose service was characterized as less than honorable) as an act of federal clemency. This requires that the person display exemplary post-service conduct and show evidence of outstanding post-service achievement in areas such as education and employment.

General Discharge

General discharges are given to service members whose performance is satisfactory but marked by a considerable departure in duty performance and conduct expected of all military members. Reasons for such a characterization of service vary but are always preceded by some form of nonjudicial punishment used by unit commanders to correct unacceptable behavior before initiating discharge action (unless the reason is homosexual conduct or drug abuse, in which case discharge is mandatory).

Commanders must disclose to the service member in writing why they are initiating discharge action, and must explain the reason for characterizing service as General (Under Honorable Conditions). The service member is normally required to sign a statement acknowledging receipt and understanding of the notification of pending discharge memorandum.

A general discharge may disqualify participation in the GI Bill, service on veteran's commissions, and other programs for which a fully honorable discharge is required. A veteran is eligible to appeal for upgrading a general discharge to an honorable discharge after six months, but only a slim percentage of the upgrades are approved.

Other Than Honorable (OTH)

An other than honorable discharge is the most severe type of administrative discharge. (An administrative discharge means it was not ordered by a military court as part of a punishment.) It represents a serious departure from the conduct and performance expected of all military members. OTH discharges are typically given to service members convicted by a civilian court in which the sentence included jail time or in which the conduct leading to the conviction brings discredit upon the service. OTH discharges are often accepted in lieu of a court-martial.

Recipients of OTH discharges are barred from reenlisting in any component of the armed forces (including the Reserves) and are normally barred from joining the Army and Air National Guard. In addition, the majority of veterans benefits, including the Montgomery GI Bill and (in most cases) VA health-care benefits, are not available to these individuals.

Bad Conduct (BCD)

Bad conduct discharges (BCD) are given to service members after conviction by a general or special court-martial in which a BCD is part of the sentence. BCDs are often preceded by a period of confinement in a military prison. The discharge itself is not executed until completion of both confinement and the appellate review process.

Dishonorable Discharge

Dishonorable discharges are handed down for what the military considers the most dishonorable of conduct. This type of discharge may be rendered only by conviction at a general court-martial for offenses such as desertion, rape, and murder. The dishonorable discharge is specified as a part of the sentence.

With this characterization of service, all veterans benefits are lost, regardless of past honorable service. This type of discharge carries a heavy stigma and makes finding a good job very difficult.

Entry-Level Separation

Another type of administrative discharge is an entry-level separation. This is an uncharacterized discharge given to individuals who separate from the service before they complete 180 days of military service, or when discharge action was initiated before 180 days of service. This type of discharge does not attempt to characterize service as good or bad. It is something of a "we don't think you fit in here" statement.

Replacing a DD214

If your DD214 is lost, request a replacement copy from the National Personnel Records Center. Generally, there is no charge for military personnel and health record information provided to veterans, next of kin, and authorized representatives. If your request involves a service fee, they will notify you of the amount.

You can request two versions of your DD214. The "long" version is a full copy of the document, containing all information about the separation. The "short" version does not include this information:

- ◆ **Character of separation**—Honorable or otherwise.

- ◆ **Authority for separation**—Under which regulation this release was made. This information is usually needed if you were asked to leave.

- ◆ **Reason for separation**—Enlistment expirations, reenlistment, and so on.

- ◆ **Reenlistment eligibility code**—Whether you were welcome to reenlist.

◆ **Separation (SPD/SPN) code**—Exactly why you were separated from the service.

◆ **Dates of time lost**—Usually time lost from unauthorized absence or time in a military jail.

You can request a copy of a DD214 in three ways:

◆ Go to eVetRecs at https://vetrecs.archives.gov/VeteranRequest/home.asp. Answer the questions. Print and sign the signature sheet, and then either fax or mail it to the National Personnel Records Center. The fax number and address are on the signature sheet.

◆ An alternative is to download a Standard Form 180 (SF-180) from www.archives. gov/research/order/standard-form-180.pdf. Fill it in and mail it to the appropriate address shown on the form, depending on your branch of service.

◆ The third way is to write to the Personnel Records Center (at the previous address) and request an SF-180, or pick one up at a local Veterans Administration office. You may photocopy the SF 180 as needed, but a certified copy must accompany a claim for VA benefits.

Correcting

People type DD214s, and people make mistakes. If after you receive a DD214 you uncover an error, you can request to have your document officially amended. To do this, submit a DD Form 149, "Application for Correction of Military Record." You must attach copies of supporting information. The form provides a place to offer to appear in person before the board to state your case. The board will call you only if that is necessary.

Army (for Active Duty Personnel)
Army Board for Correction of Military Records
1941 Jefferson Davis Highway, 2nd Floor
Arlington, VA 22202-4508

Army (for other than active duty personnel)
Army Review Boards Agency Support Division, St. Louis
9700 Page Avenue
St. Louis, MO 63132-5200

Navy and Marine Corps
Board for Correction of Naval Records
2 Navy Annex
Washington, D.C. 20370-5100

Air Force (including Army Air Corps and Army Air Forces)
Board for Correction of Air Force Records SAF/MRBR
550-C Street West, Suite 40
Randolph AFB, TX 78150-4742

Coast Guard
Board for Correction of Military
Records of the Coast Guard (C-60)
Room 4100
Department of Transportation
400 7th St. SW
Washington, D.C. 20590

The Least You Need to Know

◆ Your children lose their dependent status when they marry, turn 21, or turn 23 (if attending college).

◆ Update your DEERS information through your unit's administration office (active duty) or through a local Guard/Reserve unit office (Guard/Reserve or retiree).

◆ Retirees should know where the nearest RAPIDS office is for replacement ID cards.

◆ Obtain and safeguard a copy of your DD214 that shows your charter of service. If you lose it or it contains an error, know how to request a fresh copy of your DD214.

◆ Understand which veterans' benefits you have earned based on your type of discharge.

Part 2

Show Me the Money

Your military pay is a significant benefit. Managing your finances involves managing the money that comes in and the money that goes out. You must know what you are entitled to receive and how to verify that you are getting it. You also must know what is available to work toward, to increase your cash flow.

The most important issue is the amount of money that flows out. If you could keep everything that came in, then even someone on a military salary would feel wealthy. You can reduce some of this outflow. In certain circumstances, your income may be exempt from income taxes. Also by taking advantage of benefits that provide discounted services, you can hang on to more cash.

Finally, like all other significant life events, retirement takes planning if it is to be successful. As your military career progresses, you must know what your retirement entitlement will be. After retirement, it is a good idea to verify that you are receiving what is due you under the military pension laws.

Cash for This—Money for That

In This Chapter

◆ Determining your base pay and allowances

◆ Monitoring your deductions through your LES

◆ Keeping your pay in sync with the cost of living

◆ Initial and ongoing clothing allowance

Most civilian jobs are paid by the hour or by salary. Hourly workers are paid for actual hours worked—no work, no money. If you work more than 8 hours a day (or 40 hours per week, depending on your company's rules), you are paid an additional sum to recognize this "overtime" effort. In a salaried job, you are paid the same amount of money per pay period, no matter how much or how little you worked.

Military pay is a salary. Although many a sailor working 12-hour days, seven days per week would love to be paid by the hour, it isn't going to happen. Military service can include many long days and weekends of constant labor. So it is paid as a flat amount per month, broken into two checks.

Simplicity and the military service never seem to go together. Whereas a civilian may receive a salary, military compensation begins with a base salary (called basic pay). To that may be added allowances or any number of additional "pays," such as flight pay for aircrews, and sea pay for Coast Guard and Navy sailors aboard ship. The trick is to understand what each of these income additions are so that you can work toward earning one, or to ensure that you've received it if you've already earned it. Hopefully this chapter will take some of the mystery out of the military pay system.

Payment Then and Now

Old veterans like to spin stories about how, when they were privates, their military pay was something paid in pennies. There is some truth in this, but military pay is a matter of how much the government needs to pay to get someone to do a specific job. If people are eager to sign up, pay raises may be skipped and pay may be allowed to drift lower. If more volunteers are needed, the pot is sweetened. Many countries conscript their soldiers and pay them relatively little.

In the not-too-distant past, military personnel were paid in cash. Some young airman or soldier was tasked to draw a weapon from the arms room and meet the pay officer at the payroll office to escort the money back to the headquarters. There everyone lined up and was paid, usually one at a time. This was a long process, but one that everyone wanted to be in line for. Today everything is direct deposit. This is a great advantage. No pay lines are necessary. Everyone stays on the job. Instead of stashing large sums of money in the barracks (attracting thieves), you take out of the bank only whatever you need.

Hot Scoop _____

How does your pay stack up against that in other countries? Websites are in a country's native language, so it is hard to make a worldwide list, but here are some in English.

- ◆ Great Britain: www.army.mod.uk/servingsoldier/condofserv/mm
- ◆ Canada: www.army.forces.gc.ca/Land_Force/English/1_3_1_3.asp
- ◆ Australia: www.defence.gov.au/dpe/pac/Pay_Allow_Aug_07.pdf

Basic Pay

Basic pay is your salary for military service. If you are unmarried, live in government quarters, and eat in a government dining facility, this is likely most of what you will get. However, most service members combine it with other allowances and special pays to fill out their pay packet.

Basic pay is determined by your rank and how long you've served. The higher your rank is and the longer you've served, the fatter your check. The current Basic Pay charts are available at www.defenselink.mil/militarypay/pay/bp.

Basic pay has several categories:

◆ Enlisted—pay grades E-1 to E-9

◆ Officer—pay grades O-1 to O-10

◆ Warrant Officer—Pay grades W-1 to W_5

◆ Officers with more than four years as enlisted or warrant officers

Reading the pay charts requires finding your rank's row in the leftmost column. Next, look along the top of the chart for the column for the number of years of service. Years of service are measured from the day you first signed your military agreement papers and raised your hand to take the oath to serve. This includes all of your active duty and reserve time (including delayed entry to basic training). If you had a six-month delayed entry, then you started off with six months of service as it relates to pay (you were technically in the Reserves all that time).

For almost every rank, once you hit a certain point in your years of service, you bump into your maximum basic pay rate for that grade. For example, pay grade E-1 is paid one amount for less than four months of service and another amount for any time greater than four months. It doesn't matter how many years a service member has completed. After four months of service, there will be no increase in an E-1's basic pay unless Congress increases the entire base pay scale. However, the other pay grades increase every two years, up to a maximum.

Hot Scoop _____

Just about everyone feels that they should be paid more than they are. With the military system of basic pay and allowances, it is sometimes difficult to make a straight comparison between military and civilian pay. The Department of Defense has provided a calculator to do just that! It is online at www.dod.mil/cgi-bin/rmc.pl.

You can increase your basic pay in three ways. The first is from a promotion. The pay increase from pinning on a higher rank can be substantial. The second type of raise comes when you move to the next step in longevity, such as from six years to eight years of service. The third type of raise is the annual pay increase from Congress to reflect increases in cost of living.

Active duty service members lose their basic pay for the time periods when they are on excess leave, confinement, or unauthorized absence. Otherwise, every active duty service member is entitled to basic pay.

Cost of Living Increases

The cost of everything seems to keep going up. Just as you finally see the money coming in from a big promotion, the cost of gas shoots up and seems to eat the entire increase. To help service members maintain the purchasing power of their pay, the government provides an annual cost of living allowance (COLA) pay adjustment.

Annual military pay raises are linked to increases in private-sector wages. Annual pay raises begin with the annual increase in the *Employment Cost Index (ECI)*. To this the president recommends any additional amount. However, what counts is the amount that Congress approves in the annual defense appropriation. It is common to hear a lot of numbers bandied about, but the only one that counts is the final one that is funded by Congress.

def•i•ni•tion

The **Employment Cost Index (ECI)**, a component of the National Compensation Survey, measures quarterly changes in compensation costs for civilian workers (nonfarm private industry and state and local government workers).

The percentage of pay increase sometimes varies by rank. Portions of the increase might be targeted more toward higher-ranking personnel than the junior grades. Changes are effective on January 1 every year.

In times past, Congress has set aside the ECI-based increase and funded a lower amount. Over time, this widens the gap between military pay and civilian pay, which tends to impact retention rates.

CONUS (Continental United States) COLA

Some military personnel are assigned to high-cost areas of the nation. A civilian who is dissatisfied with the local cost of things can pick up and move. Military personnel who do this might get an MP escort back. To protect the purchasing power of personnel assigned to high-cost areas (and to prevent these folks from avoiding these assignments like the plague), the military provides an additional monthly CONUS cost-of-living allowance (COLA).

The CONUS COLA in 2007 is applied to 64 high-cost areas across the country. It compensates service members for expenses in areas where the costs exceed the national average by more than 8 percent (except for housing). (BAH has its own adjustment for the high cost of local housing.) It is a taxable allowance, with an amount added to cover an average income tax rate.

The CONUS COLA formula increases pay up to 13 percent. In 2007, the highest CONUS COLA was paid for the New York City area. The CONUS COLA is updated every January 1. You can find the CONUS COLA calculator online at perdiem.hqda.pentagon.mil/perdiem/ccform.html.

Reservists called to inactive duty for training for less than 140 days do not receive a CONUS COLA. However, if they are activated for contingency operations, they receive it beginning on the first day.

Overseas COLA

Just as a service member's paycheck decreases in purchasing power in certain areas of the United States, it can also shrink overseas. The Overseas COLA is a tax-free allowance. It is paid to more than 250,000 members at approximately 600 locations overseas, including Alaska and Hawaii.

The Overseas COLA protects your purchasing power so you can purchase about the same goods and services overseas as in the United States. It does not compensate for remoteness, hardship, or unavailability of goods and services.

The Overseas COLA is a comparison between purchasing common items in the states and purchasing the same items locally. It currently applies to more than 600 locations. A major cause of this is fluctuations in the value of the U.S. dollar in comparison to the local currency. Note that if currency rates change but local costs are still below the CONUS, no adjustment is made. The Overseas COLA is typically adjusted annually, but if currencies fluctuate widely, it can be adjusted as often as every payday.

Find the Overseas COLA calculator online at perdiem.hqda.pentagon.mil/perdiem/ocform.html.

Drill Pay

National Guard and all Reserve personnel receive their own version of basic pay called drill pay. Drill pay is pay for one drill, or a 4- to 24-hour block of training. Each weekend is considered to be four drills: two on Saturday and two on Sunday. Each participant is paid one day's basic pay (no BAH or BAS allowances) and is awarded one retirement point per drill. So if someone misses the Saturday morning drill but is present for the remainder of the weekend, he or she can still be paid for three of the drills and earn three retirement points.

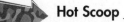

Hot Scoop _____

The website for Guard/ Reserve current drill pay is www. dod.mil/dfas/militarypay.html.

National Guard and Reserve personnel also attend two weeks of annual training (unless they are called to active duty in support of a contingency operation). These two weeks may be at any time of the year but are often during the summer. During these two weeks, they are paid the same as active duty personnel, except they receive BAH-RC/T, which is the base BAH for their rank and is not adjusted for local cost of living.

Leave

Ah, vacation, a time to kick back and recharge your personal batteries. We all look forward to a break from the usual daily grind. Active duty military personnel earn 30 days of paid leave per year, or 2.5 days per month. Leave can be used for any number of things, from tending to a family crisis back home, to vacationing someplace—different.

Leave is requested through your unit's administration section, and approval is not automatic. It depends upon current operational conditions. Leave only excuses you from duty—it does not pay to get you to your destination and back. Leave (known in the older days as a furlough) covers every day you are gone, including holidays and weekends. Most units require personnel taking leave to depart the unit area of operations and not spend their time off hanging around the barracks.

When you separate from the military, you have two options for cashing in your leave balance. The first is to stay until your discharge day and receive the basic pay for your leave days in a taxable lump sum. The other option is to spend your last military days on "terminal leave," where you are essentially discharged but receive all pay and allowances for your remaining service time. For example, if you have 30 days of leave pending, you can return home and look for a job while still drawing all military pay for those 30 days. The "terminal" designation means you are processed out of the military before departing on leave and are not required to return.

Terminal leave means that you and your family are still covered under military health-care services until your last day in the service. This may provide a useful family coverage transition between the time you leave the service and your first day on a new civilian job.

Attention!

Emergency leave requires quick action. If a family emergency arises back home, the American Red Cross can pass on emergency messages concerning the serious illness, death, or even birth of a family member. Commanding officers often use Red Cross verification of these events to determine whether emergency leave is justified. Ask a family member to contact the American Red Cross National Armed Forces Emergency Service Center at 1-877-272-7337 or www.RedCross.org. Approval of emergency leave is up to the local commander and is not automatic.

Leave and Earnings Statement (LES)

How often have looked at your paycheck and wondered, "Is this right?" "Where is the rest of it?" "Have my allotments started yet?" All of this and more is available on your personal Leave and Earnings Statement (LES). It is a comprehensive and official statement of your leave balance, tax withholding, and thrift saving plan information for the month. Active duty service members request copies of their LES through myPay. Statements are available for 12 months. National Guard and Reserve LES statements are retained for only three months. LES copies are also available from your unit's finance office. To see your LES, log into mypay.dfas.mil/mypay.aspx.

An LES is official because it represents what is currently in your pay records. If an amount is incorrect, it is your responsibility to contact your administrative office and correct it. Examples of problems might be an incorrect number of tax deductions or an incorrect leave balance.

Allowances

The military provides two primary allowances. Each is money paid in addition to basic pay. Each also comes with its own set of eligibility requirements. These allowances are for quarters and subsistence, and are provided free from federal and state income taxes, and from Social Security taxes. This saves you 20 to 30 percent of the amount.

Basic Allowance for Housing (BAH)

The government provides military personnel with quarters—a place to live. This is at least a bed, a room, and a place to store things. In some cases, military personnel do not to live in government-provided quarters, either because they prefer not to or because an adequate place to stay is not available. The Basic Allowance for Housing (BAH) provides the same benefit as the warm, dry bed in a noisy barracks.

Chapter 5 covers the BAH in greater detail, but it has five variations. In addition, service members who reside off-base with their dependents may be eligible for an Overseas Housing Allowance. Every active duty service member receives one of these BAH allowances in his or her check.

◆ BAH Without Dependents is for single service members without eligible dependents to live in civilian housing. Most services authorize this allowance for service members in pay grades E-6 and above. It is also provided to service members who do not have access to government quarters, such as recruiters.

◆ BAH With Dependents is for service members of all ranks to live in civilian rental housing. It is based on a survey of local apartment and duplex rental prices, and is based on the location of your duty station. While you live in base housing, you exchange this allowance for the quarters.

◆ BAH DIFF is an allowance to provide child support for service members who provide it to their dependents either voluntarily or because of court orders.

◆ Partial BAH is for service members without dependents who live in government quarters.

◆ BAH –RC/T is the BAH rate for service members in transit between duty stations or for Guard/Reserve called for inactive duty for training. Guard/Reserve called for contingency operations automatically receive the active duty BAH rate.

Basic Allowance for Subsistence (BAS)

Basic Allowance for Subsistence (BAS) is money to offset the cost for food for the service member where government rations are not supplied. All service members receive BAS and pay for their meals. It is adjusted annually based on the USDA food cost index. This is why the increase to BAS is different than annual increases to the basic pay amount.

For example, the 2007 BAS for enlisted service members was $279.88, but officers were granted only $192.74. Service members issued meal cards are authorized full separate rations, with the cost of meals automatically deducted.

> **Hot Scoop** _____
>
>   At one time, each branch of the armed forces had its own pay and finance centers. However, armed forces personnel were all paid essentially the same. True, each had his or her own special pays, but they all had more in common than in difference. In 1991, they were consolidated into one organization, which required fewer people to run: the Defense Finance and Accounting Service (DFAS). DFAS is the world's largest finance and accounting operation. It is found online at www.dfas.mil.

Family Separation Allowance

When service members are separated from their families, there are additional costs, such as phone calls and packages. Someone also might be needed to care for the children because a spouse is no longer there to assist. Family separation allowance provides a tax-free sum to defray some of these costs and ease the burdens of a separation on the family.

To be eligible for this money, you must be deployed for more than 30 days. The allowance is $8.33 per day or $250 per month. It begins the day you depart your normal duty station and ends the day prior to your return.

Payroll Taxes Are Unavoidable

The funny thing about military pay is that you are receiving it from money the government receives in taxes. The first thing the government does then is tax you to get some of it back.

Taxes come from different sources. Federal income and Social Security tax quickly come to mind. However, there is also state income tax (for states that do not exclude military income from taxation). City and county taxes do not apply to military pay.

Federal Taxes

Basic pay, special pay, bonuses, and incentive pay are all taxable. Some allowances, such as family separation, subsistence, and housing, are not. Federal income tax is not charged when you are in a combat zone. If you are in a war zone for a single day, that entire month's pay is tax exempt under the Combat Zone Tax Exclusion (CZTE).

CZTE is also authorized for each month you are hospitalized for over 24 consecutive hours as a result of wounds, disease, or injury incurred while serving in a combat zone. Wounded warriors may qualify for CZTE up to two years after the conflict ends if they are rehospitalized due to the same injury.

This exclusion is unlimited for enlisted members and warrant officers. However, there is a limit to how much money an officer can exempt from taxes. This is based on how much the top enlisted soldier or sailor can earn in a war zone. This is set by the base pay for the Sergeant Major of the Army, Master Chief Petty Officer of the Navy, and so on, plus hostile fire pay. In 2007, this was $6,867 per month.

Unlimited tax exemption is a great benefit for enlisted service members (aside from the personal danger to become eligible). Reenlisting in the war zone means that your entire reenlistment bonus is free from income tax. This can save you 25 percent or more of the total.

Attention!

In recognition of the difficulties in collecting records and submitting tax returns in a combat zone, the Internal Revenue Service (IRS) extends the required filing date for these returns to 180 days beyond the period of service in the combat zone. This extension is lengthened by time spent in missing-in-action status, as well as time in continuous hospitalization from injuries suffered in the combat zone.

State Taxes

Each state has a different policy when it comes to taxing military pay. The first step is to determine which state you belong to. State residency is your home of record and is initially the place indicated on your enlistment papers. When you separate from the service, this is where the military will pay you to travel to and will send your household goods. Your home state of record remains your state of legal residence unless you formally change your military records.

States that charge an income tax each have their own rules concerning military pay. State income tax for your home of record will be automatically withheld from your pay. An annual state income tax return must be submitted. Pay that is exempt from federal income tax (such as pay or bonuses earned in a war zone, or even a subsistence allowance) is also free of state income tax.

Enlisted members may change their "home of record" when they sign a new enlistment contract. Officers may not change their "home of record" except to correct an error or after a break in service. Anyone seeking to change their home of record must submit a DD Form 2058, "State of Legal Residence Certificate." You must also demonstrate that this is your new home state by living there, registering to vote, relicensing your vehicles for that state, and so on.

Clothing Allowances

The U.S. government wants its soldiers, sailors, airmen, and Marines to look sharp. Consequently, personnel spend a lot amount of money on their clothing. An initial uniform issue is provided to enlisted personnel, and then money is provided to maintain it.

Officers are expected to purchase their own uniforms and maintain them. This is a considerable expense. An initial set of uniforms will cost new officers several thousand dollars, and many a military career begins with debt. To defray some of this cost, a one-time $400 allowance is provided to officers …

- When entering active duty for more than 90 days.

- When completing at least 14 days of active duty for training in the Reserves.

Clothing Allowances

Two allowances are provided to service members to help them maintain their uniforms in top condition. These allowances are based on an estimated wear life of initial-issue uniform items; they are not intended to cover the cost of cleaning them.

Each of the services provides an initial uniform issue to all enlisted recruits. This clothing is expected to be adequate for the first six months of service. After that point, and for the next 2½ years, a cash payment for maintaining these uniforms is provided. This monthly allowance varies among services and varies according to whether you are male or female. Called the Basic Clothing Replacement Allowance, this runs between $21.65 per month (Air Force male) and $36 per month (Army female).

At the three-year mark, your clothing allowance increases over 40 percent. This is because some of the initially issued items are expected to begin wearing out and replacements must be purchased. Called the Standard Clothing Replacement Allowance, this runs between $30.83 per month (Air Force male) and $51.60 per month (Army female).

There are exceptions to these rules. The Navy provides an additional monthly Special Cash Clothing Replacement Allowance to members of the U.S. Naval Academy; the Washington, D.C., Navy band; and all Navy Chief Petty Officers.

For Your Benefits

Some tours of duty require additional uniform issues, such as a drill instructor who may be expected to change uniforms at midday to always present a crisp uniform.

The Coast Guard provides a monthly uniform allowance to Reservists. The Basic Clothing Replacement allowance for male Reservists is $3.35 per drill; females receive $3.45 per drill. The Standard Clothing Replacement allowance for male Reservists is $4.79 per drill; females receive $4.93 per drill.

Extra Clothing Allowances

Extra Clothing Allowances are paid in addition to the Basic and Standard Clothing Allowances. They are for situations in which a member may need additional uniforms or is required to have civilian clothing to perform his or her duties.

Sometimes duty requires that you wear civilian clothing, such as for courier duty or embassy duty. To provide for this new "uniform," a Civilian Clothing Allowance may be approved. This allowance applies to selected overseas assignments. It is the same amount for men and women, and for officers and enlisted personnel.

The 2007 initial Civilian Clothing Allowance is $881.30 for service members permanently stationed overseas. After that, they are allowed $24.48 per month for clothing maintenance. Service members temporarily assigned for at least 15 days in a 30-day period and requiring civilian clothes are given an initial cash allowance of $293.78. If your job requires civilian clothes for at least 30 days of a 36-month period, you are allowed $587.56 (2007 amount).

The Least You Need to Know

◆ You should know where to find the latest pay tables online and how to read them.

◆ Know when the cost of living adjustment is made.

◆ Understand the different clothing allowances that apply to you.

Chapter 4

Extra Money for Special People

In This Chapter

- ◆ Know your war zone pay entitlements
- ◆ Hazardous duty pay can be anytime, anywhere
- ◆ Sea pay to make up for the long hours
- ◆ Extra pay to keep the best medical staff around

Pay helps attract and retain people. By providing additional pay to military paychecks for participation in specific programs, the pool of service members can be encouraged to stay in the military or to move toward certain job qualifications.

Sometimes military pay seems like ordering off a menu a la carte. It starts with basic pay. Then you add in some allowances, garnish it with special pay, and then add a dash of tax-free treatment. Civilians rarely have that much confusion regarding what should be listed on their check stub. They receive a single pay (hourly or salary) and sometimes some profit sharing or bonus. That's what this chapter is all about.

Special Pay

Unlike the civilian world, the military faces a problem. Its pay system is based on a person's rank and longevity in the military. The problem is that the military also needs highly skilled people. Where an infantry captain my feel that his or her pay is adequate, a pharmacist with the same rank may not. To attract and retain highly skilled personnel, such as medical officers and lawyers, the military supplements their pay with "special pay" and retention bonuses.

Another issue involves special pay to compensate for dangerous jobs. Dangerous jobs may seem exciting at first, but once reality sets in, these trained people may want to do something else. To compensate these personnel with more income than another person of the same rank, a special pay is provided. Examples of this are HALO (High Altitude—Low Opening) parachuting, diving, and combat operations.

For Your Benefits

Special pay is the military's way to recruit and retain skilled professional to support the armed services.

Some military skills take a long time to learn. The expense of this training makes it cheaper to pay this person more than to run someone else through it. An example of this is pilots. They may complete several years of flight training, which also winnowed out the best from the rest. It is cheaper to supplement their income with special pay than it is to replace an experienced pilot with a gaggle of new trainees.

War Zone

Three special compensations are available to military personnel serving in a combat zone. Each has its own rules for stopping or continuing it when a service member is medically evacuated from the war zone. The entitlements are Hardship Duty Pay, Hostile Fire Pay, and the Combat Zone Tax Exclusion. (The previous chapter covered the Combat Zone Tax Exclusion.)

Hardship Duty Pay

Hardship Duty Pay comes in two types. Hardship Duty Pay Missions (HDP-M) is paid to active and reserve components for specific missions. HDP-M pays the full monthly rate whenever any part of the month is served fulfilling a specific mission. The individual maximum for HDP-M is $150 per month.

Hardship Duty Pay—Location (HDP-L) is payable to service members performing duty in designated areas for 30 days as hardship duty. The OIF/OEF daily rate is currently $3.33, and the monthly rate is $100. The entitlement ends the day you leave the combat zone.

Hostile Fire Pay/Imminent Danger Pay (HFP/IDP)

The monthly entitlement of $225 is paid when a member receiving basic pay performs duty for any part of a month subject to HFP/IDP. A member is entitled to IDP when assigned to designated IDP areas. You receive the full monthly benefit if you're present for a single day.

HFP is based on whether you are in or near an area that is subject to hostile fire or mine explosions. It also applies if you are killed, injured, or wounded by hostile fire, mines, or any other hostile action.

Hazardous Duty Pay

Another pay issue involves dangerous assignments. Should a sergeant safely parked behind a desk in an air-conditioned office, sleeping in a dry bed and eating hot food, be paid the same as one slipping through the mud and munching on MREs in a war zone? Dangerous assignments may be interesting at first, but sooner or later, reality sets in.

Eligibility for hazardous duty pay requires that you are MOS qualified in that skill, are filling a unit position requiring that skill, and practice it within set time frames. Holding the MOS but not being assigned to a position that requires you to perform those duties does not qualify you for hazardous duty pay. The amount of hazardous duty pay you receive depends on the category of hazardous service.

Diving Pay

Diving pay is for service members who are assigned to jobs that work occasionally under water. Various types of diving have corresponding different rates of pay. Each of the military services uses divers. Consequently, each has its own set of rules for qualifying for diving pay and for maintaining proficiency.

To be eligible for diving duty pay, you must be …

◆ Assigned by orders to an organizational billet that includes diving duty.

◆ Required to maintain proficiency as a diver by frequent and regular dives.

Attention! _____

You might think that when the job is the most dangerous, the government would be most appreciative in its pay. Not so in this case. In time of war, the president may suspend hazardous duty pay.

♦ Either actually performing diving duty in an assignment as the primary duty, or meeting the requirements to maintain proficiency while serving in an assignment for which diving is required but not the primary duty.

The maximum diving pay for officers is $240 per month. However, the maximum diving pay for enlisted service members is $340 per month. Monthly payments for diving duty are not more than two incentive payments for hazardous duty authorized.

Hazardous Duty Incentive Pay

Hazardous duty incentive pay commences on the date the member reports for the hazardous assignment and ends when he or she leaves it. Hazardous duty incentive pay is prorated to cover the actual portion of the month that the hazardous assignment is performed. This pay is also available to members of the Reserve Components who are on extended active duty (EAD) or active duty training (ADT) and who are ordered to perform any of the hazardous duties.

Hazardous duties are defined as follows:

♦ Duty involving a maritime visit and board, search, and seizure operations

♦ Duty involving parachute jumping as an essential part of military duty

♦ Duty involving frequent and regular participation in flight operation on a ship's flight deck

♦ Duty involving the demolition of explosives as a primary duty, including training for such duty

♦ Duty inside a high- or low-pressure chamber

♦ Duty as a human acceleration or deceleration experimental subject, or duty in thermal stress experiments

♦ Duty involving the servicing of aircraft or missiles with highly toxic fuels or propellants

♦ Duty involving fumigation tasks utilizing highly toxic pesticides

♦ Duty involving laboratory work utilizing live dangerous viruses or bacteria

♦ Duty involving handling of chemical munitions

♦ Duty involving use of ski-equipped aircraft on the ground in Antarctica or on the Arctic ice-pack

Hazardous duty incentive pay is $150 per month. The exception is for a High Altitude—Low Opening (HALO) parachutist who qualifies for $225 per month. Only one type of parachute duty payment is authorized at a time. A service member who receives hazardous duty incentive pay and who is injured or otherwise incapacitated as a result of performing such duty is entitled to up to three months of hazardous duty incentive pay while under medical care.

Members may receive up to two hazardous duty incentive pays for the same period. Dual hazardous duty incentive pay is limited to members who are ordered to perform specific multiple hazardous duties necessary to successfully accomplish the mission of their assigned unit. An example of dual hazardous duties is Air Force pararescue team members placed on orders to perform duties as both crew members and parachutists.

Hazardous Duty Incentive Pay—Air Crew Member

Hazardous Duty Incentive Pay—Air Crew Member is for an air weapons controller crew member aboard an airborne warning and control system aircraft (AWACS). Special pay is based on rank and the number of years of aviation service. It ranges from $150 per month to $350 per month.

Hazardous Duty Incentive Pay—Air Crew Member is for service members participating in regular aerial flight as crew members, but not in an AWACS aircraft. Pay is from $150 per month to $250 per month, depending on rank.

Sea Service Incentives

What the Air Force and Army do not realize is that when you are at sea, you are always busy. Whereas an Army artillery company may drive back to the barracks for some sleep, a ship at sea must be manned around the clock—engines working, defenses up, food made for the night crew, and so on. The days are long and endless—and no, there is not a separate crew to handle the weekends. The work never ends.

In recognition of the long hours, the long and frequent family separations, and similar considerations, a series of special pays for sea duty is provided. This additional money in a seagoing sailor's pay packets helps to keep the ship's crew full.

Career Sea Pay

Members ranked petty officer and above who receive basic pay are eligible for Career Sea Pay (CSP) when …

◆ Assigned permanently or temporarily to a ship, ship-based staff, or aviation unit, as long as the primary mission of the ship is accomplished while underway.

◆ Assigned permanently or temporarily to a vessel whose primary mission is accomplished in a port that is considered to be more than 50 miles away from the home port.

◆ Serving as a member of the off-crew as part of a two-crewed submarine.

The following are restrictions on payment:

◆ CSP is not payable to members en route and from ships outside the continental United States (OCONUS).

◆ CSP is not paid to members while onboard ships for transportation, regardless of the length of time.

◆ Midshipmen, aviation cadets, and academy cadets are not authorized CSP, and it cannot be paid to an enlisted member who is also receiving HDP-L for the same period of service.

Specific CSP rates range up to $520 per month. In addition, a CSP Premium of $100 per month is authorized for some members beginning with the thirty-seventh consecutive month of sea duty.

For Your Benefits _____

Each of the service secretaries of the Army, Navy, and Air Force sets their Career Sea Pay amount differently. For current 2007 Career Sea Pay rates for both officers and enlisted service members, as well as other incentive and special pay rates, scroll through the DFAS Pay Tables page at www.dfas.mil/militarypay/2006militarypaytables/2007MilitaryPayCharts-1.pdf.

Submarine Duty Incentive Pay

Sailors attached under orders to a submarine are eligible to receive Submarine Duty Incentive Pay. Eligibility includes sailors undergoing nuclear-powered submarine training preliminary and during rehabilitation after assignment to a nuclear-powered submarine.

It is also paid to members of a submarine operational command staff whose duties require serving on a submarine during underway operations. A minimum of 48 hours must be served every month to maintain submarine pay eligibility.

Special Skills Pay

The military needs service members with specific skills. Some of these skills may also be in high demand in the civilian world. To encourage these personnel to learn and maintain these skills and to remain in military service, a series of special skill pays is provided.

Foreign Language Proficiency Pay

Foreign Language Proficiency Pay (FLPP) is provided to service members certified as proficient in a foreign language (both written and spoken). Different rates are set for different languages, based on operational requirements. Not every language qualifies for this bonus. Each service secretary identifies the critical languages for its operations and its eligibility criteria for FLPP.

FLPP is payable in addition to all other pay and allowances. Reserve component members who meet these same criteria can receive a prorated amount of FLPP for each day of duty.

Two types of Foreign Language Proficiency Pay are given. The first is FLPP I for career linguists who are filling an organizational position as a linguist. The second type, called FLPP II, is for service members who have foreign language skills but are not assigned to a linguist position.

Members are not authorized to receive both FLPP I and FLPP II at the same time. Members may receive FLPP for multiple languages, as long as the maximum monthly FLPP does not exceed $1,000 for active duty personnel and $500 for Guard and Reserve.

Entitlement to FLPP is computed on a 30-day month. Entitlement accrues from the date of authorization through the effective date of the termination order. Payment is prorated for the portion of the month in which entitlement begins or ends.

High Deployment Pay

High Deployment Pay recognizes the personal hardship that extended deployments place on personnel. Service members who are deployed 401 days or more out of the preceding 730 days are entitled to additional pay. Time credited for deployments includes operations, exercises, unit training, home station training, and mission support temporary duty assignments. High Deployment Pay is $100 for each day over 401 days out of the preceding 730.

When counting the 401 days for eligibility, leave taken before, after, or during a deployment does not count as days away from home. Also a service member is considered deployed if hospitalized away from his or her permanent duty station.

Aviation Career Incentive Pay

Both regular and Reserve officers are eligible for Aviation Career Incentive Pay (ACIP) if they hold or are training to hold an aeronautical designation or rating, and engage in aviation service on a career basis. Each service sets its own eligibility rules and pay rate.

ACIP continues until your twelfth year of aviation service. At that point, if you have six or more years of operational flying, you will continue receiving ACIP. After 18 years of aviation service, officers with at least 9 years of operational flying continue receiving ACIP. Officers with 11 years of operational flying within 18 years of aviation service are eligible to receive continuous ACIP until their twenty-fifth year of service. ACIP ceases upon completion of 25 years of aviation service.

Career Enlisted Flight Incentive Pay

Career Enlisted Flight Incentive Pay (CEFIP) is for enlisted personnel whose duties are essential to operation of aircraft, and who are placed on orders to perform crewmember duties. Your CEFIP pay rate is based on years of aviation service. Reservists receive one-thirtieth the current monthly amount for years of aviation service for each drill performed. Pay ranges from $150 per month for less than 4 years of aviation service to $400 per month for more than 14 years of aviation service.

Overseas Extension Pay

Sometimes personnel are in short supply. Overseas Extension Pay is intended to encourage skilled service members to extend their overseas tour. Eligibility requirements include these:

◆ Entitlement to basic pay

◆ Service in a duty specialty that is in short supply

◆ A completed overseas tour of duty at a location

◆ A tour extension agreement for at least one additional year

Overseas Extension Pay may be paid either by monthly pay or as a lump-sum bonus. Monthly Overseas Extension pay is up to $80 per month or a lump sum of $2,000 per year. Early termination of overseas duty stops the monthly bonus and requires recouping unearned advance installments.

For Your Benefits

You can choose to receive either the Overseas Extension Pay, cash, or a period of special rest and recuperation (SR&R).

Special Duty Assignment Pay

Special Duty Assignment Pay (SDAP) is designed for enlisted members (pay grade E-3 or higher) whose duties are extremely difficult or involve an unusual degree of responsibility. SDAP is payable in addition to all other pay and allowances. Officers and warrant officers are not eligible for Special Duty Assignment Pay.

Each of the services determines eligibility for SDAP status. Your entitlement is reviewed annually; without recertification, the pay automatically stops on the anniversary date.

Enlisted members of the Army, Marine Corps, and Air Force are authorized to receive SDAP when on a second or subsequent enlisted term of service; a first-term member is entitled when serving an enlistment of six or more years. The Navy currently requires a combination enlistment/extension agreement for seven years. Enlisted Guard/Reserve Components duty assignments must be characterized by extremely demanding duties or duties that demand an unusual degree of responsibility.

Special Duty Assignment Pay is broken into six pay rates, ranging from $55 to $375 per month. Each service assigns rates to specific duty specialties and assignments.

Special Pay for Dental Services

Good dental health is essential for overall good service member health. To attract and retain skilled dental professionals into military service, a series of special pays are provided. Dental officers must be graduates of a dental school accredited by the American Dental Association (ADA).

Like all medical schools, dental school is expensive. Many military dentists accepted financial assistance from the Department of Defense to pay for their studies. In exchange, they must serve for a set number of years as a military dentist and are not authorized an Accession Bonus.

Variable Special Pay for Dental Officers

Variable Special Pay for Dental Officers is authorized for dental officers on active duty for at least one year. It is also paid to Reservists ordered to active duty for more than 30 days, active duty dental officers involuntarily retained under 10 USC 12305, and retired dental officers recalled to active duty for more than 30 days under 10 USC 688.

Variable Special Pay for Dental Officers starts at $250 per month if the officer is an intern or has less than three years of creditable service. Otherwise, the rate continues to increase to a monthly maximum of $1,000 for those with between 8 and 12 years of creditable service. After 18 years of service, it decreases to $667. All officers in pay grades above O6 receive a maximum of $583 per month.

Additional Special Pay for Dental Officers

Dental officers are entitled to Additional Special Pay if they are entitled to Variable Special Pay, are not serving in an initial internship or initial residency training, and sign an agreement to remain on active duty for at least one additional year. Additional Special Pay for Dental Officers is $4,000 per year for dental officers with less than 3 years of creditable service, $6,000 per year for those with between 3 and 10 years of creditable service and $15,000 per year for those with over 10 years of creditable service.

Dental Officers Board Certified Pay

Dental officers are entitled to Board Certified Pay for active duty if they are board certified and entitled to Variable Special Pay. A dental officer is considered board certified if he or she is certified by an American Dental Specialty Examining Board recognized by the ADA or is awarded a Board Certification Equivalency Certificate issued by the Department of Defense.

Eligible dental officers are paid from $208 to $500 per month, depending on the years of creditable service. A dental officer with between 10 and 18 years of creditable service is paid on a tiered system that increases every two years.

For Your Benefits

Special pay for medical professionals is designed to pay them more when they work to increase their skills.

Reserve Dental Officer Special Pay

Reserve dental officers on active duty for less than one year are entitled to Special Pay for Reserve Dental Officers. This includes active duty for training and active duty for special work. The rate payable is $350 per month and is prorated on a daily basis for actual days served.

Instead of Special Pay for Reserve Dental Officers, Reserve dental officers on active duty other than for training lasting more than 30 days, but less than one year, are entitled to Variable Special Pay, Additional Special Pay, and Board Certified Pay. Reserve dental officers who are receiving Additional Special Pay under 37 USC (b) are not required to sign an agreement to remain on active duty for at least one year.

Special Pay for Medical Services

Physicians, nurses, pharmacists, and other health-care professional are in great demand in the civilian sector. In most cases, they can make a lot of money out there. To encourage these skilled people to be here when we need them, the government provides an array of financial incentives.

Variable Special Pay for Medical Officers

Variable Special Pay for Medical Officers applies to medical officers of the Air Force, Army, Navy, and Public Health Service. It is also paid to Reservists ordered to active duty for more than 30 days, active duty medical officers who are involuntarily retained under 10 USC 12305, and retired medical officers who are recalled to active duty for more than 30 days under 10 USC 688.

Rates payable start at $100 per month for an intern and peak at $1,000 per month when an officer has between six and eight years of creditable service. The rates continue to decrease until medical officers are capped at $583 per month for grades above 0-6 or those with more than 22 years of creditable service.

Board Certified Pay

Board Certified Pay is for medical officers who are entitled to Variable Special Pay. They must also possess board certification equivalency established for specialties unique to military medicine requiring formal postgraduate medical training of at least two academic years. Rates are based on incremental increases in creditable service from $208 for less than 18 years of service to $500 for 18 or more years of service.

Additional Special Pay

Medical officers receive Additional Special Pay when authorized by the military service concerned and when not undergoing an internship or initial residency training. Additional Special Pay is $15,000 for each 12-month period. A monthly prorated amount is paid for medical officers with less than 12 months.

Incentive Special Pay (ISP)

Incentive Special Pay for Active Duty by Reserve Medical Officers is for reserve medical officers called to active duty for less than one year for annual training, active duty for training, or active duty for special work. It is $450 per month or is prorated by day for any portion of a month. Those called to active duty for more than 30 days but less than one year, for other than active duty training, are not eligible.

Multiyear Special Pay (MSP)

Multiyear Special Pay (MSP) is for medical officers in pay grades 0-6 or below who are fully qualified in a designated specialty. Medical officers can be paid for any current credential specialty as long as the MSP and ISP specialty are the same. Medical officers planning to sign an MSP agreement must ...

- ◆ Have a current, valid, unrestricted license or approved waiver.

- ◆ Have eight or more years of creditable service, or have completed all active duty service commitments resulting from medical education or training.

- ◆ Have signed an agreement to remain on active duty for an additional two to four years.

- ◆ Understand that the military service secretary can decline to accept an MSP agreement or can reduce the agreement length to less than four years.

Board Certified Pay for Nonphysician Health Care Providers

This entitlement is for officers with a post-baccalaureate degree and professional board certification in their specialty. It starts at $166 per month and runs as high as $416 per month for officers with 18 or more years of creditable service.

Diplomat Pay for Psychologists

Each military service creates its own eligibility rules for this special pay. In general, officers must have been awarded a diploma as a Diplomat in Psychology by the American Board of Professional Psychology. This entitlement pays between $166 per month and $416 per month for officers with 18 or more years of creditable service.

Nurse Corps

Incentive Special Pay (ISP) for Certified Registered Nurse Anesthetists (CRNAs) is for qualified officers called to active duty for at least one year. The ISP rate cannot exceed $15,000 per year for any contract in which the CRNA is not obligated for training. For contracts in which the CRNA is obligated for training, the ISP rate cannot exceed $6,000 per year.

CRNA officers on active duty less than one year, other than active duty for training, are eligible for ISP. Reservists ordered to active duty, other than training, for more than 30 days but less than a year are eligible, as are retirees recalled to active duty for more than 30 days under 10 USC 688.

The Least You Need to Know

- ◆ Many special pays are based on the number of years of experience doing that specialty.
- ◆ Some special pays can be received at the same time as others.
- ◆ Medical professionals may be eligible for multiple special pays at the same time.
- ◆ Special pay earned in a war zone is tax-free.

Your Military Home Away from Home

In This Chapter

- ◆ Types of government quarters
- ◆ What's in a modern military dormitory
- ◆ Your Base Allowance for Housing explained

Traditionally, the military has provided its personnel with a place to stay. The old saying was that working for Uncle Sam earned you "three hots and a cot" (three hot meals and a place to sleep). Given that civilians spend over one-fourth of their income on living accommodations, this is a significant financial benefit. This chapter explains how the government provides housing for all, or money so you can choose your own.

Government-Provided Quarters

There are three primary types of government-provided quarters. Bachelor enlisted quarters are for enlisted service members who are unmarried or unaccompanied by their dependents. These people are assigned to barracks, or dormitories. Bachelor Officer Quarters are for single or unaccompanied officers. The third type of government quarters is on-base housing for service members who live with their dependents.

Military living can be rather austere. It has ranged from large, open "squad bays" in a barracks to individual berths on a ship. Barracks accommodations provide each person with a bed, a locker for uniforms, and a footlocker for field gear. Toilets, sinks, and showers are shared in an open bay barracks. Officers and senior sergeants have fared somewhat better with individual rooms, on-base housing, or off-base housing at government expense.

The quality of government-provided quarters has long been a concern of military quality of life. Since the end of the Vietnam War conscription and the conversion to the All Volunteer Army, the armed forces have worked to replaced obsolete, substandard quarters with attractive, modern (and more energy-efficient) places for single and married service members to stay.

Simple terms like *barracks* have been replaced with terms like *dormitory* or *bachelor enlisted quarters*. This is appropriate, as the new buildings are very different from the traditional long, open room full of bunks. They are now individual living spaces with private bathrooms, private bedrooms, and shared living rooms and kitchens. This change has come with a price, of course. The old open rooms and shared latrines were quick to clean, with everyone pitching in. The new areas require more personal time to square away.

Attention!

Another roadblock to building new barracks was the number of World War II barracks still standing. These buildings had already been paid for, and it was hard to justify tearing them down just to build something else when the money was needed for so many other things.

A primary quality of life issue is the lack of privacy in a barracks. Attempts have been made to remodel barracks to two- or four-man rooms. The current standard is for a private room, to provide a place away from everyone else that can be decorated to personal tastes.

Another major quality of life concern is space to store personal belongings. After stowing all the required uniforms and equipment, there's not much space for civilian clothes, electronic devices, and other personal items. Service members with cars often use them as a footlocker and occasionally rent base storage lockers to hold everything else. The new dormitory standard calls for a walk-in closet, to provide adequate storage space for personal property.

Every service has its own guidelines for who must live on base. In some cases, mission-essential personnel must live on base so they can assemble quickly. Personnel may also be forced to live on base if there are underutilized bachelor quarters or on-base housing. However, the most common qualification for living off base is rank. There are several reasons behind this restriction. First is the cost of renting a place to live. The government provides a tax-free Basic Allowance for Housing (BAH). This is set according to rank, and in the lower ranks, it may be difficult to find adequate quarters for that amount of money. Second is the expense of furnishing and equipping off-base apartments with basics such as chairs and dishes. Third, the service member must have sufficient remaining funds to purchase and maintain reliable transportation.

Barracks/Dorms and Ship's Berths

The new-style dormitories are intended for service members who have completed their initial training. Basic training is still conducted using open-bay barracks. Many of the MOS schools also use them. However, when training is completed, you can look forward to a chance to stay in the new-style rooms. This is a "chance" because it will be many years before there are enough of the new-style quarters to accommodate everyone, everywhere.

The goal is to provide government quarters that approximate living in an "efficiency"-class apartment. This means a private bedroom that can be decorated to personal preferences. It includes a private bathroom where everything can be organized for a quick morning departure. The living room and kitchen are shared.

Another quality of life complaint about living in government quarters involves the rules you must follow. In some cases, breaking a rule can result in Non-Judicial Punishment, something the local apartment house cannot do. In fairness, these rules are intended to protect the occupants from danger and criminal activity. Common rules are these:

- Alcohol consumption is not permitted at any time in the BEQ. This rule generally does not apply to officers and senior sergeants—primarily because they are all over legal drinking age.

- Weapons of any kind are prohibited. Knives less than 4 inches long are allowed only if required for normal work duties.

- Gambling is prohibited.

- Burning candles or incense is forbidden.

- Rooms are subject to inspection without prior notice.

Each of the services addresses these quality of life requirements in a way that meets its operational philosophies. Local policies for single members living off-base depend on the availability of on-base quarters and their occupancy rate.

Air Force Quarters

The Air Force was an early leader in converting from open-bay barracks to individual rooms. The Air Force is now implementing a Dorms 4 Airmen program. Four one-person bedrooms (with private bath) are grouped together and connect into a common kitchen, washer/dryer space, and living room. Each bedroom is approximately 115 square feet plus a walk-in closet.

Air Force policy permits single sergeants with more than three years of service to reside off-base at government expense. The desirability of this depends on the availability of affordable housing within normal commuting distances.

The Navy Way

The Navy has the unique challenge because some personnel are away at sea for extended periods, and some stay ashore all the time. The Navy rules for seagoing sailors permit certain personnel to live off-base at government expense; this applies to single petty officer second class and above, and petty officer third class with more than four years of service. Land-based sailors petty officer third class and above can live off-base. Unmarried petty officer first class and above can live in town and retain their BAH while at sea (to pay for their idle apartment).

Seagoing sailors are billeted in the Home Port Ashore format, with two sailors sharing a bedroom while the ship is in port. This is because the Navy lacks sufficient facilities to provide each sailor with a private room. Besides, the room may sit idle for months at a time. Sailors who spend all of their time ashore are assigned quarters in dormitories similar to the ones for other services.

However, private rooms for all are still the goal. To achieve this, the Navy has privatized some of its single sailor quarters. (Privatized quarters are run by a civilian company.) The design is for two sailors to each have a private bedroom and bath, and share a kitchen and living room. Sailors will receive their BAH and pay rent for their quarters to the private company through an allotment. Eligibility includes at least six months remaining before your next sea rotation.

Something unique to the sea service is the quarters aboard ships, called berthing. A berthing area is where the ship's crew sleeps and stows personal items. Bunks (also called racks) are stacked up to four high, depending on the ship design. Under each rack is a small storage area for personal items (aptly called the coffin).

With the increasing number of women on ships and the trend toward private rooms ashore, this is also changing. Modern ship designs are grouping up to six sailors to a cabin, adding more personal storage space and including single-person locking bathrooms. Smaller cabins with more and smaller bathrooms will make it easier to accommodate a changing mix of men and women.

Space on a submarine is always tight, so to save idle space, there are only half as many enlisted racks as normally needed. Since crewmen are on 12 hours and off 12 hours, they take turns using the same rack. This is called "hot racking," since the mattress never has time to get cold.

Army Does It Different

The Army sees excellent housing as an important retention tool. The goal is to make single soldier quarters more like civilian housing. The standard is for two junior enlisted soldiers to each have a private bedroom and to share a bathroom, kitchen, and living room. Senior sergeants and officers have a private suite with a bedroom and a separate living room.

The Army builds dormitories in complexes of up to brigade size. Each complex includes all the living spaces, offices, dining facilities, exercise facilities, and so on required to support that unit. Headquarters for each unit have their own offices. They also include places for personnel who live outside of the complex to clean their equipment before going home.

The Army permits single staff sergeants and above to live off-base at government expense. Depending on the occupancy rate of single soldier quarters, some of the single sergeants may also move off-base at government expense.

Attention!

Recent additions to the authorized strength of the Marines and Army will delay the time when all their service members are provided quarters that meet the new standards.

The Marines Approach

The Marine Corps feels that having lower-level Marines living closely together helps to build unit cohesion. Junior-grade marines (lance corporal and below) share a bedroom and a bathroom. Corporal and above are assigned private rooms and a shared bathroom. The goal is to provide this level of military quarters to all Marines by 2012.

The Marines permit single staff sergeants and above to live off-base at government expense. Depending on the occupancy rate of single Marine quarters, some of the single sergeants and corporals may also move off-base at government expense.

Coast Guard

The Coast Guard bases are often small and not near other military installations. Rules vary among installations. Typical rules are that junior enlisted members are billeted in government-leased apartments. Single Coast Guard members ranked petty officer third class and above are entitled to either Coast Guard–leased quarters or BAH (based on funds availability). Coast Guard seamen are eligible for government-leased housing on a space-available basis. The Coast Guard shares the berthing challenges of the Navy and is seeking a similar solution.

Base Housing

Base housing is housing provided to service members and their dependents. The quality of these quarters ranges from very poor to new and modern. Building new (typically duplex) base housing units is a matter for capital improvement funds approved by Congress. The results are uneven, with some bases getting new funds this year, the other bases waiting their turn. For service members with dependent families, this makes some bases more attractive for future assignments.

Another challenge for older military bases is that some of the houses are old and historic. There are plaques outside proclaiming which famous military leaders lived there on their rise to the top—for example, houses where Generals Custer or Marshall lived at some point in their career. This makes major modifications and expansions to them difficult.

Attention!

Mission-essential personnel must live in base housing to enable a quick call to stations.

Government housing is provided for several reasons. The first is an inadequate amount of civilian housing provided when the base was built or in the current market. Second, government housing allows families of similar circumstances (all military) to work together and support each other as a community. This would be harder to do if everyone was dispersed around the country. Base housing also facilitates services such as the Exchange in providing local services at reduced prices.

You don't have to wait until you arrive at a new assignment to get on the list for base housing. Visit your local housing office and fill out an application up to one month before you are due to arrive. The effective date of the housing application at the new base will be the first day of the month prior to your arrival.

Living in base housing has many other advantages. Base housing is typically better built and has more space than comparably priced civilian rentals. Basic utilities are provided for free. This includes water, trash, natural gas, and electricity. Efforts in the past have sought to cut costs by metering utility use in individual units, but this has not been generally applied. However, it will likely be a feature of privatized housing. Any usage over a specific monthly threshold will result in a bill.

On-base housing is limited on most bases (especially the ones for which living in town is expensive). To qualify for housing, you must be residing with a dependent. In a few cases, bases may have lost major units, making on-base housing plentiful. In those cases, everyone drawing BAH with dependents is required to live in the excess housing.

The size of the housing unit you are assigned depends on your rank and the number of dependents you have. It may also depend on which list you are on (officer, senior enlisted, enlisted), as each has its own neighborhood. In general, officers in pay grade O-6 and above qualify for a four-bedroom house. Pay grades E7 through O5 qualify for a minimum of three-bedroom quarters.

Furniture is normally not provided. However, many bases have furniture for temporary free loan until your own arrives or is purchased. It may not be stylish, but the price is right. Stoves and refrigerators are usually provided with each housing unit, as are hook-ups for clothes washers and dryers.

In most cases, the local base housing authority inspects only the outside of your quarters to see how well you maintain it. However, if they believe that there is a sanitation or safety problem anywhere in the government-owned quarters, they may make a command-authorized no-notice inspection.

If you want to make a self-help improvement, you must file a request with the local base housing authority. Before you leave, you must restore the housing unit to its original condition. For example, you may add some color to the monotonous basic white living room walls, but you must repaint them the correct shade of white before you can leave. Another common request is to fence a yard to contain small children. Before you can move out, you may be required to remove it and restore the ground to its original condition.

Moving out of base housing is a challenge. The unit must be perfectly clean before the housing office will accept it. For example, you must clean everything from the folds inside the seals of the refrigerator door, and you must remove all of the oil stain on the driveway. Many people hire professional cleaners who have experience satisfying base housing inspectors to clean the place for them.

Losing Eligibility

You must leave base housing if your family circumstances change. For example, if your dependents permanently move out of your on-base quarters, you must notify base housing and prepare to vacate the premises.

If you are assigned to an unaccompanied overseas tour, you may apply for your dependents to remain in base housing while you are gone. Approval depends on the size of the base housing waiting list and other local circumstances.

Living in base housing is a privilege that can be revoked. Most housing infractions are minor and can be easily resolved. For example, if you do not cut your grass, you'll receive a "ticket" to trim things up. A serious incident can result in expulsion from base housing and possible punishment under the Uniform Code of Military Justice. Examples of this might be destroying part of the housing unit, threatening other residents, or displaying unacceptable behavior as determined by the local housing authority.

Privatized Housing

The government uses a different financial approach from the civilian world. The government includes in its capital budget all of the money to build a new housing subdivision on a base. Consider the cost to build 500 housing units, pave the streets, add water and electric, and so on. The advantage is that, at the end of the construction, everything is paid for. The problem is finding enough money at one time to make these huge purchases. There are many worthy projects and limited funds.

In the civilian world, the builder borrows the money and pays back the bank over time. So if they have 500 new units all paying in rent, they make sure that their bank payments and operating expenses are well below that amount. After 30 years of making these payments, they own the property. Using someone else's money like this allows many things to be built right now. This is the idea behind privatization. By running base housing as a self-supporting business, the government does not tie up its money in houses, and someone else has the headaches of maintaining them.

Many bases have taken this approach. Private companies are contracted to renovate, replace, or build new housing. There have been problems, but privatization as a concept is here to stay.

When a base uses a privatized housing program (some bases have both the traditional base housing and privatized operations), service members are "referred" to the privatized housing operator. They have the choice of renting from the operators or renting in town. This is different from a base housing official telling you where you will live in the housing neighborhood (whether you like the spot or not).

Your "privatized" rent equals your BAH and is paid by allotment. You sign a lease to stay there, just as with a civilian rental. Leases typically are for six months and then a month at a time after that. If your BAH increases, the allotment must increase to ensure that all of the BASH goes to the contractor.

Each privatized operation is different. If an operator's occupancy rates fall below a certain threshold, the operator is permitted to rent to retirees and, in some cases, government civilians.

Basic Allowance for Housing (BAH)

The government provides housing (*BAH*) to every service member as bachelor enlisted quarters or bachelor officer quarters. These facilities are found on every base. However, married service members prefer to reside with their spouse and children. To do this, they need housing separate from the barracks. So instead of a spot in the barracks, the government provides a tax-free housing allowance to these service members so they can rent appropriate family quarters.

How Much Do I Get?

The BAH program provides service members money to cover the costs of renting housing on the civilian market. It is set separately for each base and adjusted annually. It assumes that service members will live within a one-hour commute or 20 miles of their duty assignment.

BAH is based on your pay grade, your zip code, and whether you have dependents. It begins with a base amount that all qualified

def•i•ni•tion

Today's **BAH** is actually BAH-II. In the beginning was Basic Allowance for Quarters (BAQ), which was followed by BAH-I. Each program is a refinement of the previous one that worked to make the government housing allowance more fair to service members.

personnel of that rank receive. This amount is adjusted up to reflect the cost of the local rental market. The higher your pay grade, the larger the housing unit that you are entitled to and, thus, the greater the amount of BAH you are provided. The only distinction is with or without dependents, not in the number of dependents.

Once every year, the local rental market is surveyed and rates are adjusted either up or down. This is a problem for someone who has signed a lease. If their BAH goes down, out-of-pocket expenses increase. Also landlords typically increase rents annually to keep pace with costs.

To avoid this problem, BAH is provided with rate protection. It never goes down, but it may go up if the BAH rate increases. Rate protection means that, for as long as you are drawing BAH at that base, it will never go down, even if the local rate has declined. You receive any published BAH increase, but no decrease. Service members are entitled to the BAH rates published January 1 or the amount of housing allowance they received on December 31, whichever is larger. Rate protection continues until the service member changes duty stations, is reduced in rank, or no long has eligible dependents.

If you are promoted, your BAH is changed to the rate for your new (higher) rank. However, if the new rank's BAH is less than your old BAH amount (due to rate protections), you receive the old BAH rate instead. To determine your BAH rate, use the calculator at http://perdiem.hqda.pentagon.mil/perdiem/bah.html.

Four different types of BAH categories are available to each rank:

- BAH with dependents
- BAH without dependents
- BAH-DIFF
- BAH-RC/Transient

And a Dependent Is ...

A dependent is someone for whom the service member provides at least half of their financial support. Typically this is a spouse and children. It may also be parents, stepparents, stepchildren, and so on. A child must be less than 21 years old, or less than 23 if in full-time attendance at an institution of higher education.

Promptly report any changes in your number of dependents to your unit personnel office. For example, a divorce in which no children are involved would mean zero dependents and a movement from the BAH with dependents rate to the BAH without dependents rate. Delays in reporting this change may result in overpayments that will be collected from future pay.

BAH with Dependents

"With dependents" means that you are financially supporting a family member, whether you live with someone or far away. The amount is the same if you have 1 dependent or 20. If you live in base housing with your dependents, the government keeps your BAH in exchange for use of the housing unit and utilities. However, sometimes you will draw BAH with dependents who are not present.

- During temporary duty assignments, such as training

- During unaccompanied overseas assignments

If your dependents move away and you remain, you must vacate base housing (it is intended for families). However, you are still entitled to BAH with dependents because the military requires you to financially support your dependents.

For Your Benefits

If both a husband and wife are military members, BAH with dependents is paid to the higher-ranking member and BAH without dependents is paid to the spouse. However, if both are in the military and there are no children, they both receive the BAH without dependents rate.

BAH Without Dependents

BAH without dependents is for service members who do not have dependents and who have permission to move out of government-supplied bachelor quarters into town. This is common for assignments that are not near any military housing, such as recruiters or small military sites. BAH without dependents is available to senior enlisted personnel and officers everywhere on request.

BAH-DIFF

BAH-DIFF is paid to service members who provide child support (either court ordered or voluntary). The service member may still reside in government-provided bachelor quarters. Child support payments must be at least as much as the BAH-DIFF allowance. BAH-DIFF is usually increased annually. You cannot receive both Partial BAH and BAH-DIFF at the same time.

BAH-RC/Transient

BAH-RC/Transient is a housing allowance for personnel who are in transit or on active duty less than 30 days, such as a National Guardsman attending annual training. It also applies when an active duty service member is in transit from selected areas where no prior BAH rate existed. It is based on your rank and does not vary by geographic location.

BAH-RC/T is for only the first 30 days of active duty. After that, Guard/Reserve are paid the normal BAH for their pay grade, dependent status, and location. If Guard/Reserve are mobilized for a contingency operation, they receive active duty BAH from the first day.

Partial BAH

A member without dependents who is living in government quarters is entitled to a Partial BAH.

Overseas Housing Allowance

A uniformed service member stationed overseas (except in Alaska and Hawaii), including U.S. protectorates, who is not furnished government housing is eligible for an Overseas Housing Allowance (OHA). OHA compensates members for the majority of housing expenses. It is based on local rental surveys.

For Your Benefits

OHA rates are adjusted if currency exchange rates change more than 5 percent. This may be done as often as twice per month.

OHA is a reimbursement with three components:

◆ Rent up to a local maximum amount

◆ Utilities allowance, paid monthly

◆ Move-in Housing Allowance, which is made up of a fixed sum to make a housing unit habitable, a one-time payment to cover nonrefundable rental charges, and the costs of upgrading housing security

The OHA calculator is at http://perdiem.hqda.pentagon.mil/perdiem/allooha.html

The Least You Need to Know

- All military services view improved on-base quarters as essential to troop retention.

- Sailors can look forward to more berthing space on newer ships.

- Know which type of Basic Allowance for Housing rate you qualify for.

- Promptly report changes in the number of your dependents to your personnel office.

6

Retiring Takes Careful Planning

In This Chapter

- ◆ What military retirement really means
- ◆ Which retirement deal you get
- ◆ The finer points of retirement pay
- ◆ Government pension supplements

Of all military benefits, the most financially valuable is the chance to retire as young as 37 and draw a paycheck for the rest of your life. The amount of money paid per month depends upon several factors. If your needs are simple, that amount may be enough to get by, but most people take a full-time job and then work on obtaining a civilian retirement package as well.

Military retirement involves much more than just a check. It includes a wide range of benefits, such as medical and recreational, space-available travel, and more. All are explained in their respective chapters.

Most private businesses have quietly dropped pension plans from their benefits offerings. Aside from government jobs, civilian employers find pensions too expensive to fund and too much hassle to manage. Instead, companies provide matched savings plans or a combination of other plans. The trick is to add these plans to a military pension and Social Security, to make the grey-haired years rather cozy.

Know Your DIEM Date

Imagine the military offering someone a deal. The military will provide a specific amount of pay and benefits (like the current retirement plan) in exchange for future services. The point at which the deal is accepted (signed enlistment papers, acceptance of a commission, and so on) is where the retirement plan portion of the benefits is "frozen." This is known as a *DIEM* date.

def•i•ni•tion

> Do not confused **DIEM** with the Pay Entry Base Date (PEBD). They are determined by different rules and are used for different things. DIEM is used only to identify which retirement program a service member falls under. It does not indicate the number of years of qualifying service to earn a retirement. The Pay Entry Base Date is the actual date of original entry in the service.

Several active duty retirement programs are currently in place. The key to knowing which program you belong to is your DIEM (Date of Initial Entry to the Military) date. A DIEM (alternately known as a DIEUS—Date of Initial Entry Uniformed Services) is the first day of military service (active or Reserve). This date never changes, even if the service member leaves the service and later rejoins it.

The DIEM is the first day of …

- Delayed-entry enlistment.
- Entry to a military academy or academy prep school.
- Obligation to military service in a ROTC program.

Go Away, I'm Retired

Technically, military retirement pay is reduced pay for reduced services. It is paid once per month—and the services know where to find you if they want you to come back!

However, like all things military, each branch of the uniformed services complicates the simple in its own way.

Navy/Marines retired members with fewer than 30 years of service are transferred to the Fleet Reserve/Fleet Marine Corps Reserve until they reach 30 years. Then they are considered to be retired. The Army and Air Force consider anyone retiring with at least 20 years of service to be retired. In both cases, the pay and benefits are the same.

And speaking of benefits, Department of Defense (DoD) Directive 1352.1 says that the secretary of a military department can order any retired service member to active duty to perform duties necessary to the national defense. However, the longer someone is retired, the less likely that person is to be recalled. These DoD categories are used for recalling retirees:

- **Category I**—Nondisability military retirees under age 60, retired fewer than five years

- **Category II**—Nondisability military retirees under age 60, retired five years or more

- **Category III**—Military retirees, including those retired for disability, other than Category I or II retirees

Attention!

Unlike with civilian retirement programs, qualifying for a military retirement is an all-or-nothing affair. Unless someone is officially granted an early retirement, personnel must stay at least 20 qualifying years of service or they get nothing.

Uniformed services pensions are the government's way of saying, "Thanks for the loyal service, here's some money—good-bye." Assuming that you make it to retirement age, a pension can be worth a lot of cash. The government awards pensions for a variety of reasons.

Early Retirement

Early retirement is a manpower-management tool. Whenever the military feels that there are too many people in the upper ranks or just wants to reduce the number of people in the military, it may offer a reduced retirement at 15 years. Pay is reduced proportionally for the number of years the person retired early. Other than a smaller check, the retiree receives the rest of the regular retirement benefits. Early retirement comes along only when the military wants to shrink, so don't look for it anytime soon.

Disability Retirement

Service members who become disabled while on duty may be medically retired and receive a disability retirement. This may be from an accident or a wartime injury. Disability retirement may be temporary or permanent.

The government provides disability pensions to needy wartime veterans who are disabled due to their military service. They may also be provided to needy surviving spouses and children of wartime veterans.

Temporary Disability Retired

When service members develop a medical condition that prevents them from performing military duties, they may be recommended for a temporary disability pension. The key is the stability of the medical condition. If the condition may improve to the point at which they can resume normal duties, a temporary disability pension may be assigned instead of a permanent one. Service members in this category receive at least 50 percent (and as much as 75 percent) of their last base pay amount.

Temporary disabled pensioners must undergo a physical exam every 18 months to determine whether they can return to duty or continue in the temporary disability program. No one can remain in this status for more than five years. At that time, they are either returned to duty or transferred to permanently disabled retirement status.

Permanent Disability Retirement

Service members whom a medical board determines to be 30 percent or more disabled with no hope of returning to full duties are transferred to the Permanently Disabled Retirement program. To qualify, the service member must have at least eight years of active service, or the injury must have occurred in the line of duty. Those with limited disabilities may be retained by their service, depending on individual circumstances.

For Your Benefits

Service members with disabilities 20 percent or less are discharged. They may receive a severance compensation package. These people should contact the Veterans Administration to see if they are eligible for a disability pension. However, if they are granted a VA disability rating, they must pay back the severance pay before disability benefits begin.

Permanent disability retired pay is calculated in three ways. The Defense Finance and Accounting Service (DFAS) calculates all three ways and applies the one that provides the largest amount of retired pay. However, the minimum disability retirement is 30 percent of base pay.

1. Multiply the service member's current base pay (or the average of the highest 36 months of active duty pay) by the percent of disability.

2. Multiply the years of active service by 2.5 percent times the current base pay or the average of the highest 36 months of pay.

3. Service members with at least 20 years of service and whose disability is deemed permanent are retired permanently in disability status. Their retirement pay is calculated using whichever of the two formulas above that apply. However, the minimum retirement pay for this category is 50%.

Active Duty Retirement

Service members can retire from active duty service with as little as 20 years of service. This is quite a deal. Service members as young as 37 years old can retire at half pay for the rest of their life—or more than half pay if they choose to remain in the military longer. At 30 years of service, everyone on active duty must retire, except for a selected few provided waivers for extended service.

Just to show the world that the military can complicate something as simple as a retirement system, the military developed three different pay schemes for nondisability retirement: Final Pay, High-3, and CSB/REDUX. Eligibility is based on the service member's DIEM date.

Over time, money buys less. This is due to economic inflation, occasional price increases in things like fuel, and ever-increasing taxes. To compensate for this erosion in buying power, a cost of living adjustment (COLA) is provided. Like other kinds of colas, this one is sweet. The COLA for the Final Pay plan is set based on the Consumer Price Index (CPI).

This is a different index than the one used for active duty annual pay raises. The index used for active duty pay raises is based upon average civilian wage increases. Thus, retirement pay COLAs and annual active duty pay raises will differ.

Final Pay

Probably the easiest to understand is the "old" retirement plan. If the service person joined before September 8, 1980, retirement is 50 percent of base pay for that rank and 20 years of service. Each additional year of service increases the pension by 2.5 percent, plus any pay increase for longevity (usually every two years), plus any promotions. A service member with 25 years of service at retirement would receive 2.5 percent × 25 = 62.5 percent of base pay.

Attention!

Final Pay is 50 percent of your base pay at 20 years, plus 2.5 percent of base pay for each year between 20 and 30 years, for a maximum of 75 percent of base pay for 30 years of active service. Final Pay's annual COLA increase is equal to the CPI.

For example, if the base pay for your rank and number of years of service was $3,000 per month, at 20 years, the eligible pension would be $3,000 × 50 percent, or $1,500 per month. If you retired with 20 years of service at 60 years old and lived until you're 80, you would draw $1,500 per month for 20 years ($360,000 total). But if you retired with 25 years of service at 60 and lived to 80, you would draw $1,875 per month for 20 years ($450,000 total). So you would earn $90,000 more in retirement for five more years of service. Only you can decide the "benefit" of staying in or getting out.

High-3

The High-3 retirement plan applies to these people:

◆ Those who entered military service on or after September 8, 1980, but before August 1, 1986

◆ Those who entered on or after August 1, 1986, and declined the Career Status Bonus and REDUX retirement plan (CSB/REDUX—discussed next)

High-3 determines retirement pay as follows:

1. Start with a percentage of base pay based on number of years of service.

2. Multiply by the average of the highest 36 months of base pay—typically the last three years. (In a few cases, the highest three years of base pay may not be the last three years. For example, they may have been the ones just before a demotion.)

For High-3 retirees, the COLA is equal to the CPI.

Attention! _____

High-3 Pay is 50 percent of your highest 36 months average base pay at 20 years, plus 2.5 percent of base pay for each year between 20 and 30 years, for a maximum of 75 percent of base pay for 30 years of active service. High-3 Pay's annual COLA increase is equal to the CPI.

CSB/REDUX

So if you entered the military on or after August 1, 1986, and did not request a Career Status Bonus, you would fall under the CSB/REDUX plan. REDUX was an attempt to reduce the 20-year retirement payout, to encourage military personnel to stay in for the full 30 years. However, since there are mandatory retirement points for those below the rank of E-9 and O6, this is a pay cut without hope of gaining the full amount.

Choose carefully. Once the CSB/REDUX application is accepted, you cannot change that option. Few people feel the $30,000 is equal to what is lost.

In the fifteenth year of service, you can request a $30,000 Career Status Bonus (hello new Vette!). If you do, you must remain in the service until your twentieth year, but your retirement pay will be less than under the other plans. If you leave before your twentieth year, you must repay a prorated amount of the bonus to the government. At the service member's option, the bonus may be paid as a lump sum or in install-ments over time (to minimize taxes on it). The bonus is normally paid at the 15-year and 3-month marks.

The cash bonus is intended for long-sighted people to invest and supplement their retirement, or to address immediate needs, such as college tuition, a down payment on a retirement home, or a new bass boat. If you retire before your thirtieth year, your pension will be less than that of those who did not select the bonus. However, if you stick it out for the full 30 years, your pension will be as much as the High-3 retirement option—plus you have the extra cash up front.

For Your Benefits _____

REDUX was revised by the FY2000 National Defense Authorization Act. A $30,000 Career Status Bonus (CSB) was added for those who accept the REDUX retirement system. Individuals formerly under REDUX may now choose between the High-3 and CSB/REDUX sys-tems.

REDUX uses a different formula for calculating the amount of base pay paid as retirement pay. To begin, REDUX provides 40 percent (not 50 percent, like the other plans) of base pay for retirement at 20 years. For each year beyond 20 years, the percentage of base pay applied to retirement increases 3.5 percent. It takes 10 years for the percentage of base pay to catch up with that of the High-3 plan.

CSB/REDUX also treats COLAs differently. The COLA for a CSB/REDUX retirement is CPI minus 1 percent, noticeably less than the other plans. (If the CPI is around 3 percent, losing 1 percent is a lot. If inflation is high and the CPI is 10 percent, the impact seems less.)

Just when the whole thing starts to make sense and you know which plan to choose, there is yet another wrinkle to CSB/REDUX. When someone retiring under CSB/REDUX reaches 62 years of age, a new wrinkle is added. At that point, the retirement pay package is recalculated as if the retiree retired under High-3, to include all of the full CPI COLAs from retirement to age 62. However, from that point forward, the COLA remains at CPI minus 1 percent.

So how do they stack up? This table provides a side-by-side comparison of the three plans.

Retirement Plan	Base Pay Used	% at 20 Years	Multiplier	COLA	Re-adjustment	Bonus
Final Pay	Final Base Pay	50%	2.5% per year	CPI	None	None
High-3	Average Highest 3 years	50%	2.5% per year	CPI	None	None
CSB/ REDUX	Average Highest 3 Years	40%	3.5% per year	CPI less 1%	At 62, recalculates retirement pay as High-3 plan	$30,000 at 15th year

The Finer Points of Retirement Pay

Like everything else military, there are some "oh, by the way" variations to keep in mind.

Garnishments/Withholdings

When the courts must compel someone to pay their debts directly through a payroll deduction, it is known as a pay garnishment. Military retirement pay cannot be garnished for commercial debts, such as bank loans or car financing. However, it is fair game for garnishment to pay alimony, child support, debts owed to the government, and PX/BX deferred payment plans.

Divorce, Child Support, and Spousal Support

Divorce laws vary by state. Some states treat retired pay as joint property and divide it between the unhappy couple. Whenever the retirement check comes, think of this as your spouse's permanent reminder of your years together. Before parting company, you might move to a state that thinks the way you do.

Keep Your Pay Records Current

It is difficult for the government to send retirement checks if they do not know where you are! Ensure that DFAS is informed of any changes of address and any changes in account information for directly deposited funds. Some changes require a paper form and signature, so allow time for processing.

Contact DFAS at 1-800-321-1080 or 216-522-5955 or www.dfas.mil.

Their mailing address is:

Defense Finance and Accounting Service
Cleveland Center Retired Pay Operations (Code PPR)
PO Box 99191
Cleveland, OH 44199-1126

Foreign Employment of Retirees Can Cause Problems

Before accepting employment with a foreign government, obtain permission from the secretary of your service and the Office of Secretary of State. Otherwise, retirement pay may be withheld during the foreign employment.

Concurrent Receipt—Two Pensions at Once

The term *concurrent receipt* describes receiving both a military pension and VA disability compensation. Until 2004, recipients had to waive all or part of their military retirement pay. The law has been changed to permit the receipt of both pensions at the same time. This change is being phased in between 2004 and 2013.

Attention!

DFAS refers to this situation as concurrent retirement and disability pay.

To qualify for concurrent receipt, retired service members must have more than 20 years of service (which qualifies them for their regular pension) and be rated by the VA as 50 percent disabled or more. Concurrent receipt also applies to U.S. Code Chapter 61 medical retirees and Reserve/National Guard in retired pay status.

An alternative situation applies to people receiving 100 percent from the VA due to their unemployability code. Their pay is currently reduced, but this reduction is being phased out through 2014.

Combining Military and Federal Civil Service Retirements

In some cases, retirees from both the military and federal civil service may make more money if they waive their military pension and combine those years of service with their civilian federal service. This decision should be made in the last months before beginning the civilian service retirement. Consult both DFAS and the civilian retirement office before making this selection.

However, not everyone can do this. Combining a federal civil service pension with a military Reserve/National Guard pension is not possible.

Thrift Savings Plan (TSP)

The Thrift Savings Plan is a way of setting aside today's money for tomorrow's retirement. It gives military members the same sort of tax savings that private companies provide with their 401(k) retirement savings plans. The military plan is based on a similar plan originally created for government civilian workers.

TSP contributions should be made only if the money can stay there until retirement. It is not suitable for short-term savings. Significant tax penalties accompany early withdrawal of funds.

TSP is optional and handled as a payroll deduction. It allows contributions of up to 100 percent of pay toward the account, up to the current limits established by the Internal Revenue Service. No federal or state income tax is paid on the money deducted for TSP. These funds are taxed when the money is withdrawn at retirement.

The TSP savings plan offers a list of investments that participants can choose from. Money in a TSP account is invested in mutual funds selected by the account's owner. Participants can move money between investments as desired through the TSP website.

Enroll in the military TSP through the Defense Finance and Accounting service website: https://mypay.dfas.mil/mypay.aspx. This is the same place where you can change the monthly contribution. Another way to enroll is to submit a form TSP-U-1, available at local military finance offices.

Most people find payroll deductions the easiest way to save money. It kills them to write a check for their investments, but if the money is removed before they touch it, they don't seem to miss it. As an important bonus, more goes into the account. If $500 is sent to TSP, this is similar to reducing take-home pay by $400 because the other $100 would have gone to taxes. Therefore, more goes toward savings than if the money was received and then sent to investment. (Uncle Sam collects the taxes when the account is withdrawn—hopefully during retirement, when income is already low. And the profit from the investments grows at tax-free rates.)

Attention!

Civilian workers' contributions to TSP receive matching funds because it is a part of their retirement plan. TSP is a supplement to the military pension plan, so no matching funds are provided. But it would not be a government program if there weren't exceptions. The service secretaries are authorized to provide matching funds as an incentive for recruiting into hard-to-fill jobs. These exceptions start and stop depending on the needs of the service.

TSP has many options. Among these is the opportunity to borrow a portion of the money in the account for personal use and then repay the money, plus interest, over time. In a sense, this is a loan from you to you. However, it must be repaid according to the program's policies, or it will be assessed as an early withdrawal and will be subject to an income tax penalty.

Loans outstanding at discharge must be promptly repaid, or the money will be taxed as an early (preretirement) distribution from the account. The penalty is currently an additional 10 percent income tax (and this changes at the whim of the IRS).

When departing the military …

- ◆ If you have less than $200 in the TSP account, a check is automatically sent to you.

- ◆ If the account holds more than $200, it can remain in TSP to grow over time or for a later withdrawal. Also a portion of the account can be withdrawn, leaving the remainder in the account.

To avoid a big tax bill, roll the TSP proceeds into an individual retirement account after you leave the service. This retains the tax-deferred status. Withdrawals from TSP become taxable income. The tax-deferred status is maintained if all funds are promptly deposited into an employer's 401(k) account or a personal IRA account within 60 days. Otherwise, the funds become taxable income (plus a tax penalty).

Contact the plan administrator for the name of the institution the TSP withdrawal will be added to. The administrator can provide paperwork to keep the tax wolves at bay.

Hot Scoop _____

The latest information on TSP is available at www.tsp.gov.

The purpose of TSP is to supplement retirement pensions. The year following April 1 of the year the TSP owner reaches 70½, the owner must begin to withdraw amounts from the account monthly.

Social Security

Service members pay into Social Security (as if they have a choice) and are entitled to receive retirements from that program. Military retirement pay is not reduced when receiving Social Security benefits.

Social Security benefits are determined by a complex formula that includes such factors as lifetime earnings and inflation. Many military retirees soon tire of bass fishing and take up a civilian career. This income may significantly increase the lifetime earnings used in the Social Security calculation.

Social Security automatically provides an annual statement of personal earnings and benefits to every working citizen 25 years or older. These statements provide a year-by-year breakdown of earnings (your opportunity to suggest corrections) and the estimated benefits at retirement or in case of disability. For the latest details, contact the Social Security Administration at www.ssa.gov.

The Least You Need to Know

- ◆ Keep your contact information up-to-date at DFAS.
- ◆ Know which retirement program you qualify for.
- ◆ Stuff into TSP only money that you can afford to leave there.
- ◆ Watch the DFAS and TSP websites for the latest information.

Chapter 7

Insuring Your Family's Future

In This Chapter

- ◆ Signing up before you sign off
- ◆ Obtaining life insurance for the military family
- ◆ Converting your active duty insurance to a veteran's policy
- ◆ Securing long-term care coverage for retirees

We all dislike considering the end of our days. Often we put off planning for the financial support of those we will leave behind. The emotional pain of death is significant, but often a family's financial loss can linger for many years. Life insurance is one way to continue providing financial support to your family after your death.

Insurance can be expensive. Many military members have spouses, children, and parents to provide for. Life insurance is the largest part of financial wealth service members pass on to their survivors. The uniformed services offer low-cost term life insurance to all members who want it.

"Term" insurance is the lowest-cost form of life insurance. It gathers no cash value over the years. Term life insurance coverage is purchased for a set period of time. If you die during the term of coverage, the death benefit is paid to your beneficiary. A beneficiary is the person you designate to receive the insurance payment after you die.

These insurance programs are in addition to the military death benefit program, which pays $12,000 for the survivors of those who die while on active duty or inactive duty for training. If the death occurs in a designated combat zone or while training for combat, the death benefit is $100,000.

Serviceman's Group Life Insurance (SGLI)

Serviceman's Group Life Insurance (SGLI) is term life insurance sold to military personnel at a reduced rate. It provides for the financial needs of surviving spouses, children, and parents if the service member dies. The armed forces use a wide range of large and dangerous equipment in some rather uncivilized places. SGLI benefits are paid for death from any cause, at any time that the insurance is in force. Death does not need to be in the line of duty in a war zone.

As a group, the armed forces pose a serious insurance problem. When the bullets are flying (for a declared war, undeclared war, police action, conflict, skirmish, rescue mission, etc.), many soldiers can be killed. Consequently, insurance companies want a lot of money to cover this risk. Most private life insurance policies have a "war clause" that specifically states they will not pay for someone killed in a war. To address this need, the government created low-cost term life insurance that gathers no cash value during its existence but provides financial security in the event of a service member's death.

Eligibility

SGLI is open to these people:

- Active duty service members
- Ready Guard/Reserve members
- Commissioned Corps of the National Oceanic and Atmospheric Administration
- Public Health Service
- Cadets and midshipmen of the service academies
- Members of the Reserve Officer Training Corps

Hot Scoop

To estimate how much life insurance you might need, go to www.insurance.va.gov/sgliSite/calcuator/Lifelns101.htm.

Coverage

Use the following to determine when are you covered:

◆ If you are on active duty, or in a Reserve or National Guard unit and assigned to drill at least 12 periods per year, you are covered every day of the year. You are also covered for the first 120 days after leaving the service.

◆ If you are in the Guard or Reserve and drill only a few days of the year, you are provided part-time coverage. Part-time coverage also applies to members of the Individual Ready Reserve (IRR) who are called up for a single-day muster.

◆ If you are totally disabled when discharged, you are provided free coverage for two years.

Beneficiaries

Your first encounter with Serviceman's Group Life Insurance was likely during your first days of military service. At that time, each recruit who signed up for the coverage provided the name and contact information of the person(s) who would benefit from the insurance if the service member dies. Beneficiaries are usually a spouse and children (if any), or the service member's parents if there are no dependents.

More than one person can be designated as the beneficiary. When making this choice, be sure to specify what portion of the benefit each will receive. This can be designated as a percentage, by a specific amount, or as a fraction. Otherwise, multiple beneficiaries will receive equal shares.

You are responsible for keeping the beneficiary information up-to-date for the birth of children, a marriage, a divorce, or other life event. You make changes through your unit administrative section. You may change or cancel beneficiaries at any time. To do so, complete a new Form SGLV 8286 in your unit personnel office. It is effective on the date it is received.

With the increase in single-parent families, naming an SLGI beneficiary has become a bit more complicated. If the beneficiary is a dependent younger than 18 years old, the money must be placed in trust until he or she reaches age 18. Single parents must plan ahead to avoid the delay and expense of a court-appointed guardian by consulting with an attorney to designate a trustee of the minor beneficiary.

This leads to another complication. The trustee cannot access the money to pay for the child's care while he or she grows up. At this time, the law does not provide for early distributions from the trust fund, but the issue is in the courts. Be sure the trustee is willing to care for the child or children from his or her own financial resources.

In years past, the lazy way to designate beneficiaries was to write the words "By Law" in the beneficiary section. This means that the beneficiary of the policy is determined by the law governing estates. This practice is discouraged. However, if a specific beneficiary is not identified, SGLI goes down this list until someone is found to hand the money to:

1. The surviving spouse of the member

2. Surviving children in equal shares

3. The parents in equal shares

4. A duly appointed executor or administrator of the insured's estate

5. Other next of kin

Family SGLI (Spousal Coverage)

The Family Serviceman's Group Life Insurance program provides free insurance for children and optional term life insurance for spouses. Eligibility for spouse coverage requires that you also purchase some coverage under SGLI. A spouse can be covered for up to $100,000 or for up to the amount of your SGLI coverage, whichever is less. FSGLI automatically provides $10,000 of free term life insurance for each dependent child while you maintain SGLI coverage.

> **Attention!**
>
> Public Law 109-13 requires notifying a service member's spouse if there is a change of beneficiary designation. However, you are still free to choose anyone you want.

A service member who is married to another service member can be insured under both the FSGLI and SGLI programs at the same time. This provides a maximum coverage amount of $500,000.

What's the Cost?

Serviceman's Group Life Insurance coverage can be purchased in $50,000 increments for 7cents per month, per thousand dollars of coverage. The cost per thousand is adjusted up or down from time to time based on the program costs. It was last increased in 2006. Coverage for $400,000 costs $28 per month, plus a mandatory $1 additional per month for *Traumatic Injury Protection coverage (TSGLI)*.

Term insurance from civilian sources is priced based on the covered person's age. Costs are escalated over the years as the payout amount goes down. Roughly, SGLI is 20 percent of the cost of comparable civilian insurance. SGLI has one price for all ages (whereas civilian insurance is based on age). This makes it more of a bargain for older service members, and it is a valued benefit for Guard/Reserve members.

def•i•ni•tion

Traumatic Injury Protection coverage (TSGLI) helps severely injured Soldiers through their time of need with a one-time payment.

Spousal coverage is offered in $10,000 increments up to $100,000. The cost is based on the spouse's age. It ranges from $5.50 per month for 35 years old and younger, up to $52 per month for age 60 and over.

Individual Ready Reserve (IRR) members are charged $1.25 for $400,000 of coverage to support their one-day annual musters.

Pay Out

Casualty assistance officers provide to the deceased person's beneficiary an SGLV Form 8283, "Claim for Death Benefits." The beneficiary completes and submits this form to the Office of Serviceman's Group Life Insurance (the address is on the form) to proceed with the payout process.

SGLI benefits are payable upon the death of the covered person. The money may be paid as a lump sum or in 36 equal monthly installments, based on what you selected when identifying your beneficiary. If no option is selected, benefits are paid as a lump sum. These benefits are exempt from income tax but, based on the total value of the estate, may be subject to an estate tax. SGLI benefits are exempt from claims by creditors of the insured or creditors of the beneficiary.

SGLI does not send over an armored car full of money or mail a check. It opens an interest-bearing account and places the money in it. This puts the money in a safe place while beneficiaries decide what to do with it. The beneficiary can write drafts to make withdrawals from the account.

Serviceman's Group Life Insurance offers free Beneficiary Financial Counseling Services (BFCS) from a company called FinancialPoint. The financial counselors have no products to sell and do not receive a commission for their services. Telephone assistance is provided for 12 months. Contact FinancialPoint at 1-888-243-7351 or at BFCS@FinancialPoint.com.

FinancialPoint provides these products:

◆ Comprehensive financial-planning questionnaires and asset-management information.

◆ A customized and comprehensive financial plan with information based on an analysis of the financial data you submit.

Accelerated Payout

Sometimes the financial burden on the family of a terminally ill service member is crushing. The Accelerated Benefit Option (ABO) permits a service member's spouse to draw up to 50 percent of the SGLI benefit assigned to him or her. However, only a service member with nine months or less left to live can apply for this benefit. If the spouse is terminally ill and covered under Family SGLI, the service member can apply for accelerated payment of half of the benefit. Request accelerated payments in this way:

◆ SGLI and VGLI policyholders, use 8284, "Servicemember/Veteran Accelerated Benefits Option Form."

◆ Spouses covered under Family SGLI, use 8284A, "Servicemember Family Coverage Accelerated Benefits Option Form."

Veterans Group Life Insurance (VGLI)

Leaving military service for the disorganized world of civilians can be confusing. So many choices and things to do—without anyone to tell you what to do and when to do it! One benefit that follows you from uniform to business suit is a version of SGLI called Veterans Group Life Insurance (VGLI). VGLI converts SGLI coverage to renewable term insurance. Service members with full-time SGLI coverage are eligible for VGLI upon release from service.

Converting SGLI to VGLI requires (what else?) submitting a form (SGLV 8714—"Application for Veteran's Group Life Insurance").

Eligibility

Two different groups are eligible to convert from SGLI to VGLI. If you apply within 120 days of separation from the service, an application plus the premium is enough. If you apply after 120 days and before one year and 120 days after separation, evidence of good health may be required. Beyond one year and 120 days, you are not eligible for this program.

Cost

VGLI coverage is sold in $10,000 increments up to $400,000 or the amount of SGLI you had in force upon separation (whichever is less). Premiums are based on coverage amount desired and either your age on the 121st day after your separation or your age on the date coverage is approved, whichever is later. Premiums change whenever you move into the next age bracket. Prices are subject to change, but in 2007, if you are under 29 years old, the monthly premium is $32. However, if you are between 50 and 54 years old, the monthly rate is $160.

Insurance premiums are due monthly. You can save money by paying in advance for larger periods of time. There is a 2.5 percent discount for paying quarterly instead of monthly, a 3.75 percent discount for paying semiannually, and a 5 percent discount for paying annually.

Hot Scoop

Find out what your VGLI premiums will be at www. insurance.va.gov/sgliSite/VGLI/ VGLI%20rates.htm.

Converting Your Government Policy to a Commercial One

You have the option of converting your SGLI or VGLI policy to an individual policy of life insurance with a commercial company. You may convert up to the amount of coverage you hold. You will be issued an individual policy at the company's standard premium rate, regardless of your health. No disability or other supplemental benefits are provided on converted policies.

To convert coverage, you must …

◆ Select a company from the list of participating companies. This list is found at www.insurance.va.gov/sgliSite/forms/ParticList.htm.

◆ Apply to that company's local sales office.

◆ Obtain a letter from OSGLI verifying coverage.

◆ Give a copy of that notice to the agent who takes the application.

Traumatic Benefits Under SGLI

Traumatic Serviceman's Group Life Insurance (TSGLI) is an additional benefit by SGLI that provides payment to anyone covered by SGLI who sustains a traumatic injury that results in certain severe losses. The only way to decline TSGLI coverage is to decline basic SGLI coverage. This additional benefit is not available for Family SGLI. Payments made by TSGLI have no impact on the amount available under SGLI.

TSGLI is paid for by a mandatory $1 tacked on to the SGLI monthly fee. However, if you have part-time SGLI, the fee is $1 per year. IRR personnel on a one-day muster receive this benefit for free.

The service member is the beneficiary of this program. The payout cannot be assigned to another person, although a legal guardian may receive the cash if you are incapacitated. TSGLI provides the following:

◆ $100,000 for loss of sight in both eyes or hearing in both ears

◆ $50,000 for loss of sight in one eye

◆ $50,000 for loss of one hand at or above the wrist, or one foot at or above the ankle

◆ $50,000 for loss of thumb and index finger of same hand

To file a claim under TSGLI, you must …

◆ Be insured by SGLI.

◆ Incur a loss as a direct result of a traumatic injury.

- Have suffered the traumatic injury before midnight of the day that you separate from the uniformed services.

- Suffer a scheduled loss within two years (730 days) of the traumatic injury.

- Survive for a period of not less than seven full days from the date of the traumatic injury.

The first step of filing a claim is to obtain TSGLI Certification Form GL.2005.261. It is available from the Office of Serviceman's Group Life Insurance at 1-800-419-1473 or by e-mail at osgli.claims@prudential.com.

The second step is to work with your service department point of contact to begin the certification process. The claim form requires information from the service member (or guardian), the attending medical personnel, and the branch of service. All three sections must be completed.

If the claim is rejected, you can appeal through the service department point of contact. Submit written appeals within 12 months of the day it was denied.

Federal Long-Term Care Insurance Program (FLTCIP)

In addition to life insurance, another optional insurance program provides for long-term care. This program provides care if you can no longer perform everyday tasks due to chronic illness, injury, disability, or the aging process. Long-term care also includes supervision necessary due to a severe cognitive impairment, such as Alzheimer's disease. Long-term care is the most expensive type of care you will ever need.

Long-term care is not a cure. Care may span years—perhaps for the rest of your life—and can be expensive, depending on the type of care needed and where that care is received. Long-term care insurance is one way of helping to pay for these expenses.

Do not confuse long-term care with short-term medical care. Long-term care is not ...

- Care that you receive in the hospital or your doctor's office.

- Care you need to get well from a sickness or an injury.

- Short-term rehabilitation from an accident.

- Recuperation from surgery.

Long-term care is not just for old people. Driving and sports accidents, strokes, disabling illnesses, and a wide range of tragedies may strike people of any age. About 40 percent of the people receiving long-term care are under 64 years of age.

As your body ages, the likelihood of needing long-term care increases. In general, the longer you live, the higher your odds are of needing long-term care. Most long-term care is provided in the home rather than in a nursing home. The cost of care provided by friends and family is hard to estimate. The caregiver may have to leave a job. Perhaps a price is paid in emotional stress.

Eligibility

The Federal Long-Term Care Insurance Program (FLTCIP) is provided to a wide range of federal employees and their family members:

- Active and retired members of the uniformed services

- Active members of the Selected Reserve

- Retired "grey" Reservists, even if they are not yet receiving retirement pay

- Current spouses of eligible persons

- Adult children of living eligible persons

- Parents, parents-in-law, and stepparents of active members of the uniformed services

- Surviving spouses receiving a survivor annuity

Cost

The cost for this insurance is based on age. Once someone joins the program, his or her premium remains the same unless the Office of Personnel Management raises it.

> **Hot Scoop** _____
>
> To contact the Federal Long-Term Care Insurance Program, call 1-800-582-3337 or visit www.LTCFEDS.com.

Medicare pays a limited amount for skilled care following a hospitalization, but it does not cover care for an extended period of time. It will pay for the first 100 days of nursing home care.

FLTCIP applicants must answer questions about their health. Certain medical conditions may exclude some people from coverage. You need to apply to find out if you qualify for coverage under this program.

The Least You Need to Know

◆ Know the time limits on converting Family Serviceman's Group Life Insurance (SGLI) to Veterans Group Life Insurance (VGLI).

◆ Think carefully about the many benefits of signing up for the Federal Long-Term Care Insurance Program (FLTCIP).

◆ If you or your spouse becomes terminally ill, you can request an advance payout from SGLI to help with expenses.

◆ Except for SGLI, insurance premiums are based on your age.

Chapter 8

A Helping Hand in a Personal Crisis

In This Chapter

- ◆ Finding financial help and advice in a crisis
- ◆ Understanding what the relief agencies will not help with
- ◆ Sending an emergency message to wherever the service member may be
- ◆ Identifying scholarship money for spouses and dependents

Life comes at you fast. Family emergencies emerge, financial crises erupt, and a whole range of problems can complicate simple living. Organizations are available to assist military families through their trouble—if you reach out to them.

In general, these organizations are here to help eligible groups and their immediate families through urgent financial crises. The Red Cross helps everyone, whereas each of the services has its own relief organization. However, none of these groups is financed to provide long-term assistance or to help people maintain a lifestyle they cannot afford on their military income.

To verify the extent of financial need, each agency will request personal financial information on incomes and debts owed. This verifies that the financial need is real and determines whether the assistance will be an interest-free loan (most common assistance) or a grant (gift). In a crisis, much must be done and emotions run high. Do not sell yourself short. All of these organizations are biased toward helping. If the need arises, do not hesitate to contact your service's relief society and let them decide whether they can help.

All of these organizations are funded by the generous donations from the general public. They do not receive any funds from the government. Also they never check to see if you are a donor when they evaluate your need for assistance. They just want to help.

American Red Cross

The American Red Cross has a long history of supporting the armed forces. Financed by voluntary contributions of time and money, the Red Cross provides free assistance. The Red Cross provides personal counseling, financial counseling, and referrals. Working closely with other military aid agencies, the Red Cross can provide or find the right information or social service assistance.

The Red Cross is ready to help 24/7. Family members are not required to go through their military sponsor to request Red Cross services. They are welcome to contact the Red Cross at any time.

Emergency Notification

Family emergencies arise in their own time. When a member of the U.S. armed forces is far from home, the American Red Cross can pass on emergency messages concerning the serious illness, death, or even birth of a family member. These messages are rapidly communicated to the farthest outposts and ships at sea. Commanding officers often use Red Cross verification of these events to determine whether emergency leave is justified.

Emergency notification by the Red Cross does not guarantee that someone will be released on emergency leave; that decision is up to the commander.

Emergency notifications can be sent at any time of day, any day of the year. They can be initiated by either service members or their family back home.

> **Hot Scoop**
>
> Contact the American Red Cross National Armed Forces Emergency Service Center at 1-877-272-7337 or at www. RedCross.org.

A specific delivery time is not guaranteed, but this type of message is usually handled as a high priority. The first step is to locate a nearby Red Cross office through the local telephone book or to contact the National Armed Forces Emergency Service Center at 1-877-272-7337. Alternatives are to look up the local Red Cross chapter via www.RedCross.org.

To send an emergency message, the Red Cross needs essential information for locating the service member.

- Full name
- Branch of service and rank
- Military address
- Any information on where the service member may be
- Social Security number (if known)

The Red Cross also provides financial assistance. Funds may be needed to cover emergency-leave travel expenses, food and shelter, urgent health expenses, or even the burial of a close family member. Financial assistance may be an interest-free loan or a grant. Requests for emergency assistance must demonstrate a true financial need.

Guard and Reserve

You don't have to be on active duty to benefit from the Red Cross Armed Forces Emergency Services. Guard and Reserve members are encouraged to learn about the services available to them from the Red Cross during mobilization. Families should learn the process for requesting Red Cross emergency communications and assistance before they need it. During a mobilization, everything is rushed and time is hard to find to provide this information. Also Red Cross services are available to everyone in their local communities, even if they are not mobilized.

Service to Veterans

Sometimes the variety of veteran services available and the piles of forms required to obtain them from the Department of Veteran Affairs can be overwhelming. The Red Cross's Service to Veterans program can help. The Red Cross works with Veterans Affairs, the veteran, and the veteran's family to help them get the benefits they deserve. The Red Cross explains how to fill out the forms and obtains the necessary supporting information for filing a successful claim. The Red Cross does not bypass the Veterans Affairs process. It helps the veteran make more sense of it and work through it. It can also help to prepare appeals.

Not every Red Cross chapter has its own veterans' counselor. Applicants may be referred to the program's headquarters for assistance.

Army Emergency Relief

Army Emergency Relief (AER) was founded in 1942 as a nonprofit organization dedicated to "Helping the Army Take Care of Its Own" and its families. It provides funds to major commands and installation commanders for emergency financial assistance to soldiers, retired soldiers, and their families. Army Emergency Relief also assists widows and orphans of soldiers who die on active duty or after they have retired.

Army Emergency Relief provides financial assistance for a wide range of hardships, such as for emergency vehicle repairs, for medical expenses, or when someone's pay is delayed. However, some things do not pass muster as "emergency assistance":

Hot Scoop _____

Army Emergency Relief can be reached at www.aerhq. org.

- ◆ Financing a lifestyle beyond a soldier's income
- ◆ Paying legal expenses or fines
- ◆ Financing nonemergency leave or vacation
- ◆ Buying a car

AER provides scholarships for a first undergraduate degree for spouses and children of soldiers, based on financial need. Recipients may renew their scholarships annually. Application instructions are updated annually, so allow time to prepare documents before the deadline.

- ◆ The M. G. James Ursano scholarship fund assists children of soldiers for a first undergraduate degree, vocational training, or preparation for a military academy. It is awarded annually for up to four years. The soldier sponsor and student must both be recorded in DEERS.

- ◆ The Overseas Spouse Education Assistance Program is for spouses of active duty Army soldiers only. If the applicant's status changes, you must notify Army Relief immediately. The spouse must physically reside at the sponsor's overseas residence during the school term.

◆ The Stateside Spouse Education Assistance Program is a need-based education assistance program for spouses (or surviving spouses of soldiers who died on active duty or after retirement). Applicants must be accepted as full-time students in an accredited institution.

You need not be near an Army facility to receive assistance from Army Relief. There are reciprocal agreements with the Air Force Aid Society, Navy–Marine Corps Relief Society, Coast Guard Mutual Assistance, and Red Cross. If necessary, contact these agencies, and they will help contact Army Emergency Relief and provide funds for them. It is all about serving the emergency needs of soldiers.

Navy–Marine Corps Relief Society

The Navy–Marine Corps Relief Society was founded in 1904 and is sponsored by the Department of the Navy. It has almost 250 offices worldwide on shore and afloat. The Society depends on volunteers to support its many services. Navy Relief works closely with the local command structure to identify service members in need.

As a nonprofit charity, the Navy–Marine Corps Relief Society depends on the generosity of donors to finance its programs. Funds are primarily raised during an annual drive among active duty service members and retirees. All proceeds are returned to the members through its many services. The society's small core of employees is paid out of the Reserve Fund established during World War II.

The Navy–Marine Corps Relief Society provides financial, educational, and other assistance to …

◆ Active duty and retired U.S. Navy and Marine Corps personnel.

◆ Surviving immediate family members of sailors and Marines who died on active duty or after military retirement.

◆ Uniformed members of the National Oceanic and Atmospheric Administration (NOAA) and their eligible family members.

◆ Indigent mothers (65 years or older) of deceased service members, based on financial need.

◆ Unremarried former spouses whose marriage to a service member lasted for at least 20 years while the service member was on active duty.

The Navy–Marine Corps Relief Society provides a wide range of services to eligible recipients:

◆ Interest-free loans and grants to meet emergency needs

◆ Needs-based scholarships and interest-free loans for educational purposes

◆ Budget-counseling services, such as when a new baby arrives, to plan financial self-sufficiency

◆ Infant layettes (junior sea bags) for future sailors and Marines

◆ Visiting nurse services

 **Hot Scoop** _____

Learn more about the Navy–Marine Corps Relief Society at www.nmcrs.org.

The Navy–Marine Corps Relief Society assistance is for emergencies. It does not provide funds for non-essentials such as vacations, legal expenses, fines, or taxes. Service members are expected to budget their funds and live within their means. However, if an emergency arises, let the Navy–Marine Corps Relief Society decide whether you are eligible.

Air Force Aid Society

The Air Force Aid Society, founded in 1942 as the Army Air Forces Relief Society, is the official charity of the U.S. Air Force. It supports Air Force personnel and their families by providing emergency financial support and assistance in financing their education. The Air Force Aid Society helps individuals with personal emergencies and also helps commanders solve personnel problems in their units.

The Air Force Aid Society is a nonprofit organization. The Air Force community annually demonstrates its support through contributions that are used solely for emergency assistance. The Air Force Aid Society does not receive appropriated or nonappropriated government funds.

The Air Force Aid Society assists active duty Air Force personnel and their families. It also is available to help spouses and dependent-age children of Air Force personnel who died on active duty or after retirement. Air National Guard and Air Force Reserve personnel on extended active duty for over 15 days under Title 10, U.S. Code, may also apply.

The Air Force Aid Society strives to provide timely response to personal emergencies with minimal paperwork. Emergency assistance combines an assessment of the emergency situation and an evaluation of the applicant's overall financial situation. The result may be an interest-free loan (repaid by allotment), a grant, or a combination of both. Individuals are encouraged to apply for assistance whenever they feel an emergency situation exists. Each case is evaluated on its own merits.

Financial assistance is given when a qualifying individual cannot otherwise pay for basic needs that are essential to continued personal effectiveness as an Air Force member. It is generally limited to relatively short-term periods. Travel funds may be provided for an emergency leave or if the service member is stranded and trying to return from leave. Active duty members faced with funeral expenses for immediate family members may seek assistance if there is no other means of paying for the burial. This assistance is provided on a case-by-case basis and is usually a loan.

The Air Force Aid Society cannot take the place of sound financial judgment by Air Force personnel. Funds are not awarded to pay for a lifestyle beyond the airman's means, for fines, for nonessential needs, or for an extended period of time.

The Air Force Aid Society also provides assistance through agreements with other relief agencies. If you are not near an Air Force installation, you can contact the American Red Cross or other service relief agencies that can provide immediate assistance or pass the request on to the Air Force Aid Society.

 Hot Scoop _____

Learn more about the Air Force Aid Society at www.afas. org.

Air National Guard or Air Force Reserve personnel away from home stationed on extended active duty 15 days or more under Title 10 USC are eligible for emergency assistance when the emergency is incident to an active duty tour. The Air Force Aid Society responds to emergency situations but not long-standing problems caused by previous employment, poor home maintenance, or a serious mortgage delinquency.

The Air Force Aid Society's education fund provides $2,000 need-based grants to active duty dependent children pursuing an undergraduate degree. Eligible sponsors are active duty servicemen, active Guard/Reserve members, or retired and deceased Air Force members. Dependent children of retired Reservists with more than 20 qualifying years are also eligible to compete for these grants.

Another education fund provides assistance to the spouses of active duty airmen who have accompanied them overseas. The General George Brown Spouse Tuition Assistance Program awards up to $1,500 in tuition assistance annually to successful applicants.

Coast Guard Mutual Assistance

Coast Guard Mutual Assistance is a nonprofit organization that provides financial assistance to the Coast Guard community. Coast Guard Mutual Assistance strives to meet the valid and verified needs of eligible participants and their immediate family. Assistance is provided through counseling, short-term interest-free loans, financial grants, and referrals to other agencies.

Almost everyone associated with the U.S. Coast Guard and their immediate family members are eligible to request assistance. The Coast Guard Mutual Assistance offers aid to these people:

- Coast Guard active duty service members, retired military personnel, and civilian employees

- Commissioned officers of the Public Health Service serving with the Coast Guard

- Coast Guard Reservists (selected and stand-by in an active status)

- Coast Guard Auxiliary members

- Family members of these categories

Hot Scoop

Contact the Coast Guard Mutual Assistance Headquarters at 1-800-881-2462, Monday through Friday 7A.M. to 4P.M. Eastern Standard Time.

Coast Guard Mutual Assistance handles all applications as confidential information. The goal is to provide speedy service to eligible participants in their time of need. Assistance may be requested for many different needs:

- Emergency housing
- Necessary unplanned expensive medical needs
- Emergency travel
- Funeral expenses
- Loss of funds or property

Coast Guard Mutual Assistance does not provide funds for the following:

- ◆ Purchase, rental, or lease of motor vehicles

- ◆ Marriage costs

- ◆ Expenses resulting from disciplinary action, including court fees, fines, judgments, liens, bail, or legal fees, except to prevent privation of immediate family members

- ◆ Legal expenses, including fees for divorce, child custody, or other domestic issues

If the sponsor is not available, the spouse can still request assistance by providing a power of attorney. (Most assistance is an interest-free loan that is repaid through a payroll allotment, so a power of attorney is needed.) Such need must be for essentials to solve a temporary problem.

Each case is considered on its own merits. Coast Guard Mutual Assistance may provide a one-time emergency loan of up to $200 to the spouse if there is no power of attorney or you cannot be contacted.

The Least You Need to Know

- ◆ The American Red Cross can pass on messages about family emergencies to soldiers, sailors, airmen, and Marines wherever they may be.

- ◆ Each service has a relief society ready to help in an emergency.

- ◆ The service relief societies also provide scholarships for spouses and dependents.

- ◆ When in doubt about eligibility for financial assistance, always ask.

Part 3

Noncash Benefits

Family health insurance has long been in the news. It is expensive—unless you are on active duty. Depending on which of the plans you choose, it may be free or at a much lower cost than a similar civilian-sponsored plan. Even Guard/Reservists are eligible for coverage, based on their military service.

Probably the most unappreciated military benefit is the Exchange system. The Post (or Base) Exchange provides everything from low-cost movie theaters to barracks or shipboard vending machines, to liquor sales, to even new car sales (for active duty service members serving overseas or at sea). Approximately two-thirds of the profits from the Exchange system are used for Morale Welfare and Recreation programs; the rest is used for facility maintenance or construction.

Morale Welfare and Recreation programs provide activities to keep the minds and bodies of service members active. Most of these activities are also open to National Guard and Reserve members, and retirees and their dependents. They include vacation resorts, hobby shops, organized sports, aero clubs, riding stables, and many other activities.

Chapter 9

TRICARE: The Military's Medical Plan

In This Chapter

◆ Picking a TRICARE health-care program

◆ Enrolling in the TRICARE Dental Program

◆ Saving through the TRICARE mail-order pharmacy

TRICARE is the military's comprehensive (and complex) medical support plan for service members and their families. It attempts to accommodate personal preferences and the far-flung places that service members, retirees, and their families live and work.

Heath care is a very personal thing. Many people prefer to pick their own physician and establish a trust relationship with them. The least expensive TRICARE options do not directly accommodate this (although you may see the same group of faces). TRICARE offers a range of choices from no (or low) cost with fewer choices, to a higher cost with more choices.

TRICARE eligibility is based on information in the Defense Enrollment Eligibility Reporting System (DEERS). All family members must be listed in DEERS before they are eligible for TRICARE coverage. It is your responsibility to keep DEERS records current. Family events such as marriage, births, divorce, deaths, and adoptions require prompt DEERS updates.

TRICARE Comes in Many Varieties

People come in many sizes, with many different personal situations and preferences. Rather than provide a single one-size-fits-all program, TRICARE comes in several different versions. Participants can choose from the various types to fit their lifestyle.

Like other benefits Congress provides, TRICARE is constantly changing. The latest rules governing TRICARE can be found on its website at www.tricareonline.com. The site also provides access to frequently asked questions, forms, and resources. If the website does not have the answers, you can always call stateside customer service at 1-800-600-9332.

TRICARE Prime

TRICARE Prime is the most popular TRICARE option for active duty families. It operates similarly to a health maintenance organization (HMO). Prime participants receive most of their care from military treatment facilities. TRICARE Prime has limited options of selecting a specific physician. It is not available in all areas and requires a minimum one-year enrollment.

Active duty service members (and Guard/Reserve on active duty more than 30 days) are automatically enrolled. Their family members are not. Each family member must fill out enrollment forms before receiving benefits under this program. Newborns are automatically covered by TRICARE Prime for their first 60 days. After that, they must be registered in DEERS and formally enrolled in the program.

TRICARE Prime is the lowest-cost TRICARE option. It does not charge an enrollment fee or require participants to submit claims. TRICARE Prime participants must first seek help at a military treatment facility. This option does not charge fees for visiting military treatment facilities. Active duty personnel do not pay a fee for civilian doctor visits. TRICARE Prime has no deductibles. There is a $12 co-pay for dependents to see a civilian doctor.

TRICARE Prime assigns a primary care manager as your health-care point of contact. It arranges all visits to specialists. If your primary care manager does not arrange a specialist's visit, you may be billed expensive point of service (POS) option charges. Travel costs for specialists arranged by your primary care manager more than 100 miles away from the primary health-care facility may be reimbursed.

The point of service option allows use of TRICARE-authorized providers into or out of network without a referral. However, POS claims are subject to outpatient deductibles of $300 per individual and $600 per family. Also there is a 50 percent cost-share for claims and excess charges up to 15 percent over the allowed amount. The cost-share is applied even if the enrollment year catastrophic cap has been met.

Attention!

Emergency care is not subject to point of service option charges.

Costs for TRICARE Prime are as follows:

◆ Annual deductible: None

◆ Annual enrollment fee: None

◆ Civilian outpatient visit: No cost

◆ Civilian inpatient admission: No cost

◆ Civilian inpatient behavioral health: No cost

◆ Civilian inpatient skilled nursing facility care: No per-diem charge per admission

TRICARE Prime participants also have vision coverage. As with other TRICARE Prime services, active duty members are served by the military treatment facilities. Required eyeglasses for active duty participants are covered.

Family members are covered for annual eye exams by a TRICARE-authorized optometrist or ophthalmologist. Eyeglasses are cost-shared for certain diagnoses.

TRICARE Standard

TRICARE Standard is the basic health-care program. It does not require an annual enrollment fee and is the most expensive TRICARE option. Unless active duty families (recorded in DEERS) choose a different TRICARE option, they are automatically signed up for TRICARE Standard.

TRICARE Standard is a fee-for-service plan that allows beneficiaries to see any TRICARE-certified provider they want. In exchange for this flexibility, it charges the patient greater out-of-pocket expenses. TRICARE Standard requires a yearly deductible before it begins cost-sharing. Co-payments or cost-shares for outpatient care, medications, and inpatient care may also be required.

Costs for TRICARE Standard are as follows:

- Annual deductible: $150 per individual or $300 per family for E-5 and above; $50/100 for E-4 and below

- Annual enrollment fee: None

- Civilian outpatient visit: 20 percent of allowed charges for covered service

- Civilian inpatient admission: Greater of $25 or $14.35 per day

- Civilian inpatient behavioral health: Greater of $20 per day or $25 per admission

- Civilian inpatient skilled nursing facility care: $11 per day ($25 minimum) charge per admission

TRICARE Standard places the burden of filing insurance claims on your shoulders (although some providers may do this for you). Use DD Form 2642 to submit a claim. Submit all claims separately. It is important to fill out the claims form correctly and completely. Be sure to attach any supporting documents. Otherwise, your claim may be denied and you become responsible for paying the full bill. Make copies of everything before submitting a claim. Claims may become lost somewhere in processing.

TRICARE Standard pays for only medically necessary care and services provided at an "appropriate level of care." (Be sure the claim indicates this.) Claims that don't meet this definition will be denied.

A health-care provider must be certified under TRICARE Standard for the government to share your cost. Always verify that your health-care provider is certified before a visit. Participating providers agree to accept TRICARE payment and any cost-share. They may also charge an additional 15 percent, which you are responsible for paying.

The lowest costs come from using military treatment facilities. However, other groups have priority over TRICARE Standard participants, and capacity is limited. Active duty personnel (who are covered by TRICARE Prime) always have priority in military treatment facilities.

Sometimes paperwork gets mixed up and you must appeal a TRICARE decision. The appeals process depends on why a claim was denied. You are notified of the appeals process when you receive a written claim denial.

When submitting an appeal, stand in the TRICARE claims clerk's shoes for a moment. You can require them to search for everything (which may cause a significant delay in a response), or you can send copies of everything so it is all in front of them from the beginning. (Always keep a copy for your future reference.) Address appeal correspondence to:

TRICARE Management Activity
Appeals, Hearings, and Claims Collection Division
16401 E. Centretech Parkway
Aurora, CO 80011-9066

TRICARE Extra

TRICARE Extra is a lower-cost option for TRICARE Standard beneficiaries. You give up some of the flexibility of choosing a health-care provider, and TRICARE Extra saves you money and the pain of filing claim forms.

TRICARE Extra is a preferred provider plan that contracts with health-care organizations to supply services at a discounted price. Your health care is provided by an in-network provider that costs you 5 percent less than TRICARE Standard's outpatient visit fee. Under this program, the health-care provider files the necessary claims. TRICARE Extra charges the same deductibles as TRICARE Standard.

Since there is no formal enrollment into the program, there is no special entitlement ID card. Your uniformed services ID card is proof of eligibility. TRICARE Extra is not available overseas or to active duty service members.

Costs for TRICARE Extra are as follows:

◆ Annual deductible: $150 per individual or $300 per family for E-5 and above; $50/100 for E-4 and below

◆ Annual enrollment fee: None

◆ Civilian outpatient visit: 15 percent of negotiated fee (5 percent less than TRICARE Standard)

◆ Civilian inpatient admission: Greater of $25 or $14.35 per day

◆ Civilian inpatient behavioral health: Greater of $20 per day or $25 per admission

◆ Civilian inpatient skilled nursing facility care: $11 per day ($25 minimum) charge per admission

For Your Benefits

Always save every health-care payment receipt. You never know when these documents will be needed to correct billing errors or to prove payment (long after the fact).

TRICARE Prime Remote

TRICARE Prime Remote provides health-care coverage through civilian providers. It is available for active duty members and families in distant U.S. locations. A distant location is one where the active duty member both lives and works more than 50 miles or a one-hour drive from the nearest military treatment facility. Eligibility is based on the sponsor's residential address in DEERS. Check your eligibility for TRICARE Prime Remote at www.tricare.osd.mil/tpr.

Guard and Reserve members activated for more than 30 consecutive days are also eligible. Family members of activated Guard and Reserve members may enroll if they reside with their sponsor. The sponsor does not need to be enrolled in this version of TRICARE. If family members choose not to enroll in TRICARE Prime Remote, they are always covered by TRICARE Standard and TRICARE Extra (neither requires enrollment).

Just like TRICARE Prime, TRICARE Prime Remote enrollees are assigned a primary care manager (PCM) if network primary care providers are available within the drive-time standards. PCMs provide preventive services, care for routine illnesses or injuries, and manage referrals to specialists or hospitals as required. If no network primary care providers are available, you may use any TRICARE-authorized provider.

TRICARE Coverage for Retirees

At some point, old sailors, airmen, and soldiers must leave the service to slowly fade away. Two different TRICARE programs are available for retirees. The first program covers retirees not yet eligible for Medicare (under 65 years of age). The second program includes those who are eligible for Medicare. It is important to understand the rules for each to ensure that the best care is provided for the least cost.

Attention!

Retirees are not eligible for vision benefits under TRICARE Standard or Extra.

TRICARE Prime retirees and their family members are covered for biennial eye examinations by a TRICARE-authorized optometrist or ophthalmologist. Eyeglasses for certain diagnoses are cost-shared with authorization under exclusions and limitations. Retirees and their family members are not responsible for any co-payments for vision care if it is through a TRICARE network provider.

Retired but Less Than 65 Years Old

Most active duty personnel retire before they turn 65 (usually long before they turn 65). This group is eligible for TRICARE Prime, TRICARE Standard, and TRICARE Extra. However, whereas active duty members receive TRICARE Prime for free, retirees must pay for this service. The annual enrollment fee for retirees is $230 (individual) or $460 (family). There is also a co-pay to see a civilian doctor. Access to military treatment facilities may be limited.

Retired Guard and Reserve members who are over 60 and less than 65 years of age (and their families) are also eligible for this program. They must be drawing retirement pay and must enroll in the program before coverage can begin.

TRICARE For Life (TFL)

Once retirees become eligible for Medicare, they must change to the TRICARE For Life (TFL) program. To continue using TRICARE after age 65, Medicare-eligible beneficiaries must be enrolled in Medicare Part B. This includes participants who reside overseas, even though Medicare will not pay for the foreign medical services.

TRICARE For Life coverage for those who reached 65 years of age before April 1, 2001, includes use of the pharmacy benefit without Medicare Part B. Participants in TRICARE for Life have no premiums. However, there may be costs for participating in Medicare Part B. TRICARE For Life is treated as the " second payer" after Medicare. It also provides benefits that may not be covered under Medicare. Under these programs, providers participating in Medicare and TRICARE file all of the necessary claims. Participants receive a statement of benefits from TRICARE detailing what they paid.

Medicare usually does not provide benefits overseas. However, Medicare is available in the U.S. territories (Guam, Puerto Rico, the U.S. Virgin Islands, American Samoa, and the Northern Mariana Islands). In all other overseas cases, military retirees and their families must use TRICARE Standard.

For Your Benefits

Persons who have received the Medal of Honor and their family members are eligible for TRICARE For Life.

Widows or widowers of service members lose their TRICARE coverage if they remarry. Former spouses of retired military members are also eligible for TRICARE For Life if they were divorced after their spouse completed eligibility for retirement before the divorce. If they remarry, they lose their TRICARE eligibility. They also lose coverage while covered by an employer-sponsored health plan.

Military retirees who need treatment of service-connected conditions may choose to be treated under TRICARE or to get civilian health care that's paid for by the VA—but not both.

Some services, such as custodial care, are not covered by either Medicare or TRICARE. The entire cost of noncovered services falls on the participant.

TRICARE Global Remote Overseas (TGRO)

TRICARE Global Remote Overseas provides TRICARE Overseas Program Prime benefits to active duty members and their family members assigned to a remote overseas location. This benefit is also available to Guard/Reserve members (on active duty more than 30 consecutive days) and their families who are residing in a remote overseas location. This service is provided by an organization called International SOS Assistance, Inc.

A TRICARE Global Remote Overseas call center in each overseas area coordinates host-nation assistance. They help in the location of urgent, emergency, and dental care in their service area. If an in-network service provider is used, there is no need to file claims.

Service members must enroll in TRICARE Global Remote Overseas. The service member must initiate family member enrollment. Submit an enrollment application for each family member and attach a copy of orders demonstrating command sponsorship of accompanying family members.

Family members not enrolled in TRICARE Global Remote Overseas are covered by TRICARE Overseas Program Standard. You are responsible for co-payments and annual deductibles. You must also pay for services when received. Submit claims for reimbursement to the regional TRICARE Global Remote Overseas office.

Hot Scoop

Get the latest information and updates on TRICARE Global Remote Overseas from www.tricare.mil/overseas.

TRICARE Global Remote Overseas also coordinates dental care for active duty personnel, but not their families. That is provided under the TRICARE Dental Program.

Transitional Assistance Management Program (TAMP)

All good things come to an end, and at some point, everyone must transition from military service back to the disorderly world of civilians. The Transitional Assistance Management Program (TAMP) provides uninterrupted health-care transition for service members and their families.

In some cases, several months may be required to find suitable employment. Also civilian health insurance programs vary widely on when they take effect. This can create a gap in medical care coverage for you and your family. TAMP fills this gap by extending your TRICARE coverage.

These groups are eligible under TAMP:

◆ Service members who are involuntarily separated from active duty. In this case, family members are eligible, also.

◆ National Guard and Reserve members separated from active duty after being called up in support of a contingency operation for an active duty period of more than 30 days (and their family members).

◆ Members separated from active duty after involuntary retention in support of a contingency operation (and their family members).

◆ Members separated from active duty following a voluntary agreement to stay on active duty for less than one year in support of a contingency mission (and their family members).

TAMP continues TRICARE coverage for 180 days following separation. If you wish to continue TRICARE Prime coverage, you must submit a new TRICARE Prime enrollment application (if it is available in your area). Otherwise, you can use TRICARE Standard or Extra benefits. The TRICARE Prime Remote and TRICARE Prime Remote for Active Duty Family Members Programs are not available under TAMP.

Continued Health Care Benefit Program (CHCBP)

Individuals who lose their TRICARE coverage are eligible for temporary health-care coverage under the Continued Health Care Benefit Program. You have 60 days to apply after loss of TRICARE coverage. If you are separating from the uniformed services, your Continued Health Care Benefit Program coverage runs for up to 18 months. In other categories, such as for unremarried spouses, coverage runs for up to 36 months.

You may not need to change your physician. The program uses existing TRICARE providers and follows the TRICARE Standard program rules. If you have questions about coverage or limitations, contact a local TRICARE Service Center.

Premiums are $933 per quarter for individuals and $1,996 per quarter for a family. The first quarter's premium must accompany the enrollment application (DD Form 2837).

CHCBP is administered by Humana Military Healthcare Services, Inc. For enrollment information, contact:

Humana Military Healthcare Services, Inc.
P.O. Box 740072
Louisville, KY 40201
1-800-444-5445
www.humana-military.com/chcbp/main.htm

TRICARE Dental

TRICARE Dental is organized much differently than the TRICARE health-care programs. It is open to dependents of active duty members, Selected Reserve and Individual Ready Reserve sponsors, and their families. Active duty service members receive care through their local military dental facilities. As with all TRICARE programs, enrollment eligibility is verified through DEERS.

Hot Scoop

For the latest information on costs, participant rules, forms, and more, visit the United Concordia website at www. TRICAREdentalprogram.com.

TRICARE Dental is run by United Concordia, one of the nation's largest dental insurance companies. United Concordia has prenegotiated rates and coverage guidelines with dentists across the country. New enrollees receive a list of participating dentists. However, if participants are located in remote locations, they may submit a waiver of nonavailability to use a local source.

TRICARE Dental Costs

TRICARE Dental tries to offer something for everyone. Three categories of participants exist: active duty, Selected Reserve, and Individual Ready Reserve. Costs are based on who is being covered, and within the three participant categories are different service options, each with its own fee.

◆ Active duty service members receive free coverage. Coverage for a single family member is $11.05 per month; coverage for more than one family member costs $27.63 per month.

◆ Selected Reserve members pay $11.05 for themselves or $27.63 for a single family member if the sponsor declines to participate. All family members can be covered for $60.07, or the family and the sponsor can be covered for $80.12 per month.

◆ Individual Ready Reserve members pay $27.63 for themselves or a single family member if the sponsor declines to participate. All family members can be covered for $69.07, or the family and the sponsor can be covered for $96.70 per month.

Enrolling

Eligible participants must submit an enrollment form along with the first month's payment to begin coverage. Timing is everything. Enrollment forms received before the 20th of the month begin coverage on the first day of the following month. Enrollments received after the 20th take force the month following the next month.

TRICARE Dental enrollment requires an initial 12-month commitment. Thereafter, enrollment is on a month-by-month basis. Of course, significant life changes such as divorce and marriage may be exceptions to the 12-month rule. Contact United Concordia at 1-888-622-2256 for any questions involving enrollment rules. If you decide to stop participation in TRICARE Dental, you must officially request disenrollment.

Dental Coverage Overseas

TRICARE Dental provides coverage outside the continental United States. If a uniformed services dental facility is not available, members can receive treatment from local sources. Refer to the TRICARE Dental Outside of the Continental United States (OCONUS) provider listing. If adequate care is not available from someone on the list, submit a nonavailability and referral form to use a local source.

In many cases, using an OCONUS dentist requires that you pay for services and then submit a claim for reimbursement. Submit claims within 60 days to:

United Concordia
TDP OCONUS Dental Unit
P.O. Box 69418,
Harrisburg, PA 17106-9418

Include the completed claim form (called an Attending Dentist's Statement, available from www.TRICAREdentalprogram.com), the dentist's statement of charges, and a copy of the nonavailability form. Be sure to keep copies of everything submitted.

TRICARE Retiree Dental Program

The TRICARE Retiree Dental Program is the dental program for retired uniformed service members and their families. Unlike other programs, it is also available for Guard and Reserve "grey area" retires who have retired but are not yet drawing a retirement check. This program is also available to surviving family members of active duty members and to Medal of Honor recipients and their families.

The TRICARE Retiree Dental Program is managed by Delta Dental of California. Delta Dental handles all enrollments and claims. This program is similar to the TRICARE Dental plan, in that it requires a 12-month initial enrollment period. After that, members are continued in the program on a month-by-month basis.

The annual deductible (May 1 through April 30) is $50 per person and $150 deductible per family. The annual maximum coverage is $1,200 per person. The deductible and maximum do not apply to the diagnostic and preventive services, which are covered at 100 percent, or to dental accident procedures or orthodontia.

The TRICARE Retiree Dental Program offers three choices for dental care:

◆ Use a dentist from the Delta Dental Select and Delta Dental PPO networks. The dental care provider submits all claims, and the participant pays only the co-pay amount.

◆ Use a dentist from the Delta Dental Premier Network. The dental care provider submits the claims and will not charge more than the agreed Delta Dental fees. Co-payments and deductibles still apply.

◆ Use any licensed dentist you choose, but you are responsible for paying the bill, filing the claim, and paying any differences between the Delta Dental allowable charges and the dentist's fee.

Hot Scoop

For the latest TRICARE Retiree Dental Program information, call 1-888-838-8737 or visit www.trdp.org.

TRICARE Pharmacy (Better Living Through Chemistry)

Health-care coverage can be expensive. Modern health care depends upon modern medicines, which can also be very expensive. A valuable part of TRICARE support is its pharmacy benefit. All TRICARE-eligible participants can benefit from this program.

DoD policy is to substitute generic medications for brand-name medications, when available. If you insist on receiving the brand-name medication, you must pay the full cost of the prescription, and you will not be reimbursed for out-of-pocket expenses.

To learn more about any medication, check for generic equivalents, and even learn about common food and drug interactions, beneficiaries may use the many pharmacy resources, including the Rx Checker, available under the TRICARE Online General Health Information link at www.tricareonline.com. For more information on policies, formularies, and prescribing limitations, visit www.pec.ha.osd.mil.

Hot Scoop _____

TRICARE programs sometimes change. Get the latest information from www.tricare.mil/pharmacy.

TRICARE Retail Pharmacy (TRRX) Program

The TRICARE Retail Pharmacy (TRRX) Program provides local service to participants, no matter where in the United States they reside. Locate a TRICARE retail network pharmacy near you. Present the pharmacist with your uniformed services ID card and a TRICARE retail pharmacy information card. (Replacement cards are available from Express-Scripts.) Prescriptions can be filled for up to a 30-day supply at $3 per generic and $9 per brand-name item.

Hot Scoop _____

A list of the TRICARE network pharmacies is available at www.tricare.osd.mil/pharmacy/retailnetwork.cfm.

Participants can use a non-network pharmacy to fill their prescriptions, but it can be expensive. Beneficiaries must pay the full retail price for the item and then file a claim for reimbursement. Reimbursement does not begin until the TRICARE annual deductible amount has been fulfilled. After that, reimbursement is 80 percent of the retail price. The reimbursement claim form is DD Form 2642. As always, make copies of claims before submitting them, and be sure to attach all relevant receipts and documentation.

Drugs by Mail

TRICARE mail order is the least expensive way to obtain medicine. The suggested technique is to obtain a 30-day supply of a prescription from the local pharmacy and then mail-order the rest. Prescription drugs are $3 for a 90-day supply of generic drugs and $9 for a 90-day supply of brand-name prescriptions.

Some medicines must be taken for an extended period of time, such as those for asthma, high blood pressure, or high cholesterol. A mail-order pharmacy can conveniently drop off a 90-day supply of most medicine right at your front door.

TRICARE Mail Order Pharmacy is administered by a contractor called Express-Scripts. The first step is to register every eligible family member with Express-Scripts. It is a good idea to do this before the need exists. The enrollment stays active until needed.

To sign up for TRICARE Mail Order Pharmacy, either call or write:

◆ Call 1-866-363-8667 or (OCONUS) 1-866-275-4732.

◆ You can enroll online or download a registration form and mail it. Obtain the form from www.express-scripts.com/custom/dod/ben_message. Mail the completed form to:

Express-Scripts, Inc.
P.O. Box 52150
Phoenix, AZ 85072

Once you are registered, mail your health-care provider's written prescription along with your co-pay to the Express-Scripts address. Active duty personnel do not co-pay for this service. All others must enclose the correct co-pay for each prescription ordered. Payment may be by check, money order, or credit card. There is no charge for shipping. Turnaround time for an order is about two weeks.

Attention!

Only prescriptions written by a U.S. physician are honored.

To order by mail from overseas, you must have an APO/FPO address. Prescriptions cannot be mailed to a private foreign address.

For medicines taken regularly, there is a big savings to ordering a 90-day supply. However, most prescriptions are enough for only 30 days. To obtain the full amount (assuming that this much is required), request that the prescription include at least two refills. Keep in mind that some medicines are strictly controlled and may not be available in more than a 30-day supply.

Prescriptions can be filled by fax if sent from a physician's office. The Express-Scripts fax number is 1-877-895-1900. Prescriptions faxed from any place other than the doctor's office are not accepted. Wait 48 hours after the fax is sent, and then log on to your Express-Scripts account and charge the co-pay to your credit card.

The Least You Need to Know

- ◆ Know how to obtain a referral from TRICARE to avoid point of service charges.
- ◆ If you travel overseas for vacation or assignment with dependents, understand how TRICARE works in your area.
- ◆ Understand what you are eligible for by researching the TRICARE website.
- ◆ Preregister with TRICARE Pharmacy to ensure that coverage flows smoothly.

Legal Paper Shuffling

In This Chapter

- ◆ Drawing up wills and other formal papers
- ◆ Using powers of attorney
- ◆ Adding to the family: adoption
- ◆ Becoming a citizen

Legal services are one of those things that many people do not think about—unless they are in trouble. However, the military provides free legal services to active duty and retired service members. (Guard/Reserve members may be able to use this service if they are quick about it during active duty for training.)

Free legal services for creating documents are a real dollar savings. Such things as wills and powers of attorney, to name few, can be created for no cost. However, do not look for free lawyers to handle your divorce or to stand next to you in traffic court; this they cannot do.

No one likes legal paperwork, with all its archaic jargon, but it is a necessary evil for most people, not the least servicemen and women. When Reserve units are called into action, it is important for members to have their affairs in order. If something happens, the result is worse for the family than it would have been if the paperwork had been up-to-date.

Important documents and the decisions regarding them should be completed in your own good time, not in a confused rush at the last moment before a deployment.

Of course, there are happy kinds of annoying paperwork, too. These include adding to your family through adoption or welcoming a family member as a naturalized citizen. This chapter guides you in where to look and talks a bit about how to go through the processes, as well as how to keep your paperwork disaster safe and relatively hassle free.

What to Do When You're Gone: Wills

A last will and testament indicates your desires for your legacy and estate. This is a common document for many Americans to create, especially if they are aging or sense that their life is drawing to a close. Unfortunately, the very nature of a military career makes a will a necessary commodity. When a deployment comes out of nowhere, such as in the case of the Gulf War or after September 11, 2001, you don't want to spend your last bit of time with your family frantically throwing together a will. A will needs to be thought out, carefully drawn up, witnessed, and stored in a safe place.

For Your Benefits

Here are some words that may pop up in this chapter or in drawing up your will—make sure you're familiar with them:

beneficiary   The person or organization getting your stuff, as designated in your will.

estate   Basically, your stuff. Everything you own.

executor   Also sometimes known as the personal representative. This person is the one who will be in charge of your estate and the distribution of it, with your will as his guide.

framing   The writing of a will.

testator   You. The person the will is being written by and for.

Figuring Out Who Gets Your Junk or Your Bills

Deciding on beneficiaries can be a difficult task, especially when it's something you don't want to think about. Sit down in a quiet place and make a list of your most valuable possessions—things that are monetarily, emotionally, or personally valuable. Make sure that you clearly spell out anything you think might be argued over. In a military family, special items such as uniforms, medals, awards, and your veteran flag may be topics of arguments. Things of monetary value could be cars, houses, stocks, real estate, insurance policies, collectors' items, jewelry (including your wedding band), and large quantities of money. Items of personal value might include something like an afghan knitted by your grandmother, your Great-Aunt Bertha's tacky costume jewelry, or china dishes—things that would fetch little to no money on the second-hand market but that are priceless to you.

If you have underage children and are a single parent, your will should indicate a guardian. Also if any property or money left to the children cannot be reached until they are of age, someone must manage it or a trust fund must be set up.

The next step is to think about whom you want to give these things to, or who you think might benefit the most from having them. Try to be in a calm state of mind—for example, not feuding with a child or sibling you might normally give something to—so that you can make the best possible decision. Also if for some reason you are ill or in an unsettled mental state while making up the will, it can be contested.

When you've made the list, consider putting it aside for a few days and coming back to it. Then look it over and decide if you still agree with what is written. Something else to consider is who you want to be the executor of your will. Distribution of property can become an emotional issue. Do you want this to be done by a friend, a family member, or an attorney?

Ready for the next step?

Getting It Done

All the thinking and planning is worthless if you don't actually make up a real will. You can choose to frame your own will or have a lawyer do it for you.

For Your Benefits

A will is a will—legal paperwork doesn't differ much for any citizen, military or otherwise. However, military personnel can use the services of a military lawyer free of charge. Also you don't have to do it in your free time. With permission from your commanding officer, you can do it at almost any time, on the military's time. Also as you're about to read, the military offers worksheets to simplify the potentially confusing process.

Now you can go through the process with a lawyer and get a very personalized will, carefully thinking out wording and so on, or you can make a simple but functional will using a worksheet provided by the military. This form is a foolproof way of making up a will; all you have to do is fill in the blanks. Of course, all of the prior considering of who gets what also comes into play in this type of framing, so don't leave that out if you choose this route! Careful, don't think that this form is a will by itself. You have to give the form to a lawyer and have an actual will drawn up. If you're wondering what the worksheet looks like or what might be asked on it (so you can be prepared to fill out an official copy), just search for it online. Type "military will worksheet form" into your preferred search engine, and several options should come up. Click away!

Making It Official

A witness must be present and must sign a copy of the will. This person can be someone you know or perhaps someone provided by your lawyer, but it absolutely cannot be someone who is getting anything in your will. The witness must be a third party with no personal interest in the document.

Keeping It Safe Until It's Needed

A will is replaceable; however, it's better to just keep it safe from the beginning. You can keep documents safe in many places. One place to consider is a safety deposit box at your bank, but if you choose that option, be sure that it can be accessed in case of your death. Some lockboxes are sealed upon death, depending on state law.

If you don't have a safety deposit box or don't want to get one, buy a fire-safe container. This is, in most cases, a safe where you can keep other valuable items or documents as well. Your executor should know how to access the will. This means having access to your safety deposit box, the code to your safe, or a way to get to wherever you decide to keep it.

Copies and Revisions

It is legal to make copies of your will and give them to people to hold on to (perhaps your family, a close friend, or even a religious leader). When making the copies, do not remove any staples from your master copy of the document. Staple the new pages together. Make certain that all of the copies are clearly labeled "COPY" on each page. Do not attach any extra documents to the original or the copies.

A will can be a one-and-done process, but many people choose to keep theirs updated. You may want to consider reviewing it on a yearly basis, considering births, deaths, marriages, and divorces of your family or friends named in your will. If you need to revise your will, compose a new document instead of writing corrections to the existing one. Do not edit it yourself because crossing out and writing in casts doubt on the contents of the document.

If you have any copies distributed, gather them and destroy them only after the new one is complete. Do not leave any copies or the original of your former will intact; this can invalidate your current will. Burn, shred, or destroy by some other means all former wills.

Medical Care If You Can't Decide for Yourself: Living Wills

Living wills have become increasingly popular as medicine advances. These documents, also known as advance medical directives, state your feelings on how you should be treated if you are unable to make decisions for yourself. Incapacitation can take many forms: a coma, brain damage, Alzheimer's disease, or a permanent vegetative state, for example. The result of all of them is that you are unable to talk to doctors or your family and make decisions for yourself.

Making up a living will can help your family or doctors in the field know what you want to be done for you. With the current state of battlefield medicine, brain damage and comas due to bombs are more common than in the past, and living wills are more relevant than ever.

Okay, So What Exactly Does It Do?

If you are unconscious or somehow unable to make decisions or communicate your wishes to a doctor or family members, a living will clearly states what you want to happen in that situation. Usually living wills come to the table when you have sustained severe physical or mental damage, and recovery is unlikely. Decisions can range from not wanting to be a financial burden on your family and wanting them to "pull the plug," to wanting the best treatment available, to simply being uncomfortable with the thought of being brain-dead, with a preference for actual death.

Without a living will, all of these decisions are put on your family (if you have a health-care power of attorney—explained in the next section—in place). Your family must decide what they think you would want, or what they can afford. This can put a lot pressure on families mentally and emotionally, sometimes creating rifts when there are disagreements over decisions. If the decisions made are yours, they can't argue. You may want to talk to your family before or after you make up your living will. Let them know your intentions. Make sure they understand that this is what you want. That should help them cope if it is ever necessary to actually use the directive.

If a living will clearly states that you do not wish to be on life support for the rest of your life, it will clear your family and doctors of any possible criminal lawsuits. Also in a living will, you can state preferences such as whether you would like your organs donated.

Get Your Number 2 Pencil: Writing a Living Will

Normally, drafting a living will is a tricky thing, with specific language that must be used and a certain format that must be followed. To make this easier, the military provides a worksheet. All living wills that come out of military law offices are recognized as legal and lawful. Just as when writing a normal will with the military, you just need to find time to visit a military lawyer, who will explain the worksheet. Fill it out and hand it back in, and the lawyer will make up an official advance medical directive for you.

Storing Your Advance Medical Directive

Now that you've got your living will, where do you keep it? It's no good if it can't be readily accessed when it's needed! As with a normal will, you can make copies and distribute them. Keep one with your important documents at home in that fire-safe box we talked about, one in a safety deposit box at the bank (yours or a close family member's), one with your lawyer, and one with your regular doctor, in your medical file. It might be wise to carry a small card in your wallet that mentions the existence of your advance medical directive and where it can be located in case it is needed. Keep this card with your identification and insurance cards in your wallet—don't tuck it into a back corner where it will never be found.

I Give You the Power of Me ...

A power of attorney (POA) is a potent thing. It allows someone to legally act as you. This is similar to the president handing over control to the vice president so he can undergo surgery. The vice president becomes the president for a limited amount of time, in case anything important occurs. With a POA signed by you, a person can do anything in your name, and any responsibility for their actions falls on you. Therefore, be careful when choosing whom you relinquish your decisions to. Make sure you trust that person not to abuse your trust.

For Your Benefits

There is legal jargon for powers of attorney, too. In this case, you, the person giving power to someone else, are called the "principal" or "grantor," and the person whom you give the power of your legal identity is called the "agent." It is possible that you will have a primary agent and a secondary agent. This is a nice back-up plan, especially for medical powers of attorney, in case your primary agent can't be reached during the critical time.

Don't let this deter you from having a power of attorney because, in the right situation, it can be very useful. For example, if you are incapacitated and require medical care, someone can make decisions for you if he or she has a power of attorney concerning your health care. Or if you are deployed out of the country and must leave your family behind, you can leave a POA for your spouse to do things that you may have had to be there for (such as selling a car that has a title in your name). A whole Idiot's Guide could be written on powers of attorney, in all their various forms and intricacies. Here we address some of the POAs you are most likely to need or encounter due to your military status.

A Bit of Info for All POAs

As previously mentioned, a power of attorney is a very powerful document. The rule of thumb here is, "Never use a general power of attorney when a special one will do!" Be careful in choosing whom you want to give this power to. In most cases, people choose to give the power to their spouse or a close family member. Once a power of attorney is given, it is extremely difficult to take back, so if it is necessary to have one, it is best to specify a limited amount of time or special circumstances in which it is active.

Two basic types of powers of attorney exist. The first is general, which gives people all power over anything that might require them to legally be you. This document enables them to do anything in your name. It's the most complete and, therefore, the easiest to abuse. The other type is specific or limited powers of attorney, which give the agent the power to do only certain things and/or under certain circumstances.

Most lawyers suggest this type, as it gets the job done most of the time and is much more difficult to exploit.

You can make as many copies of a POA as you want. It is advisable to keep at least one in a very safe place, such as a lockbox or a fire-proof box at your home. Also give a copy to the person you are granting power of attorney and one to your secondary person. Consider leaving one with your lawyer. If the POA is medically related, give one to your normal doctor and have one put in your medical file.

It's a good idea to build an expiration date or circumstance into your powers of attorney. They automatically expire upon the death of the grantor (you) or agent. It's better safe than sorry. You can always get another one made up, but they're very hard to revoke if you change your mind about your agent or if you wanted the POA available only for while you were out of the country or your kid was on a field trip—temporary conditions.

Health-Care Powers of Attorney

A living will kicks in only if you're determined to be terminally ill or injured, with death standing over your shoulder. What if you're only unconscious or unable to communicate? That's where a health-care power of attorney (HCPA) comes in. An HCPA transfers the power of decisions from you to the person of your choosing in case you are unable to make medical decisions concerning yourself. In simple terms, it does the exact same thing as a normal power of attorney, except that it is limited to medical situations.

As with any power of attorney or medical paperwork, it's useless if it's not there when it's needed. Make sure that there is a copy in your medical file and also with your agent, as well as one in a safe place at your house or in a lockbox. We suggested that you keep a card in your wallet mentioning that you have a living will, and on that same card you might want to mention your health-care power of attorney and how to contact your doctor and/or agent. Make sure this card is located with important information in your wallet, such as your identification, driver's license, insurance card, and Social Security card. If it's in some odd pocket with pictures of your children or frequent-buyer's cards you never use, it is unlikely to be found.

Military Special Power of Attorney

As with many other potentially complicated and confusing forms for legal documents, the government provides a worksheet to service members for this particular POA. A military special power of attorney is a type of limited POA that gives your agent (in most circumstances, your significant other) power of attorney while you are away on military duties.

If you are declared to be missing, missing in action, or a prisoner of war, your military special power of attorney will not expire, even if it is set to. It will remain valid through the time you have returned to the United States military, plus 60 days. This can be a real help to your family and is a service clause not included in a normal power of attorney.

The best part about the military special POA is that it is extremely simplified to be filled out via worksheet, so it doesn't fit normal government standards and requirements for a power of attorney. The government has exempted the military from these standards, and any power of attorney made up through the military with this worksheet is as valid as one made up with civilian lawyers, and is treated the same.

Adding to Your Family Through Adoption

Adoption can be a wonderful way to add to your family. Unfortunately, on top of the difficulties adopting within the United States or outside of it are the exorbitant fees. Also having frequent changes of address, and parents who may be absent more than present or who can't attend a number of competency or preparation meetings with agencies or psychiatrists, isn't usually a plus with adoption agencies. Agencies rarely place a child in a home that will move across state lines, let alone frequently in or out of the country!

It's not all downsides, though. Adoption agencies recognize that military families seeking to adopt generally are some of the most eager and easiest to work with. They also know that military education, medical, and general finance benefits are beneficial to the child as well as the parents. No need to fear—Uncle Sam is here! He will help you add to the family by smoothing out a few wrinkles in the ordeal.

Adoption Benefits for Military Families

Enough of hearing about the roadblocks of adoption into a military family, which you probably are all too familiar with by now. Let's have some of the benefits available to you because you are in the service of your country.

Military families who are adopting children may be eligible for reimbursement of up to $2,000 a year per child to help pay for adoption expenses. The money can be used to help pay for adoption fees charged by a foreign agency, placement or counseling fees, legal fees and services that cannot be taken care of in a military court or with military legal aid, and medical expenses for a newborn or the birthmother. This money is given out after the adoption is finalized, and only if the adoption was done through a state adoption agency or a nonprofit private agency. Unfortunately, this money cannot be used for travel expenses within the country or internationally. If you are adopting more than one child, there is a maximum of $5,000 in reimbursement per family, per year, even if both parents are in the military.

If you are adopting a disabled child, you may be eligible for up to $1,000 a month in monetary assistance to help you with your child's extra costs, under the military's Program for Persons with Disabilities. Also families who adopt children with special needs are assigned to duty stations where the child's medical or educational needs can be met, thanks to the Exceptional Family Member Program.

As soon as a child is placed in your home, even if the adoption is not yet finalized, your soon-to-be son or daughter is eligible for free military medical care. It can take a long time to finalize adoptions, in some cases, and this can be very helpful to families who go through that long wait period between placement and legal adoption.

Getting Leave for Your Adoption

As of January 1, 2006, service members are granted 21 days of nonchargeable leave following the placement of their child in their home. Unfortunately, if two service members are married and adopting, only one of those parents gets the leave, so it's up to you to pick which one. As with the reimbursement for fees accompanying and leading to adoption, this leave applies only if you meet the qualifications (which are pretty much that you adopt from a nonprofit agency). Of course, if the other parent is entitled to leave and is allowed it, that person can take time off, which counts against his or her annual allowed leave.

Websites to Answer Questions and Provide Support

We've included some useful links to find out more about the programs mentioned here. Also several provide more in-depth information, tips, and support for military families who are trying to add to their families through adoption.

- ◆ **www.militaryhomefront.dod.mil**—Here you can find information about the Exceptional Family Member Program (EFMP) in the "Troops and Families" section.

◆ www.nmfa.org/site/PageServer?pagename=reus_adoptionintro—This is the National Military Family Association article on military adoption, with helpful links.

◆ http://groups.yahoo.com/group/AdoptionSupportGroupForMilitaryFamilies— This is an Internet group for discussing what you've gone through, and tips for and from others about how they went about adopting their children. This group for military families was recommended in the May 2005 issue of the National Military Family Association newsletter.

Citizenship for You and Your Family

Although you are fighting for the United States, you may not be a citizen, a fact that the service member next to you might not even know. Since the U.S. military doesn't require you to be a citizen, just a legal resident, it at least provides a way for you and your family to be naturalized or not deported, in some circumstances.

Even if you are a legal resident and are fighting or stationed abroad, and leaving your (legal, but not citizen) family at home, some worries might be in the back of your mind. This chapter can help get you and your family on the way to naturalization, as well as set your mind at ease that they're safe from deportation while you're away.

Serving Your Country with a Green Card

About 35,000 other service members serve this country without having real citizenship. The government can help you by speeding up your application process, covering fees, and letting you file paperwork while abroad. U.S. Immigration and Customs Enforcement has also postponed deportation of immigrants on active duty until they are discharged. The government wants to do all it can to keep you happy and in the service.

For the most part, the military and government acknowledge that service members are more at peace when they do not worry about their family members. Immigrants serving in the military, or even legal citizens who have family who are illegal aliens or have only temporary permission, are constantly worried about their family while they are away. Will they be deported? What if something happens to the service members? Unfortunately, there's no special help the government can provide. Strict immigration and illegal alien laws apply as much to members of military families as to families of civilians.

Requirements for Citizenship

To become a citizen of the United States of America, you must fit the following requirements:

◆ You have been a lawful permanent resident for five years.

◆ You have been a lawful permanent resident for three years, have been married to a U.S. citizen for those (three) years, *and* continue to be married to that citizen.

◆ You are the lawful permanent resident child of U.S. citizen parents.

◆ You have qualifying service in the U.S. armed forces. ("Qualifying service" consists of three years of service on active duty while in a lawful permanent resident status *or* any length of service on active duty during time of war, regardless of resident status.)

If you meet one of those requirements, you also must be a person of good moral character; be able to read, write, and speak the English language; and demonstrate a knowledge and understanding of the history and form of government of the United States.

For Your Benefits _____

If one of the following describes you, you must take the U.S. History test in your native language, and you don't have to take the English test:

◆ You are over 50 years old and have been a lawful permanent resident for 20 years or more.

◆ You are over 55 years old and have been a lawful permanent resident for 15 years or more.

◆ You are over 65 years old and have been a lawful permanent resident for 20 years or more. Also if this applies to you, you are able to take an easy version of the history test in your native language.

◆ You have a learning disability that prevents you from learning history or the English language. Proof of this disability from a doctor is required by Immigration.

Next, you fill out an Application for Naturalization and submit it to your state Immigration and Naturalization Service (INS) office. If you have previous or current military service, you must fill out INS Form G-325B, "Biography," and submit it to have your service records checked. For civilians, it can take one to two years after the paperwork is filed before citizenship is granted. For active duty service members who file with the help of the military, the turnaround time is four to eight months.

How Does the Military Help Me?

Active duty service members are eligible for expedited naturalization through a special agreement between the INS and the DoD. The military will help you prepare and process your Application for Naturalization, as well as your INS Form G-325, "Military Biography." You will need to go to your local Legal Service Office and prepare an INS Form N-426, "Request for Certification of Military Service." Your command will help you assemble the applications and forms, make an appointment for fingerprinting, and forward the whole packet to the INS processing facility for military applications. The processing facility for military naturalization applications does not depend on where the service member is stationed, unlike normal processing facilities, which are in the state where the person requesting citizenship is living. These hurried services are *not* available to inactive members of the military.

Legalizing and Naturalizing Family Members

So maybe the military can't help your family by speeding up their naturalization process, as it can with yours, but you can help. At the very least, begin by making sure that your family members are legal residents. You can place a request for a green card through the INS. This is much easier if your family entered the country legally under a visa of some sort. Beyond that, if your family is eligible for citizenship, you can, of course, use military legal assistance free of charge for consultation and aid in filing your paperwork.

 **Hot Scoop**

Numerous websites claim to be sites where you can download immigration forms. These are *not* affiliated with United States Citizenship and Immigration Services (USCIS), the official organization that distributes information and forms. Some of these websites are scams, but the most common problem is that their forms are out-of-date and don't have the latest version with the newest information and wording. USCIS always has the latest forms and information, so be sure to go there for your immigration form needs. Using out-of-date paperwork can hinder and even halt your progress to citizenship. The official website of USCIS is www.USCIS.gov. That's easy to remember, right?

If you have a child who is not a citizen of the United States by birth and who is under 18 years of age and unmarried, that child can become a citizen through you. If both of the parents become naturalized as citizens of the United States, or if you are a single parent with sole custody of the child and you become naturalized, your children automatically become naturalized citizens when they reach the age of 18, if they were already legal residents at that time. This also applies if one parent became naturalized before February 21, 2001, and the child was under 18 and unmarried and a legal resident at that time.

If you're reading this section looking for a quick way for your spouse to become a citizen, you can skip this paragraph. It's not the best way to become a citizen when there are other options. In 2003, as Congress was streamlining the naturalization process for immigrant service members, it granted citizenship to noncitizen service members who had already been killed in combat in the war on terror and extended eligibility to their surviving spouses. As previously stated, there are better and happier ways to become a citizen, but sometimes you have to take what you can get when tragedy has already struck.

The Least You Need to Know

- ◆ It's important to have a plan for death, just in case.

- ◆ Be prepared for medical emergencies with a living will or health-care power of attorney.

- ◆ The military can help with adoption expenses and you get leave, but be careful to adopt from a nonprofit organization if you want the benefits.

- ◆ Becoming a citizen is easier than you think, so go for it!

Chapter 11

Shopping with Military Style

In This Chapter

- ◆ Who is eligible to shop, and where
- ◆ How the Exchanges fund base recreation
- ◆ Commissaries for your groceries

Post Exchanges and commissaries seem so "ordinary," and what can be said about them? In terms of military benefits, a lot. Both are an important part of a service member's total military compensation package. Understanding how these enterprises work and their many programs is essential if you are going to get the most out of them. This chapter helps you understand the extensive services offered by the Exchange and commissary systems.

Post (or Base) Exchange

The purpose of the Exchange system is to provide high-quality merchandise to military personnel at a reasonable price. Secondarily, the profits from these sales are used to finance the Morale Welfare and Recreation (MWR) programs at the local base. For most service members, probably their least understood military benefit is their local Base Exchange. It is a large and complex organization striving to support military operations across the world, including in the midst of war zones.

The local Exchange is a handy thing for a young sailor, Marine, airman, or soldier. Exchanges are located near the barracks (not everyone has a car), carry all the essential things a young military person would need, and charge reasonable prices. In fact, these merchandise marts, barber shops, movie theaters, snack bars, dry cleaners, telecommunications centers, and more are so handy that they are taken for granted as just a normal part of the military scenery.

Essentially, an Exchange is a department-type retail store on a military base. Whether it is called a PX (Post Exchange) or a BX (Base Exchange), it is essentially the same thing. Each service operates its own Exchange system. The Air Force long ago split off from the Army. However, their Exchanges are combined into a single unit called the Army and Air Force Exchange Service (AAFES). AAFES is the largest of the four Exchange systems.

The other Exchanges are the Navy Exchange Service (NEX), Marine Corps Exchange (MCX), and Coast Guard Exchange (CGEx). Separate Exchanges give each branch of service the freedom to offer products that support their unique operating environment. The Exchange systems are almost entirely self-funded and receive very little appropriated funds. Profits from sales are used to pay salaries and facilities expenses.

To find the latest information on your local Exchange, such as sales programs, rebates, or even part-time employment, check online here:

- Navy Exchange: www.navy-nex.com
- Army and Air Force Exchange: www.aafes.com
- Coast Guard Exchange: www.cg-exchange.com
- Marine Corps Exchange: www.usmc-mccs.org/shopping

Eligibility for the PX

At one time you had to show your military ID just to get past the PX doorkeeper. That is long gone. Now everyone can walk straight into an Exchange. You must prove your eligibility to shop at the Exchange only if you are purchasing something. Eligible patrons are identified in DoD Instruction 1330.21, "Armed Services Exchange Regulations" as follows:

- Active duty, Reserve, or National Guard uniformed personnel, or retired uniformed Personnel, and their dependents. This includes the former Lighthouse Service (officers, crew, light, and depot keepers), officers and crews of vessels of the National Geodetic Survey, commissioned officers of the Environmental

Science Service Administration, commissioned officers of the Public Health Service, commissioned officers of the National Oceanic and Atmospheric Administration, and PHS Reserve officers.

◆ Medal of Honor recipients and their dependents.

◆ Honorably discharged veterans of the uniformed services who have a 100 percent service-connected disability, and their dependents.

◆ Foreign-country military, when on duty in CONUS, and their dependents.

◆ Red Cross personnel assigned to duty outside of CONUS, Alaska, Hawaii, and Puerto Rico, with an activity of the military service, and their dependents.

◆ U.S. civilian DoD employees or government contractors who are assigned to duty outside of CONUS, Alaska, and Hawaii, and their dependents.

◆ NOAA wage marine personnel and retired wage marine personnel.

◆ USO personnel when stationed outside of the United States.

◆ Delayed Entry Program (DEP) or Delayed Training Program (DTP) enlisted.

◆ U.S. citizen employees of the Armed Forces Exchanges (active and retired), and their dependents.

The Exchange Is Big Business

Most people think of the Exchange as a big store. However, that is only the main facility. A base's Exchange system encompasses many other things, including barber shops, gas stations, a Class Six store, fast food stands, convenience stores, the base movie theaters, and usually a car repair service. Just as military personnel are a reflection of the society that they came from, the Exchange is reflection of current retail trends.

The main Exchange has evolved over the years from a standalone facility to mini-malls that also host commercial retail operations to provide greater choice to service members. For example, Exchanges typically include an office of a bank and a "name brand" fast food outlet. Both are owned by some other organization than the Exchange but must follow the Exchange's customer service guidelines.

Exchanges are self-supporting and receive little financial help from the government. Unlike commissaries, Exchanges are 98 percent self-funded. The government assistance received is in the form of a small number of military personnel and free use of land. As an agency of the Department of Defense, Exchanges do not pay taxes, which also gives them a cost advantage that they pass on to their customers. The government also pays to transport supplies to overseas Exchanges so that goods from home can be offered at affordable prices.

Profits from the Exchange system are used to finance new construction and remodel existing facilities. However, true to its founding principle, the Exchange system returns two-thirds of its profits to the soldiers, sailors, airmen, and Marines who buy from it. In 2006, the Army and Air Force Exchange System (AAFES) alone provided $236 million to the MWR funds. So the next time you buy a soft drink from a barrack's or ship's vending machine, or get a haircut at the base barber shop, you are indirectly contributing to the base recreation funds.

For Your Benefits

The Exchange system takes its mission to support the uniformed services seriously. It is one of the major employers of military family members. This makes sense: as military families move from post to post, they bring their skills and experiences to the local Exchange. They come in the door already trained with a known work record. AAFES estimates that military family members make up 31 percent of its workforce.

Catalog and Online Sales

Catalog sales allow a retail operation to offer goods for sale to people who cannot walk into the store (many active duty, Guard/Reserve members, and retirees live far from an Exchange). Catalogs also allow a store to offer a wider range of goods than might fit into their doors. To a great extent, online sales have eclipsed catalog sales. It is cheaper to create web pages than it is to print thousands of copies of full-color catalogs that may never be seriously looked at.

The Exchange systems offer a series of catalogs either focused on a topic, such as electronics or fitness, or geared to a season, such as fall and winter." Catalogs are sold for a small fee, but they come with coupons that more than cover the purchase price. Catalog orders can be placed at the local Exchange, and the merchandise will be delivered directly to your home.

The Online Exchange store is a combined effort that supports all the Exchanges. This is convenient for ordering goods that are not locally available or for ordering a gift to be shipped directly to a special person. In addition to merchandise offered by the

Exchanges, the Online Mall offers goods by other stores affiliated with the Exchange. To ensure that only authorized patrons order from the Exchange online shopping, you must log into the web pages. The logon verifies your identity through DEERS. Online sales are found online at thor.milexch.com.

PX Down Range

To fulfill its pledge to support its customers, the Exchange service goes wherever the troops go. This includes forward bases in the Middle East, Iraq, and Afghanistan. Staffed by volunteers, they provide an important part of morale support in difficult circumstances. Their goods and services provide a touch of home to personnel in hostile areas. These Exchanges are managed by AAFES, with staff support from the Marine Corps Exchange system.

Forward-deployed Exchanges make the most of available resources. They might set up in prefabricated buildings, tents, or trailers. For widely dispersed personnel, the Exchange may use a mobile store. This allows them to deliver much-appreciated goods even to the remote outposts.

A forward-deployed Exchange has limited space. However, it attempts to provide some sort of fast food service from a major American chain (such as Popeye's, Burger King, or Dairy Queen). It includes a phone center so that patrons can e-mail or call home; a barber/beauty shop and a gift shop stocked with local merchandise are other common services.

To find out what is available at your next visit to Southwest or Central Asia, check out www.aafes.com/downrange/home.htm.

Attention!

The Marines are the only service with a primary MOS for Exchange officers (4130) and MWR specialists (4133). These personnel are trained to operate tactical field Exchanges and Warrior Express Service Teams in support of Marines in the field who do not have access to a regular Exchange.

Exchange Shopping Overseas

Overseas Exchanges far from hostile fire have long supported the many overseas units in Europe and the Far East. Being far from home in a strange land can make someone a bit homesick. The overseas Exchanges bring a piece of home to you. They provide American merchandise that would be unavailable or unaffordable through the local markets. This includes American food, publications, clothes, snacks, and more.

Shopping privileges are also generally extended in overseas locations to U.S. government civilian employees who are assigned overseas and their dependents. Shopping privileges can vary overseas, according to applicable status-of-forces agreements with host nations. In some countries, this requires rationing to prevent merchandise from being resold on the local civilian market to circumvent the local tax authority.

Navy Exchange System

With over 100 sites around the world, the Navy Exchange system plays an important part in the quality of a sailor's life, both on land and while at sea. The Navy Exchange plows 70 percent of its profits into its Morale Welfare and Recreation programs. The remaining profits are used for new Exchange construction and for remodeling existing facilities.

The Navy Exchange System is wide reaching. It is configured to support the unique challenges facing sailors in their many duty locations. It includes the Navy Lodge chain of temporary lodging facilities, the Navy Uniform Program, the Ships Store program, and telecommunications centers. To find the Navy Exchange near you, check out www.nexnet.nexweb.org/pls/nexstore/nx_storefinder.

Ship Stores

The Ship Store program provides quality goods to sailors afloat. These stores stock personal comfort items and provide services necessary for day-to-day living. A well-run Ship Store is essential to a crew's morale, especially during long deployments.

Ship Stores and Navy Exchanges are separate programs under the Navy Exchange Service Command. There are 155 Ship Stores on various Navy and Coast Guard ships. Each store carries basic items, such as toothpaste and towels, as well as snacks and consumer electronics. Space is limited, so a range of goods is preferred over a large number of choices. Other shipboard Exchange services include barber shops and vending machines. Ship stores are financed through appropriated funds. Profits from sales are retained on board to support that ship's Morale, Welfare, and Recreation programs.

NEX Telecommunications

All sailors have some loved ones that they want to talk to. The NEX Telecommunications programs are provided ashore, afloat, and off-base through partnerships with telecommunications companies.

The Ashore Program provides pay phones, prepaid telephone cards, service in quarters such as barracks and Navy Lodges, voice mail, and Internet service. The Afloat Personal Telecommunications Program (APTS) provides personal calling from Navy Ships using satellite communications.

Attention!

As can be expected, prices for the same item may vary between the Exchanges of different services. Prices and selection may differ significantly. When shopping online, take a few minutes to check out similar items offered in the other online catalogs.

Marine Corps Exchange (MCX)

MCX provides a wide range of services to support the entire Marine community (active, Reserve, and retired). These include vending machines, dry cleaning, and telecommunications—and, of course, how could a Marine base survive without its busy barber shops? Purchasing merchandise or services from the MCX is your way to contribute to the local MWR funds.

To find a Marine Corps Exchange near you, check online at www.usmc-mccs.org/shopping/mcxlocation.cfm?sid=shop&smid=4.

Coast Guard Exchange

By the nature of their mission, Coast Guard bases may not be near a major military base. Some of the bases can be in remote locations. To ensure that their personnel are provided the same services, the Coast Guard has its own Exchange system. The Coast Guard Exchange System (CGES) provides the same types of products as the other Exchanges, plus items specific to the Coast Guard and Homeland Security. Profits are turned over to unit MWR funds.

You can locate the nearest of 24 Coast Guard Exchanges online at www.cg-exchange.com/CGESWebSite.nsf/LocationsPG?OpenPage.

Military Star Card

To assist military personnel with obtaining credit that they can use responsibly, the Exchange systems have teamed together to offer the Military Star card. All of the Exchanges accept this card. Military Star offers competitive rates, no annual or late fees, and online bill paying (a nice feature for units that move frequently). Using your Military Star card for catalog or online purchases entitles you to free shipments.

Service members in forward-deployed locations have found the card to be easier to manage than cash. (ATMs can be a bit difficult to locate in some of the native villages.) Personnel use the Military Star card for purchases at tactical field Exchanges and then later pay their bills online using a one-time debit from their checking account to their Military Star account.

Current plans call for a Military Star Rewards MasterCard credit card that would also be good outside of the Exchange system. Points are awarded for purchases that can be redeemed later for prizes. For more information on Military Star cards or to apply for a card, log into your online Exchange web link and then check online at odin.aafes.com/starcard.

A unique feature about a Star Card is that if your unit is deployed, your interest rate is eligible for a reduction to 6 percent. This is not automatic. You must provide either a copy of your orders or a letter containing your name, your Social Security number, and your length/dates of deployment. No payments are required, and you can continue to use the account, although a monthly allotment is recommended to keep the balance from rising too far.

Class Six Stores

With all of this talk about tax-free sales at the Exchange and commissary, what about at the base liquor store? Known in the civilian world as the ABC store, State Liquor Store, or Package Sales, a Class Six store sells beer, wine, and liquor to service members who are at least of legal age to consume these beverages for the state the base is in. (The term "Class Six" comes from the military supply classification for personal demand and comfort items.)

Class Six stores overseas are governed by the local Status of Forces Agreements (SOFA) with the local government. Many governments (including the U.S. government) tax liquor heavily, with additional taxes on imports. Merchandise sold through a Class Six store is intended only for the use of authorized patrons and is not for resale or to be given as gifts. Selling Class Six merchandise on the local market is illegal and is prosecuted by both base authorities and local law enforcement.

Cheap Movie Seats

The local base theater is a service offered by the Exchange system that everyone can enjoy. Sometimes overseas life can be somewhat short of diversions. Base theaters offer first-run movies at reduced prices. Movies rotate through daily, making even daily runs to the movie theater practical.

The Navy and Coast Guard use local websites to list the movie schedule for their bases. To find out what is scheduled on Marine, Army, and Air Force bases, check online here:

◆ Marine Corps: www.usmc-mccs.org/fitnessrec/theaters.cfm

◆ Army and Air Force: www.aafes.com/ems/default.asp

Your Shopping Basket

If you are serving an assignment overseas, you have an opportunity to purchase a new car or motorcycle at a reduced price. AAFES offers these vehicles to all services through its Exchange New Car Sales (ENCS). AAFES has arranged with Ford, DaimlerChrysler, and Harley-Davidson to sell their products to you at a guaranteed low price—if you meet the following criteria:

◆ You are an active duty member of the U.S. military, or a DoD employee or contractor.

◆ You are assigned overseas outside of the 50 United States for 30 consecutive days or more (90 days or more for eligibility to purchase a Harley-Davidson product). This includes Navy personnel serving on ships in international waters or overseas.

ENCS and Navy Auto Source sales personnel are there to guide you through the process. Discuss with them what you are looking for, and they will explain your options to you. Unlike a car dealer in the United States, there is no aging inventory to push on customers. You can choose the vehicle and options you want to buy. Sales personnel will answer questions about any of the vehicles in the program. If you do not see what you want in a standard model, they can help you configure a build-to-order vehicle.

For Your Benefits

The ENCS dealer may have a small inventory of vehicles used as models. These may be available for local sale.

Unless you are sitting on a pile of bonus money, you will need to borrow enough to pay for your new vehicle. Your ENCS representative may assist you in applying for loans. Possible sources are the auto manufacturer's finance division, credit unions, or your bank. Where you get the loan is up to you. The ENCS representative will determine the deposit necessary to secure your purchase. This should be less than $1,000.

Your order is summarized into a Buyer's Offer. This document lists the price of the basic vehicle, options, freight, and other costs associated with the transaction. All prices are subject to ENCS's price review process. When this is completed, ENCS mails you an Order Acceptance. Compare your offer to the acceptance. You have 10 days to object to document differences. The Order Acceptance is the binding contract.

You have two options for vehicle delivery. Vehicles can be delivered to the CONUS dealer of your choice. The dealer will clean and prepare the vehicle for delivery according to the manufacturer standards. The dealer may also assist in submitting the appropriate tax forms and obtaining license tags. The cost of these services is prepaid in your original order. Alternatively, if you are authorized to have a privately owned vehicle at your overseas duty station, you may have it delivered there.

The Order Acceptance document details when and where your final payment is due. In general, the final payment is due when you pick up your state-side delivered vehicle. If the vehicle is to be delivered overseas, you must submit the final payment 21 days before it is delivered to the shipping terminal (who will ship the vehicle to you). Final payment must include local taxes and vehicle registration fees.

New vehicles sold through ENCS are covered by the manufacturer's warranty. If you are not satisfied with the manufacturer's support, AAFES may intercede to assist you. If you need this assistance, call 1-800-527-6790, ext. 3119.

To find the latest details, such as eligibility criteria, rebates, and program rules, check online at www.encs.com. This website also contains information on ENCS representatives who are permanently located at many major overseas Exchanges.

The Navy Exchange calls its version of this program the Naval Auto Source. It can be found at www.navyauto.com. The Navy Exchange program works together with the ENCS program but is tuned to meet the unique needs of sailors. The dealers for the Navy Auto Source program can be found online at www.navyauto.com/locations.aspx?id=260. You can also call them at 1-877-MYNAVYCAR (1-877-696-2892) or e-mail them at navyinfo@navyauto.com.

If your location does not have an ENCS office, contact ENCS at:

Overseas Military Sales Corporation
ATTN: Customer Relations
100 Crossways Park West
Woodbury, NY 11797-2084
Phone: 1-800-669-6183 or 516-921-2800
Fax: 516-677-3701

Complaints About the Exchange System

In recent years, the major discount stores have offered high-quality goods at prices lower than the Exchanges. The Exchanges have responded with a Price Match Guarantee stating that they will match the locally advertised price for identical items within 14 days. This does not include double or triple coupons, or clearance items. Check with the local Exchange for details.

The Exchange is legally required to charge prices for tobacco and alcohol that are somewhat comparable to local prices. Guidelines are set by DoD Instruction 1330.9.

Exchanges have been accused of censorship in the sale of printed materials. The Exchanges carefully select publications that they will sell, as do all commercial enterprises. They carefully review adult material and any magazines or books that deal with controversial subjects. If a patron desires these materials, they can be obtained from other sources. However, the Exchange cannot possibly stock every item available and must choose which ones it will offer. Although the Exchange supports an adult-aged military, it also supports families who shop there.

Commissary

The uniformed services provide a significant cost savings benefit through the world-wide system of commissary stores. These stores, operated by the Defense Commissary Agency (DeCA), provide groceries to military personnel, retirees, and their families. DeCA was formed in 1990 as a consolidation of the commissary organizations of the individual services. You can find information about the commissary system online at www.commissaries.com.

Commissaries obtain the best prices for quality food and pass on the savings to service members. Annual commissary sales now exceed $5 billion. A typical commissary is similar in service and product offerings to a supermarket and carries approximately 11,000 items.

Authorized patrons do not pay any sales tax. However, a 5 percent surcharge is added to all purchases. This surcharge pays for the construction of new commissary buildings and the remodeling of existing ones. The 5 percent surcharge has not been increased since 1983. With shoppers saving an average 30 percent on their purchases, it is easy to see why admission to the base commissary is a valued part of military pay and benefits.

Unlike the Exchange system, commissary employees are U.S. government employees. However, the baggers are not. Commissary baggers work only for tips. They are frequently military dependents working to make some supplemental income. An exception to this rule has been at Fort Leavenworth, where trustees from the disciplinary barracks have been used as baggers in the past.

For Your Benefits

Military service members need to ensure that their laundry detergent doesn't have optical brighteners when it comes to proper care and cleaning of ACUs. Commissaries help them make the right selection with signs listing products considered safe for ACUs.

Although prices at the commissaries are low overall, some items, like bread and milk, may be more expensive than at a regular grocery store. This is because most civilian stores use them as loss leaders to pull shoppers into the store, expecting them to also purchase other things. Some of the best savings are processed food, such as frozen dinners and breakfast cereals. Make your own comparison by shopping at a local store and then your local commissary.

Eligibility for Commissary

Eligibility for admission to a commissary in the 50 states and territories is open to active duty, Guard/Reserve, and retired personnel, and their dependents, as described in DEERS. Other eligible patrons include Medal of Honor recipients and 100 percent service-disabled veterans. At one time, Guard and Reserve members were limited to 24 commissary visits per year, but that rule has been rescinded. They now have unlimited visits.

Overseas Commissaries

An overseas commissary can be a big savings for military personnel. It provides American foods usually at prices significantly less than on the local market.

Overseas commissaries are governed by the local Status of Forces Agreement (SOFA). This agreement determines who may use the commissary and what may be sold. These agreements may vary by country, so if in doubt, ask the local commissary what is permitted. For example, the local SOFA may restrict retirees from using the local commissary because they are not there on orders. Just as commissaries overseas stock American food for the benefit of service members, the stateside commissaries stock foreign foods for homesick foreign-born spouses.

Virtual Commissary

No matter where you go, there seems to be some way to reach out to the Internet. The commissary has recognized this by creating a Virtual Commissary for gift purchasing. The Virtual Commissary offers prepackaged gift baskets containing products from DeCA's business partners at commissary prices. Once you select the gift, you are transferred to the manufacturer's website to include shipping charges.

When you first access the Virtual Commissary, you are asked to download a DoD security certificate. This acknowledges to your computer that the Virtual Commissary is a trusted site and avoids incorrect warning messages that it is not. The website to access the Virtual Commissary is www.commissaries.com/log_in/html/vcintro.cfm.

Most (but not all) sales by Exchanges are free of local sales or VAT taxes because the sales take place on military reservations (exceptions may include gasoline sales in the United States and sales by concessionaires licensed by the Exchange).

The Least You Need to Know

- You can save a lot of money by shopping at the commissary.
- The Exchange system is a major employer of military spouses and children.
- All of the Exchanges share the same online store.
- You can get a great price on a new vehicle if you order it while overseas or at sea.

12

Money-Stretching Things to Do Around the Base

In This Chapter

◆ Things to learn in your spare time

◆ Sports around the base

◆ Hobby shops for your creative side

◆ Off-base recreation spots

Okay, the duty day is over—now what? You can sit around the squad bay, ship, or Air Force dormitory and stare at the walls, or rise up and make good use of your time. A military base offers many interesting things to do, if you only go out looking for them. Of course, the larger the base, the more there is to do. However, never let anything like that discourage you. Get up! Get Started!

So Much to Do—So Little Time

Activities can be broken into several major categories. The first is those that help you gain more education. Some day you will pass back into the unorganized world of civilians and must be prepared for one of the big-paying jobs. Another is physical activity, from martial arts to organized sports or even a relaxing game of golf. A third category is hobby and crafts, which involves such things as car repair, ceramics, wood shop, or outdoor activities such as fishing. All this and more is available if you go looking for it.

These activities are open to all service members, their dependents, and usually retirees. They provide positive outlets for spare time at a nominal price. Young families have many affordable things to do. Riding stables, scuba diving opportunities, and Rod and Gun Clubs are available. Many retirees living near a military base use these facilities because they are significantly cheaper than their commercial counterparts.

The station's Morale, Welfare, and Recreation (MWR) organization typically operates the recreation programs. The same group may be called the Marine Corps Community Services (MCCS) or an Air Force Services Squadron. MWR programs are dual-funded by appropriated and nonappropriated funds. The appropriated funds typically are provided to build new facilities; the nonappropriated funds come from a share of the PX and commissary profits. Funds also come from sales at popular activities, such as the club system, bowling alleys, and movies. Recreation and family support is also available through the local USO Center and the branch of the Armed Services YMCA.

Are there any other nearby military bases? MWR activities are open to all service members, so another service at a nearby location might offer the activity you would like most. To find all there is to do locally, start with either that base's website or the MWR website for that uniformed service. The MWR websites are listed here:

- www.mwr.navy.mil
- www.armymwr.com
- www.usmc-mccs.org
- www.uscg.mil/MWR
- www.usafservices.com

Education

One of the best long-term activities for soaking up spare time is to gain a college degree or other professional credentials. Whether you'll be applying for a new job or competing for a promotion (inside or outside of the military), completed college credit will pay you back again and again for the rest of your life.

Try a Little Night School

Colleges are big business, and like fast food restaurants, they cling to military bases. In its simplest form, a college classroom needs only a place for the students to sit, an instructor, and perhaps a blackboard (although many use a projector and PowerPoint slides). This fits in nicely with military bases, which have classrooms everywhere that are empty in the evenings.

Another education alternative is an Internet-based course. Some of these courses can be completed at your leisure—others must follow a prescribed schedule (although you can participate at any time of the day). The primary requirement is access to a personal computer with an Internet connection. Chapters 14 and 15 are devoted to your college options and paying for them. Some classes, such as those in foreign languages, geography, or military history, may have immediate value by enhancing your military skills.

You can also earn civilian skills certifications, such as computer skills, quality control, welding qualifications, or even materials management. Finally, many military correspondence courses are available to help with promotions—and they are free.

Read a Book at the Base Library

A library is an important part of every person's lifelong learning process. Why spend your money for a book to read once and then store away? A library holds (in written, audio, and video form) the hard-won knowledge of others, including military history, the feats of great heroes, fictional works for entertainment, and more. Why not learn the easy way? Pick up a movie to watch later. Borrow a book on tape (or CD) to listen to on the long journey to your hometown. Oh yes, and the library is free!

Libraries have evolved from stacks of books and eerily quiet rooms into a place full of activities. A popular library service is free Internet connections. Groups also often are organized to critique popular works and discuss the work of various authors.

> **Hot Scoop**
>
> You can find out about things to do on a base in several places. The base newspaper likely has stories and local announcements seeking new people to join. The base telephone directory should list places that are rarely heard about but still open for you to join in.

Sports of All Types

Face it, exercising is a lot like work. Most of us do it because we must, not because it is a lot of fun. However, sports are a lot of fun and, by the way, a great workout. Military bases are full of sports that you can join in, no matter what your skill level. You only have to step up and ask.

Of course, the simplest sport is running (no special equipment or special exercise facility is required). Here again, the military has a benefit. Bases tend to have a lot of green space and woodland available. Instead of pounding down paved roads to the detriment of your knees, you can run on trails through the woods. Depending on your location, there is usually a gravel and dirt road around the perimeter wire of the base itself. This long stretch of dirt track is easier on the legs and combines running with a stroll through the woods. (A tank trail will do just as nicely.)

Shoot a Round of Golf

It seems like whenever the military builds a base, it first plants the flag and next builds a golf course! Golf has a well-deserved reputation as a rich person's game. A round of golf at a commercial course can be an expensive afternoon. However, military golf courses charge only a fraction of a commercial course fee. On some bases, the fees are prorated by rank. Learning to play golf reasonably well is also a useful civilian business skill. Many business deals have been sealed during a game.

Golf provides fitness and an escape from a stuffy office into a well-kept green space. Combined with walking the course, the surroundings refresh the mind while improving fitness. Most courses provide lessons for beginners (highly recommended) and rent clubs. Although the Pro Shop may have rows of expensive clubs for sale, novices should stick with an inexpensive set until they develop their own playing style.

Military golf courses include a driving range and a putting practice green. Even if the line at the tees is too long or time is not available for a round of golf, hitting a couple of buckets of balls on driving range will surely loosen up the muscles for a full workout later.

Martial Arts of All Types

Rarely does a military base not offer multiple martial arts classes. Mastering this art not only improves military skills, but also promotes fitness in a fun way. Judo, karate, and even boxing may be available at the local military gym. Fees usually cover membership to the national certifying organization and a payment for the instructor. Martial arts address the whole person and encourage healthy habits to enhance fitness.

Before settling into a particular martial arts program, take time to try several different ones. Select an instructor and style of martial arts that suits your fitness level and time available. The programs offered on base are usually less expensive since the MWR provides the building and equipment.

Team Sports of All Types

From the battalion football team to a squad's mud volleyball team, sports are everywhere—and, yes, rarely cost the participants anything. You can borrow equipment from the local MWR office. It may be in rough shape, but it is serviceable and the price is right.

Military units have long promoted sports for their fitness value as well as their entertainment utility. Pitting the baseball teams of two adjacent units is just one way to build espirit de corps and to encourage teamwork. Forming your own team is as easy as posting a notice on a bulletin board.

Most bases have an organized sports program open to anyone. These intramural sports" cover a range of different sports, such as basketball, racquetball, volleyball, softball, skeet and trap shooting, football, bowling, and tennis. In some cases, given the dispersal of units around large bases, the intramural sports may be local and the leagues made up of the various intramural groups.

Athletes who have mastered intramural level sports can request to move up to the base-level competition, sometimes called "varsity" sports. These competitors are now in a much tougher game but are in a position to take on the best teams of the various services. Often their unit will release them from some of their military duties to train for special matches. The highest level of military sport competition is the Olympics. Although this is an admirable accomplishment, it is quite a stretch for someone who is just trying to soak up some spare time around the ship.

Swimming Pools—Grown-Up Style

Sometimes your fitness routine gets into a rut. Consider alternating it with a workout in the base pool. Most bases have swimming pools—in many cases, indoors. Pools are used for a variety of training purposes. After mission requirements are satisfied, they are available for sport and fitness. Typically, a swimming pool is free to service members and available to military dependents for a nominal fee.

Some bases form swimming clubs, much as they do running clubs. Swimming for distance is excellent fitness. Members keep logs of their exercise and are awarded small prizes for completing 50 miles or more. Pools may also offer water aerobics, water polo, and water running.

At the Beach

Is your base located on the coast? Does it own a stretch of beach? What better place to practice sea kayaking, scuba, snorkeling, surf fishing, or surfing? Step away from the predictable, controlled environment of a swimming pool and go into the deep water to swim with the hungry fish! You can borrow or rent equipment from the local MWR Equipment Checkout Center. Classes such as snorkeling, surfing, and sea kayak safety are usually available for a low fee that covers the cost of maintaining the equipment.

If your base is not on the coast, gather some friends and strike out for an ocean-facing military base. MWR facilities are open to all service members, retirees, and their dependents. To find out what is available at other bases, look up their web page and search for the MWR.

Outdoor Recreation

Military bases have a lot of land for training areas and as a buffer between danger areas and the rest of the world. Often this extra ground provides opportunities for the outdoorsman. Outdoors activities may be managed through a Rod and Gun Club or directly through the game warden. These organizations are open to service members, retirees, and their dependents. They provide a self-policing group that enjoys the outdoors and appreciates the lightly used nature of the bases.

An Army MWR website that describes military outdoor recreation sites coast to coast is www.pathsacrossamerica.com.

Borrow What You Need

Camping and other outdoor activities require some equipment. However, this equipment can add up to a lot of money—then again, given the small amount of space each person is allotted in a barracks or ship, there's no place to store this gear. MWR addresses this through its equipment checkout and rental program.

Equipment checkout centers are a benefit available to all service members, retirees, and their dependents. They rent or loan a wide variety of outdoor recreation equipment on a daily or weekly basis. Items range from party and BBQ equipment, to indoor and outdoor sports and recreation equipment, to fully rigged boats, barbecue grills, and camping supplies. If the checkout center is near the ocean, they may have scuba equipment for rent. If they are near the mountains, they may offer ski equipment and snowboards. The list will reflect what people have found locally useful in the past.

Some equipment requires prior training on its use. Safety regulations may require a brief explanation of how to properly operate the equipment before its release. If larger equipment, such as an RV or camping trailer, is checked out, time must be allotted to learn the proper way to operate the unique device. Check with your MWR equipment checkout center for a full list of what is available and the price to rent it. You will be amazed by what is available.

Practice Fire and Maneuver in a Paintball Arena

What's the use in being a warrior if you can't play like one? Some MWR activities offer a complete paintball program in which participants can practice their stealth and rapid assault, and feel the sting of a paintball when they err.

An MWR paintball operation begins with a designated playing field with enough obstacles to keep the game interesting. It also offers rental equipment and lots of supplies, such as air and paintballs. Tournaments can be arranged to prove who has the sharpest skills. Units or groups may also rent the playing fields for parties.

Fishing Those Seldom-Touched Ponds

Low ground collects water. If you have a lot of ground, you will likely have ponds or streams. Both of these can be a fisherman's dream since, unlike the public waters, they are not heavily fished. The key to base fishing is to understand the local regulations, to avoid problems with the game warden.

For example, most stations require both a base fishing license and a state fishing license. The money generated by license fees is used to stock ponds and other wildlife maintenance. The base permit should include a description of the local regulations for using fishing on government property.

For Your Benefits

Bases along the coasts may offer great surf fishing. Check local regulations about licensing requirements and rules governing crabbing and digging for shellfish.

Sometimes near campgrounds, the base provides a well-stocked "kiddie pond" for use by children 12 and under. These catch-and-release ponds are usually stocked with blue gill, crappie, and bass, for easy catching.

Shooting Ranges for All Types of Weapons and Contests

Firearms and the military kind of go hand in hand, so it is natural that during off hours, someone might like to practice with weapons. Bases establish shooting ranges to support mission training requirements. They either permit recreational users to fire on them after hours or provide a separate range for their use.

Ranges are normally managed by volunteers from the base Rod and Gun Club. This ensures that the grass is mowed, the trash is emptied, and someone responsible will enforce safety requirements, such as mandatory eye and ear protection.

Membership in a base Rod and Gun Club is open to anyone in the military community. Most charge an annual membership fee to cover expenses and range usage fees. Fees may be prorated based on the member's rank. On the larger bases, the Rod and Gun Club may rent weapons and sell ammunition.

Shooting at targets is fine for awhile, but then most people want to move up to local competition. Rod and Gun Clubs frequently organize matches for recreational shooters, based on the type of weapons used, type of target, and so on. If this is your sport, this is a great place to socialize with likeminded people while polishing your military marksmanship. Rod and Gun Clubs may offer state-certified hunting classes (if locally required). For many shooters, target practice goes hand in hand with hunting. Other times, it is just relaxing to make things go bang.

A popular form of shotgun target practice is skeet and trap. Consider taking some lessons offered by the Trap and Skeet members to quickly learn the finer points. These can be arranged through the Rod and Gun Club office. Most ranges rent weapons to beginners. The shooting range cost is for the ammunition and the targets.

Rod and Gun Clubs also operate the base recreational archery ranges. Costs are substantially less than on a firing range since arrows are not nearly as messy. As with firearms, archery competitions and lessons are arranged through the Rod and Gun Club. Archery supplies may also be sold. Practice your archery to be ready for hunting season set aside for archers.

Hunting

All of those fences and guards around military bases serve one very vital function. They keep the civilian hunters away from the base and leave the animals for us to hunt! Most military bases have lots of wildlife. Elk, turkey, bear, and deer are just some of the larger game found on military bases. Most bases organize hunts and offer first priority for assignment of hunting areas to service members.

Prices for hunting permits vary widely between bases—even in the same geographic areas. Each base sets its own fee schedule. It pays to shop around before buying a base hunting permit. Also most bases require that you also possess a valid state permit for the game you are hunting.

If you do not have a personal firearm at the base, the Rod and Gun Club may rent firearms to you. If you bring your own weapons, they must be registered with the base provost marshal's office, and their storage must conform to base rules. A base hunting permit is usually required before hunting on base. The Rod and Gun Club may provide any safety training required to obtain a base hunting permit.

Marinas

Marinas are a handy place to launch or dock watercraft. However, there are still plenty of things for a boatless service member to enjoy. Begin by taking a watercraft safety course. This will qualify you to rent boats, such as small sailing craft, canoes, and kayaks—all of which are available at low rates. For marinas located on the ocean, a popular activity is organizing a deep-sea fishing trip. Large boat fishing trips may also be arranged on the Great Lakes.

A popular marina service is scuba diving lessons. These programs require participants to pay fees to cover the equipment maintenance and payment to the instructor. Scuba training often opens the door to organized ocean dives to many interesting places. Of course, equipment is available for checkout or rental from the MWR equipment checkout center.

For Your Benefits

It is prudent to reserve watercraft as early as possible. As with anything else, the most desirable boats will be rented quickly, leaving the rest to whoever walks up.

Riding Stables

For many people, horses are valued companions. Bases often provide boarding stables, riding arenas, and riding trails for a nominal fee. In some cases, to encourage others in their equestrian pursuits, they also offer horses for rent and riding instruction. Given the wide-open spaces on most bases, the riding trails, scenic views, and wildlife encountered can be extensive.

Base stables can provide other services to military horse owners. They can purchase feed and bedding in bulk, saving service members money. They can also negotiate a reduced price with local farriers.

The range of equestrian activities is limited only by your imagination. Some stables offer "pony parties" for young children. Fort Leavenworth offers humane fox hunts, where members on horseback follow the hounds across the countryside but are careful not to injure the object of their chase. Other places form a mounted color guard to enliven base festivities.

If you would like to learn how to ride a horse, ask about lessons at the base stables. Someone there can provide contact information for local instructors and answer basic questions about the type of instruction you may want (such as English- or Western-style riding lessons).

Campgrounds

An infantryman might ask, why would you want to pay someone so you can go camping when Uncle Sam pays me to do it all the time? Likely because camping can be a lot of fun if you don't have to stand middle-of-the-night guard duty and crawl through swamps. Camping just needs a place to pitch a tent, and a tent to pitch. MWR services can help with both of these.

The first step is to locate a campsite. Most bases have some available, but you will need to work through your local MWR office to reserve one. Some have only simple facilities, while others have flushing toilets and showers. Also remember that you can use the campsites provided by the other services. To find a military campground in your state, check online at the Army MWR site (www.pathsacrossamerica.com) or the Coast Guard site (www.uscg.mil/MWR/Cottages/RecreationalLodging.htm).

Next, make a list of everything needed to make your camping experience a low-stress event. Check out tents, sleeping bags, lanterns, camp stoves, and similar equipment from the MWR equipment checkout point. Review the equipment's assembly and

proper use with the attendant. MWR
operations at larger bases may also rent RVs
and camping trailers, if you have completed
a training course on their safe and proper
operation. As with all military gear, you must
clean it up before returning it.

For Your Benefits _____

Most military campgrounds
are adjacent to a fishing
pond, so remember to bring your
tackle box.

Base Services

Base services are all of those other MWR activities that make it such an all-
encompassing operation. This includes recreational lodging (explained in Chapter 13),
food service, clubs for all ranks, and youth programs in support of military families.

Clubs

Enlisted and officer clubs are a popular gathering spot for unit members. Generally
located near your quarters, they provide a ready source of entertainment. Clubs range
from off-hour establishments in the midst of the barracks to full-service enterprises
providing a range of services to members and their families. They provide food, entertainment, and a convenient gathering place for unit members. Military clubs provide
entertainment areas with big-screen TVs, a variety of table games, and game centers
with Xbox, PlayStation and other systems.

What better place to watch the "big game" than on a club's big screen? Better yet, the
club pays for the cable TV access to the major sports networks. With their facilities,
a club is like a tailgate party without the parking lot. Most clubs follow a variety of
sports, based on the season.

Eligibility for a club membership varies according to the branch of military service
and local circumstances. A small base may have an all-ranks club, or a larger one may
have different clubs for different ranks. Clubs are generally open to active duty or
retired service members, or DoD civilian employees. Normally, a club member whose
monthly dues are current can visit similar clubs on other bases for no additional fee.

Hobby Shops for Arts and Crafts

Arts and crafts skills development programs offer a wide variety of craft activities,
which can include framing, engraving, ceramics, woodworking, pottery, photography,
jewelry making, and fine arts. Instructional classes in each of the locally supported

crafts are available. Each craft shop provides the necessary tools and work surfaces to complete the projects offered. Skilled staff members provide advice as requested.

Most craft shops require that you attend a brief safety lecture before you can use the facility. For woodworking, for example, a separate safety briefing may be required for each large piece of equipment that you operate.

Craft materials can be inexpensive or can bite deeply into your wallet. For example, hardwood lumber to make a presentation box might be expensive, while clay for ceramics would cost much less. The craft shops will sell materials for your project at a reduced cost.

Auto Repair Self-Service Center

One of the most popular (and money-stretching) hobby activities is the automotive repair center. The centers provide tools and work bays supporting auto maintenance and repair for service members who have the skill and inclination to attempt it. Lifts racks are available for oil change and lube service. Tire balancer and front-end alignment machines are typically also available. Auto service advisors are on-site to assist with use of technical equipment and to help ensure the safety of all patrons.

Classes on basic automotive maintenance are available for a small fee. (Often one of the student's vehicles is chosen to act as the class example, which means it benefits from free expert work.) Automotive classes address such services as oil changes, tune-ups, front-end alignment, tire balancing, and dent removal. A reference library of automobile repair information is also available for use by all patrons.

Some auto self-service centers divide their auto shops into auto body and auto mechanical repairs. Auto body includes fender repair, dent removal, panel replacement, vehicle preparation for repainting, and more. Larger bases also provide a paint booth for painting over the repairs.

Auto self-service centers are open to active duty and retired military and their dependents during posted hours. Service and usage fees are charged for the auto activities. This pays for an attendant to manage the site and ensure safety rules are followed, reduce loss of tools, and more. Some of the repair centers also sell common repair parts (oil filters, fasteners, and so on). You might be able to rent storage lockers, to save time hauling things back and forth to your home.

Not everyone can afford a late-model vehicle. Auto center services provide pretrip vehicle inspections for service members. These inspections ensure the safety of all passengers for the journey.

Finally, auto hobby shops help to preserve the environment. They provide collection points for used antifreeze, motor oil, containers, and filters for proper disposal.

Discounts to Main Events

Sometimes just getting off base for awhile or taking the family for a trip (where someone else fights the traffic) can be relaxing. MWR offices frequently organize one-day or short vacation trips to nearby sites and recreation areas. How about a white-water rafting weekend? Perhaps a day trip to see all the sites of a major city? They may also organize a bus to carry a load of football fans to see the big game. MWR negotiates the best price, saving you money.

MWR sells discount tickets to your favorite places. This includes all of the major amusement parks and local attractions (varies by where your base is located). Special group excursions to popular events such as NASCAR races, major-league baseball games, and other sporting events can be arranged.

On some bases, this MWR activity is known as Information, Ticketing, and Reservations (ITR), or Information Tickets and Travel (ITT). It is your one-stop travel agency online:

- www.mwr.navy.mil/mwrprgms/itt.html
- www.public.afsv.net/Travel
- www.uscg.mil/MWR/Cottages/RecreationalLodging.htm
- www.usmc-mccs.org/itt/?sid=rf
- www.armymwr.com/portal/travel/itroffices

Aero Club

Have you ever wanted to learn to fly an airplane? To soar up into the clouds, leaving your worries behind even for a little while? Join your base *Aero Club!* Aero Clubs provide an opportunity to develop aeronautical skills in piloting, navigation, mechanics, and other related areas. An Aero Club gives military aviators a place to maintain pilot proficiency skills while assigned to nonflying billets. They encourage awareness of aviation techniques and issues, and provide a recreational facility for low-cost, safe, light aircraft operations.

def•i•ni•tion

A military **Aero Club** is a bit different. Pilots must learn about security measures required for flying onto a military base.

Aero Clubs typically require a monthly membership fee (to cover aircraft and ground equipment expenses). Aircraft are available for rent at a cost less than at a commercial flying school. Aero Clubs own a small group of aircraft that the members share. Aircraft are rented by the engine hour "wet" (means full of fuel). Of course, before pilots can rent a specific aircraft, they must prove their expertise to safely operate it though a checkout ride with an instructor.

Your first step is to take a sample flying lesson to see if is this sport is for you. For about $50, you will get a half-hour flying lesson, with you doing most of the flying. Aero Clubs often offer advanced flying lessons and appropriate ground school for instrument and commercial pilot ratings.

USO

One of the more iconic symbols of military recreation is the United Services Organizations, better known as the USO. Formed just before World War II, the USO is famous for its support to U.S. military members around the world.

The USO is a private, nonprofit organization that provides members of all services morale, welfare, and recreation–type services. The guiding vision of the USO is to extend a touch of home to the military. The USO currently operates more than 130 centers worldwide, in major cities, near military bases, and in major airports.

These centers are staffed primarily by volunteers and depend on donations to finance their operations. Most USO sites have their own website to highlight local programs and events. These websites can be found at www.uso.org/whoweare/findyourlocaluso/uslocations.

Entertainment

Bringing entertainment to the troops is one of the USO's most famous activities. Around the world and even in the war zones, the USO brings a bit of America to the nation's warriors. Famous people shake hands, sign autographs, tour facilities, and help service members and their families feel a little closer to home. USO carefully mixes entertainers from many different backgrounds and with a variety of talents. Performances often take place in an airplane hanger, on flatbed trucks, and in military tents and bunkers.

No one does these tours to get rich—they do it because they want to. The top performers and their support staff volunteer their time, and receive only travel expenses and a small daily stipend. USO tours can be anywhere the U.S. military goes. For the latest tour information, check online at www.uso.org/whatwedo/entertainment.

USO Airport Centers

A USO sign at an airport is a welcome signal for a tired military traveler in a strange place. It means a safe haven to rest, someone to provide directions about the airport, and some free snacks (instead of expensive airport food). Airport USO centers provide a safe place to sleep between flights. Airport USO centers are also equipped to handle the special needs of military families with young children.

Airport USO centers usually occupy space donated by the airport, so no two facilities are alike. Where possible, they try to provide free Internet/email access, a library with takeaway books, and magazines. Books can be taken from one center and dropped at the next (a very useful benefit when traveling between airports serviced by the USO).

USO Service Centers

USO service centers provide ways for service members to remain in contact with their families through telephone as well as Internet and e-mail access. USO centers provide a safe place for service members and their families to play games, participate in family support groups, and enjoy a touch of home through a holiday program. Each center provides programs and services geared to the unique needs of the local military community. Libraries and reading rooms are available in most USO centers. Many popular magazines are also provided.

A stranger in a strange place can be quite lonely. The USO sponsors tours to help service members become more familiar with their new environment and the local culture. Tours may be to local cultural sites or to nearby famous locations. The USO also offers language classes to help you become more comfortable in the new situation.

Another way to help new people is to show them around. The USO provides information on local activities, as well as referrals for local lodging.

USO centers may provide free tickets or reduced rates to theatres, movies, sporting and museum events, and sightseeing tours. For example, the famous New York City USO Canteen located on Times Square (www.usonyc.org) sometimes has free tickets to the New York theaters, sporting events, and other activities. Availability is based on donations, often made on short notice. The website also provides information about live television shows in the New York City area and how to obtain tickets to be a part of the audience.

USO and the Military Family

USO centers offer a sense of community to mobile military families. Activities vary by location but include bingo nights, video game tournaments, holiday programs, family support groups, and free dinner nights. These activities also give families an opportunity to meet other military families in that area.

Moving to a new area is often a difficult transition. Many USO centers offer orientation programs, to introduce new residents to the local culture and community. They may also provide military families new to an area with community welcome packets. These include maps, cultural and entertainment information, restaurant listings, and information on local services and programs offered by the surrounding military installations. The USO also provides referrals and follow-up services for those who need family counseling assistance.

USO centers are family friendly, providing nursery facilities and children's play areas. They offer a quiet place with changing tables and portable cribs. Children's play areas provide a place for kids to watch movies and play with fun, educational toys.

The USO can help military families locate both short- and long-term housing in the area. Emergency housing can also be arranged for military members and their families.

Armed Services YMCA

The nonprofit Armed Services YMCA (ASYMCA) is a member of the YMCA of the United States. It has provides support services to military service members and their families. The ASYMCA is open to the entire military community but focuses on assisting junior enlisted service members and their families. ASYMCA operates at 34 locations worldwide.

ASYMCA programs include child care, hospital assistance, spouse support services, computer training classes, health and wellness services, holiday meals, and much more. ASYMCA keeps children and adults active to build and maintain a healthy lifestyle.

Military families move about, which imposes social difficulties on children. New schools, new friends, new everything can disrupt a child's stable growth. ASYMCA operates Operation Hero for children from 6 to 12 years of age who are experiencing temporary difficulty in school, both socially and academically. It provides after-school tutoring and mentoring assistance in small groups

To locate the Armed Services YMCA center near you, check online at www.asymca. org/a3.html.

The Least You Need to Know

- Sports of all kinds are available for those who want to join in.

- The local MWR activity loans or rents a wide range of recreational equipment.

- A variety of hobby and craft shops are available on your base.

- The USO and ASYMCA offer MWR-like services.

13

Planning a Family Vacation (On the Cheap)

In This Chapter

- ◆ How to fly free as a space-available passenger
- ◆ Where to find the military resorts
- ◆ Stretching vacation dollars
- ◆ Condos at military discounted prices

If you pay attention to no other chapter, listen to this one. Many money-stretching vacation options are available to you—if you reach out and use them.

Planning a vacation involves three critical elements. First is the amount of time available. With 30 days of annual leave, this should not be a significant constraint. Second is interest in a great place to visit. This can be to sit back and relax by the beach or to tour the local culture. The third element that humbles the other two is cost. Covering the expense of a family vacation on a military income is tough. This chapter shows many ways to reduce this third constraint.

A Free Flight to Vacationland

Few civilians realize the extensive network of scheduled flights that occur between military bases. Often these flights carry priority cargo or things that are better off not shipped using public carriers. Sometimes they provide for the regular rotation of personnel between the United States and its many far-flung bases.

It did not take too many partially full cargo flights in the early days for some bright person to realize that any excess space could be used for travelers "hitching a ride." In the beginning, it was mainly a matter of asking the pilot if you could fly along in the back. Eventually, an organized system was developed to be sure that available space was used for the highest-priority additional passengers.

Space-available travel is free. However, there is a head tax on CONUS outbound or federal inspection fee on CONUS inbound international commercial charters. Avoid peak travel months of December, January, June, and July.

Flying space available is just that—flying in the available space. At each stop, the aircraft's load is evaluated to determine how much space is available for the next leg. You might be bumped off the flight if a higher-priority passenger wants to get on. Then you must wait for the next one or finish your journey using a commercial carrier.

Flying space available requires time, patience, and some spare cash. Sometimes the journey is a bigger adventure than the destination. Be sure to have sufficient funds available to complete travel using commercial transportation, if necessary. Even waiting for the next flight may require an overnight stay with the expense of a hotel room and meals.

For Your Benefits

Before starting out on a space-available flight, do a quick financial check. If the cost of travel to and from your home to the military air terminal is high, it may be cheaper to book a commercial ticket directly to your destination.

Space-available travel is not for the faint hearted. There are no stewardesses pushing drink carts along the aisles, and services in the smaller terminals may be sparse. Also the type of aircraft available may be cold and shaky, and have uncomfortable seats. So if you want predictable travel, buy an airline ticket. If adventure is in your soul, space available is the way to go.

Facilities at space available passenger terminals depend on the terminal's size and location. Some may include a branch Exchange store, a barber shop, baggage lockers, or a nursery. Some terminals also provide a USO lounge. Remember that most terminals close at night; you must leave and find lodging.

Arranging Flights

Step one, of course, is to find a base that provides regular passenger service. A document at www.amc.af.mil/shared/media/document/AFD-060328-001.doc provides a list of terminals.

With a gateway selected, register at the terminal's Passenger Service Centers (in person, by e-mail, or by fax). You must present travel documents when you are selected for the next available seat. These documents include up-to-date uniformed services ID cards, passports, immunization records, and visas (when required).

During registration, you may select up to five destination countries. Consider selecting "All" as your last option. This may open a seat in the right direction, but not exactly the destination you had in mind. At that point, you can switch to commercial or compete for a space-available hop to your desired destination. It also opens the option of flying to some unique and interesting destinations. Passengers remain on the registration list for up to 60 days or until selected for travel. Be ready to go and in the vicinity of the terminal during "show time," which is typically three hours before departure.

Space-available seats are typically identified between 30 minutes and three hours before a flight. Check with the Passenger Service Center for the space available show time whenever departing the terminal. Always be ready for immediate processing and boarding.

Upon registration, you are assigned a category of travel and compete for seats within that category based on the date and time of registration. This date and time of sign-up are yours through to your destination. All flights are one-way. You will receive a new date and time when registering for your return travel. You may be able to sign up prior to arrival at a destination by use of fax, mail, or e-mail.

Service members (except the Marine Corps) are not required to travel in uniform. Appropriate civilian attire is permitted, if it is in good taste and does not in conflict with accepted attire in the overseas country of departure, transit, or destination. Also, it should also be capable of keeping you warm on a chilly military aircraft.

Eligibility for Flights

Active duty and retired service members may fly anywhere the Department of Defense has flights operating. Guard/Reserve members may fly to, from, and between all 50 states, Puerto Rico, the Virgin Islands, Guam, and American Samoa.

Attention! _____

Personnel on official orders are in a funded travel status and should not be flying space available.

Flying space available from a foreign point into the United States may be difficult. Entry into the United States for nonactive duty personnel (those traveling on passports) may require passage through a terminal that has appropriate Immigration facilities, which means returning through a civilian airport.

Space Available Priority Categories

Space-available passengers are divided into six priority categories. In most cases, family members must be accompanied by their sponsor. Base operations will assign the seats in order of category. The lower the category number, the greater your chances are of getting on the aircraft. This is a partial listing of eligible individuals and their category of travel.

Category 1—Emergency leave unfunded travel for uniformed services members, U.S. citizens or employees of the American Red Cross stationed overseas, employees of the Uniformed Services/Non-appropriated Fund (NAF) activities, and dependents of all of these categories.

Category 2—Sponsors in an environmental morale leave (EML) status and their dependents traveling with them, also in EML status. "Sponsors" includes the following:

- Uniformed services members

- U.S. citizen civilian employees of the armed forces who are eligible for government-funded transportation to the United States at tour completion (including NAF employees)

- American Red Cross full-time, paid personnel on duty with a DoD component overseas

- USO professional staff personnel on duty with the uniformed services

- DODDS teachers during the school year and for employer-approved training during recess periods

Category 3—Ordinary Leave and Others:

- Uniformed services members and their dependents in a leave or pass status, other than emergency leave

- Uniformed services members traveling under permissive TDY orders for a house-hunting incident to a pending PCS

- Medal of Honor recipients and their dependents (when accompanied by their sponsor)

- Foreign cadets and midshipmen attending U.S. service academies, in a leave status

- Foreign Exchange Service members and their dependents on permanent duty with the Department of Defense, when in a leave status

Category 4—Unaccompanied dependents on EML and DODDS teachers on EML during summer

Category 5—Permissive TDY (non-house-hunting) students, dependents, and others

Category 6—Retired uniformed services members and their dependents when accompanying them, and command-sponsored dependents stationed overseas with their sponsor

Baggage Allowance

Even though you are assigned to sit in a cargo plane, space for luggage may be limited. Pack light and do not place valuables in checked luggage. The amount of baggage permitted may be limited due to the type of aircraft and how full it is.

Each passenger is allowed to check two pieces of baggage, 70 pounds each, up to 62 linear inches in size (the sum of the length, width, and height). Family members may pool their baggage allowances. Each passenger is permitted to hand-carry one article (small baggage, backpack, and so on) and one personal item (purse, briefcase, and so on) for storage in the passenger cabin area. Hand-carried items must be no longer than 45 linear inches and must fit under the passenger's seat or in the overhead compartment, if available.

Discounted Commercial Travel

Space-available air travel flies only between military facilities. If your journey does not begin and end near one, it is likely cheaper to pursue a military discount from a commercial carrier. When traveling, keep all your options open, and you will be less likely to be stuck somewhere you don't want to be.

For long distances, air is usually the best choice, if the air fares are reasonable. Rail and bus companies stop occasionally along the way, which greatly lengthens the journey. Of course, a leisurely trip can be a vacation in itself.

Rail Travel

Passenger rail travel is available but is not commonly used in the United States. Still, it is a great option when the East Coast is closed due to fog. The seats are much larger than an airline seat and are easier to sleep in for overnight travel.

Amtrak offers active duty U.S. military personnel and their dependents a 10 percent discount off most Amtrak rail fares in the United States. However, there are some limitations, so ask the ticket agent before booking the ticket. Also you must present your active duty United States Armed Forces ID card when buying the ticket.

Bus Travel

Just as there are different types of airlines focusing on a specific route, the same holds true for buses. Whereas Greyhound runs intercity routes coast to coast, regional bus lines may be your choice for shorter interstate distances. Each bus line sets its own rates and discounts.

If you travel for any distance on an instate highway, you will likely see a Greyhound bus. Just as airports provide a link between major cities, these intercity (and interstate) buses link the rest of the country. Airfares between large cities can be affordable. But if you add flying from the large airport to the much smaller local airport near your destination, the cost can be significantly higher. In the western states where large airports are far between, this can be very expensive.

Greyhound offers active duty and retired military personnel and their dependent family members a 10 percent discount off the Greyhound unrestricted fare. Another option for military personnel is to travel on Greyhound for a maximum fare of $198 round-trip anywhere in the continental United States. Check out the latest fares at www.greyhound.com.

A 25 percent discount on one-way fares is available to U.S. Veterans Administration Hospital patients assigned by the U.S. Veterans Administration to military hospitals, or patients assigned by the U.S. Veterans Administration to civil and state institutions when traveling at their own expense. To qualify, the patient must present a completed original Veterans Administration Request for Reduced Rate Transportation Form (VA-Form 3068) to the ticket agent at time of purchase. Copies are not accepted for this discount.

Commercial Air Travel

Purchasing an airline ticket is a delicate art. With luck, the round-trip ticket will be less than $200 for anywhere in the CONUS. Usually, this means purchasing the ticket two weeks or more in advance and watching for special pricing for specific flights.

But if the purchase must be completed at the last minute or is for a busy holiday period, the price per ticket can be several times the best rate. Fortunately, the major airlines offer some sort of military discounts as a courtesy to their military customers. (Discount airlines believe they are already offering their best rates to everyone and may not have a military discount.) Each carrier has its own requirements to obtain a reduced rate, so you might want to shop around. These discounts are for active duty personnel. If you are a member of the Guard/Reserve on extended active duty, you need a copy of your orders and time to explain to the ticket agent why you do not have an active duty ID card.

Obtaining a military discount involves either finding that category online or asking a ticket agent. Either way, you must prove your entitlement to the discount. Your uniformed services ID card is the preferred method. Usually these discounts include your dependents (they need their ID cards also). Discounts are often extended for a few days past your separation from the uniformed services.

> **For Your Benefits**
>
> Military personnel on emergency leave can often obtain low airfares if they show their emergency leave orders to the ticket agent. If you are on emergency leave, always tell the ticketing agent. The agent may also advance you to the top of the standby list.

Kick Back at a Military Resort

In basic training, recruits are told that if the military wanted you to have something, they would have issued it to you. The next best thing to that is when the military sells it to you at a discount. That is what you can get from the various military-only resorts located around the world. Uncle Sam has created a system of hotels and campgrounds that are available to most people in the military community. These resorts are open to active duty personnel, Guard/Reserve members, retirees, and in many cases, DoD civilian employees and the families of authorized patrons. Always verify your eligibility to use a specific facility before making a reservation.

On the big end of the discounted hotels are the full-featured Armed Forces Recreation Centers located in Hawaii, Germany, Japan, Korea, Florida, and Virginia. They provide high-quality and affordable vacations. Each has its own reservations center and its own twist on who is eligible.

In the middle tier are the local recreation facilities. These include beach houses, mountain cabins, lakeside cabins, and a wide range in between. Reservations are usually handled at the local base.

For the budget-minded, most military bases have their own temporary lodging facilities for incoming families, visitors, or other authorized patrons. So if you want to stay near, say, Panama City Beach but want to save money on hotel bills (and have a less rowdy place to sleep), you might check into the Tyndall Air Force Base's Sand Dollar Inn," which is just 18 miles from the beach.

Attention!

Some of the resorts hold a block of rooms open to accommodate service members on R&R from Southwest Asia.

Typically, lodging in any of these facilities is based on your rank, duty status, room size, and/or room location. The higher your rank, the more the room will cost. Also, the rooms are allocated based on a priority system. Typically, it runs from active duty at the top to Guard/Reserve, to retired, and, in some cases, to also include DoD civilians. Always make reservations far in advance because these facilities are often full.

To streamline the room reservation process for their many sites, the Air Force and Navy are combining their reservation websites. Check them out online at www. dodlodging.net. This page includes a link to their eligibility, policies, and standards. You can also contact DoD Lodging at 1-877-782-4681.

Shades of Green

Imagine a 586-room hotel right on the grounds of Walt Disney World in Florida, sandwiched between golf courses—a place that is close to everything and still affordable for a young military family. Imagine a true resort that includes complimentary buses to the Walt Disney World Resort transportation center. This place is called Shades of Green.

Shades of Green facilities offer guest rooms that meet the Americans with Disabilities Act (ADA) standards. This includes standard oversized rooms, oversized elevators, special transportation options, and multiple ramps for full resort access.

A ticket office in the lobby offers reduced-priced admission tickets to the many attractions in the area. Two PGA Championship Golf Courses, operated by Disney World, are located just outside the hotel's door. Military discounted greens fee are $55 plus tax (includes cart). Check with Shades of Green Guest Services for the latest rates and additional information.

Room rates are broken into three categories:

Category 1: E-1 through E-5

Category 2: E-6 through E-9, O-1 through O-3, WO-1 to CW-3, Widows, Medal of Honor recipients, 100 percent disabled veterans and cadets

Category 3: O-4 through O-10, CW-4 and CW-5, active and retired Department of Defense civilians, foreign military assigned to a U.S. military installation only

Rates through September 30, 2008 (Subject to Change)

Room Type	Category #1	Category #2	Category #3
Standard Room	$ 89.00	$111.00	$119.00
Poolside Room	$ 99.00	$121.00	$129.00
Family Jr. Suite	$250.00	$250.00	$250.00
Family Suite	$275.00	$275.00	$275.00

You can make a reservation in several ways. The easiest is online. As you fill in the online reservation information, the calendar indicates which room types are available for a given day. Given its high occupancy rate, you can see which types of rooms are available for a given date. Reservations can be made up to one year in advance. Look up Shades of Green online at www.shadesofgreen.org.

Reservations can be called in Monday through Friday, from 8:30 A.M. to 5:00 P.M. (Eastern Standard Time), at 1-888-593-2242. For the shortest hold time, call on Wednesday or Thursday afternoons. You can also e-mail your request to reservation@shadesofgreen.org.

Finally, you can post a letter requesting reservations to:

> Shades of Green Reservations
> PO Box 22789
> Lake Bucna Vista, FL 32830-2789

Attention!

The resort hotels fill up quickly and stay full, so make your reservations as far in advance as possible.

Cape Henry Inn and Beach Club

The Cape Henry Inn and Beach Club is located on Fort Story near Virginia Beach, Virginia. It offers beachfront accommodations, outdoor cabanas at each of the two swimming pools, and beachside cabanas at the end of the boardwalk overlooking the Chesapeake Bay.

The Cape Henry Inn offers a wide range of accommodations options, from traditional hotel rooms (many overlooking Chesapeake Bay) to family-sized cottages that accommodate up to eight people. There are also bungalows that permit smoking and pets. One- and two-bedroom log cabins that accommodate up to eight people are also available.

These facilities are open to active duty, retired, and Guard/Reserve personnel, and DoD civilians. Unlike other military recreation facilities, the Cape Henry Inn has the same price for all ranks. Rates vary by the season: winter (November 1–March 31), spring (April 1–May 14), summer (May 15–September 14), and fall (September 15–October 31). Reservations are taken on a first-come, first-served basis and may be made up to 52 weeks in advance.

For example, for a two-person room in the inn, the room costs $85 per night in the spring, $95 per night in the summer, $75 per night in the fall, and $40 per night in the winter. The two-person log cabin costs $100 per night in the spring, $110 per night in the summer, $90 per night in the fall, and $80 per night in the winter.

All rates are based on two adults (18 and older) in the room. Add $10 per night for each additional adult.

Reservations can be made online at www.capehenryinn.com/booking.htm. They can also be called in to 757-422-8818 or made by fax at 757-422-6397. The address of the facility is:

> The Cape Henry Inn and Beach Club
> 1116 Kwajalein Road
> Ft. Story, VA 23459-5034

Hale Koa Hotel

Imagine a vacation in Hawaii for yourself or for your entire family. Imagine kicking back on the beach right outside your hotel. The Hale Koa Hotel is the answer to all of this and more. The 817-room Hale Koa is located on 72 acres fronting Waikiki

Beach. It offers a range of resort services, from in-house entertainment to snorkel and surf equipment rental. The Hale Koa features its own branch military Exchange.

Rates are based on your military rank or civilian grade at the time of check-in. The rate for a retired military member is based on the rank you held at the time of your retirement. The Hale Koa Hotel requires a deposit equivalent to a one-night stay. The credit card provided on your reservation is automatically charged this deposit.

You room rate is based on your category and room type. Through September 2008, the cheapest room is $83 per night for an E-5 or below "standard" room (plus any taxes). That same room would cost a general officer $24 per night more.

Category 1: E-1 through E-5

Category 2: E-6 through E-9, O-1 through O-3, WO-1 to CW-3, widows, Medal of Honor recipients, 100 percent disabled veterans

Category 3: O-4 through O-10, CW-4 and CW-5, active and retired Department of Defense civilians

Category 4: Foreign military assigned to a U.S. military installation only or with U.S. travel orders

The Hale Koa has seven classes of rooms, ranging from standard to deluxe oceanfront.

Rates through September 30, 2008 (Subject to Change)

Room Type	Category #1	Category #2	Category #3	Category #4
Standard Room	$83	$99	$107	$142
Deluxe Oceanfront	$154	$183	$202	$268

You can make your reservation in several ways. The easiest is online. The web pages display the full range of room options and costs. As you fill in the online reservation information, the calendar indicates which room types are available for a given day. Find the Hale Koa hotel online at www.halekoa.com.

If you prefer to call in your reservations, call 1-800-367-6027 (from CONUS) Monday to Saturday from 8:00 A.M. to 4:00 P.M. (Hawaii Standard Time). The telephone reservations desk is closed on federal holidays. Reservations may also be e-mailed to reservations@halekoa.com.

Finally, you can mail reservations to:

> Hale Koa Hotel, Honolulu
> 2055 Kalia Road
> Honolulu, HI 96815

Dragon Hill Lodge

If a Korean adventure is more to your taste, consider staying at the 394-room Dragon Hill Resort in the heart of Seoul, Korea. The Dragon Hill is located on Yongsan South Post in Seoul, South Korea, just north of the Han River. Visiting personnel active duty and retired, and DoD civilians can gain access to the installations by showing their DoD identification cards.

Each room has a queen-size bed and a sleeper sofa, a private bath, and a color television with satellite channels. Maximum occupancy is four persons per room.

The hotel offers tours to learn more about the Korean arts, history, and culture. There is even a day trip available to see the Demilitarized Zone with North Korea (from a safe distance).

The Dragon Hill Lodge is available to active duty, retired military, dependents, DoD civilians, and all foreign non-Korean military with orders to USFK. All patrons must present either a DD Form 1173 or a DD Form 2.

Reservations can be secured online through www.dragonhilllodge.com. There is also a 24-hour telephone reservation hot line at (011-82-2) 7918-222. The advantage of these approaches is that you can instantly confirm room availability for your desired dates.

Reservations can also be arranged by e-mail at reservations@dhl.korea.army.mil.

Category 1: E-1 through E-5

Category 2: E-6 through E-9, O-1 through O-3, WO-1 to CW-3

Category 3: O-4 through O-10, CW-4 and CW-5, active and retired Department of Defense civilians, retired military

Category 4: All military and civilians on PCS/TLA

Category 5: All military and civilians on TDY

Rates for a single room are $59 for Category 1, $70 for Category 2, and $82 for Category 3. Add $19 for each additional person in the room, up to the maximum of four people per room. Authorized military and civilian personnel on PCS/TLA pay $150 per room and an additional amount for each person (ask for your total room rate when making reservations). Authorized military and civilian personnel on TDY pay $220 per room plus $30 more per person.

Room reservations are accepted up to 365 days before departure date for PCS (TLA) only. Reservations from personnel on leave, pass, or TDY are accepted only six months in advance of checkout date.

The Edelweiss Lodge

High in the Bavarian Alps near Garmisch sits the 330-room Edelweiss Lodge and Resort. Located 56 miles from Munich, the Edelweiss Lodge offers an array of guest amenities, entertainment, and recreation activities. Enjoy a sightseeing tour, spend a day on the slopes, or just revel in the majestic Alpine views. The Edelweiss Lodge is a destination for all seasons.

Authorized patrons include active duty service members, military retirees, Reservists, Guardsmen, current DoD civilian employees assigned to EUCOM and Coast Guard civilian employees, foreign military on orders assigned at a U.S. military installation, family members of authorized patrons, and other supporters of the DoD. Room rates are determined by pay grade.

Category 1: E1 through E5

Category 2: E6 through E9, WO-1 through CWO-3, O1 through O3, widows, and 100 percent disabled veterans

Category 3: CWO4 through CWO5, O4 through O10, all civilians, SES, and NATO

There are five classes of rooms, ranging from a standard room with queen-sized beds ($84 per night for Category 1) to Deluxe Loft Suites at $239 per night for all categories. All suites are the same price for all ranks and must be booked through the Vacation Planning Center at (011-49) 8821-9440 from the United States, or (49) 8821-9440 from Europe. The Vacation Planning Center is open Monday through Friday from 8 A.M. to 5 P.M. local time (except U.S. holidays).

Reservations can be made online at www.EdelweissLodgeandResort.com. Phone reservations are available from Monday through Friday, 8 A.M. to 5 P.M. (Central Europe Time). Call from Europe to (00-49) 8821-9440, or from the United States to (011-49) 8821-9440. Reservations may also be e-mailed to vacation@edelweisslodgeandresort.com

The New Sanno Hotel

Located in the heart of Tokyo, one of the world's most expensive cities, is a bargain that is available only to the world's most exclusive organization—the U.S. military. The 149-room facility offers a range of accommodations, from a single room with a queen bed and shower to a Japanese-style room. The Family room holds a maximum of four people. If there are more than four people in the party, additional rooms are required.

The New Sanno Hotel offers a range of services, such as an in-house APO post office and a Navy branch Exchange. There is also concierge service and travel desk for advice on what to do in Tokyo and how to get there. The concierge can explain the use of trains, subways, and buses in and around Tokyo.

Eligibility to use the New Sanno Hotel is rigorously controlled by the Status of Forces Agreement. It is limited to the following:

◆ Active duty personnel and/or their dependents

◆ Retirees with military retirement ID cards (spouses must be accompanied by sponsors)

◆ Reserve component of military

◆ Disabled veterans with DAV ID cards (DD-Form 1173/2765)

◆ DoD civilians stationed in Japan and/or their dependents, or from outside Japan on funded or nonfunded TDY orders or EML orders to Japan

◆ Public Health Service personnel on funded TDY orders to Japan

Room rates are broken into three categories:

◆ Junior Grade—E1 to E5, and G1 to G5.

◆ Mid-Grade—E6 to O3, WO1 to W4, G6 to G11.

◆ Senior Grade—All other military ranks and G ratings. Also anyone on TDY, retirees, Reservists, and disabled veterans.

Room rates (subject to change) range from $48 for a Junior Grade single room, to $58 for a Senior Grade person to use that same room. The most expensive room is a Japanese Suite for $66 for a Junior Grade person, and $87 for a Senior Grade person. The other room types fall in between. A complete breakdown of the room types is available on the New Sanno website. All reservations must be accompanied with one night's room rate. This can be charged to a credit card or paid by a mailed-in check.

Reservations can be called in from Japan to (03) 3440-7871 and from outside of Japan at 81-3-3440-7871. Reservations can also be e-mailed to room_rsv@thenewsanno.com.

Rooms can be reserved up to one year in advance online at https://ssl.thenewsanno.com/reservations.html. The maximum reservation permitted is for 14 days. Exceptions must be approved by the facility management.

Military Hotels

Each military base of significant size has some sort of on-base hotel, known as a Temporary Lodging Facility. These hotels provide short-term accommodations for military members, their families, and guests. These are usually available to military travelers at a reasonable price.

The cost for staying at these facilities varies but is generally significantly less than a commercial hotel rate. Occasionally, they offer equipped kitchenettes, a free DVD library, video games—things for which a commercial hotel charges extra.

Military lodging is not available in all places. In some cases, it is available only to active duty personnel. Availability depends on how heavily it is occupied. However, never let that stop you from asking. Take time to call the facility and, if necessary, be placed on a waiting list. Hotel reservations can usually be cancelled for no penalty if done at least a full day in advance. Drop the expensive hotel and head for the base.

 Attention!

Note that, when on an active military base, you should pay attention to the threat level and listen for announced alerts.

Army Lodging

The Army has a series of bases around the world, and some of them are quite large. As would be expected, these larger bases provide some of the largest temporary lodging facilities. Locate the Army lodging nearest your destination at www.armymwr.com/portal/travel/lodging/.

Eligibility for Army lodging is based on a priority system. Priority One includes all of the active duty personnel who need it for military business. Priority Two is generally referred to as space available. Each facility determines how far in advance it will accept reservations from space available patrons. In an operational emergency, space available customers may be evicted. Within each priority, reservations and assignments are made on a first-come, first-served basis without regard to rate or rank.

Priority One (reservations can be made anytime):

◆ Military, DoD civilian, or family member on TDY orders

◆ Contract personnel with a letter of identification (LOI) or official orders

◆ Military, DoD civilian, or family member on PCS orders

◆ Reserve personnel on IDT, IDTT, AT, or ADT status (must be at least 50 miles from home to installation)

◆ Foreign military under the PEP, IMET, or FMT programs

Priority Two (space available—reservations can be made up to five days in advance):

◆ Military, retired personnel, or family members (must be at least 18 years old), on leave

◆ Personnel on orders/official business from other governmental agencies

◆ Guests of the installation, as determined by the region or installation commander

◆ Medal of Honor recipients and 100 percent disabled vets, with proper ID

◆ Relative or guest of an active duty member assigned to the installation

◆ Relative or guest of an active duty member in a DoD medical facility

◆ Foreign military in the PEP, IMET, or FMT program, on leave

◆ Reservists residing within a 50-mile radius of assigned installation

Navy Lodges

Forty-one Navy Lodges are located around the world, many of them near terrific vacation destinations. When you think Navy, you think water, ocean, and the beaches. There are Navy Lodges in Hawaii, in foreign locations, and even in the Nevada desert.

Navy Lodges rates average 40 percent less than comparable commercial accommodations, but have the same amenities. Navy Lodges are located near all the base services, such as the Exchange, and offer discounted tickets for area attractions at great prices.

Reservations can be made by calling 1-800-Navy Inn, via the web page www. Navy-Lodge.com, or by directly calling the Navy Lodge of your choice.

Reservations are accepted for all eligible personnel on an as-received basis. Rooms may be reserved in the following timeframes:

- Reservations and room assignments are made without regard to rank or rate, or time of reservations. Active duty and Guard/Reserve personnel on PCS can reserve their rooms at any time.

- Sixty-day advance reservation can be made by active duty on leave, surviving spouses, and delayed-entry program participants. This option is also open to retirees awaiting medical treatment.

- Thirty-day advance reservations are for vacationing Guard/Reserve, retired personnel, and their families.

Coast Guard

Some of the most interesting recreational facilities are offered through the U.S. Coast Guard. How about a week in a lighthouse keeper's house (West Chop Lighthouse Recreational Housing Facility on Martha's Vineyard, Massachusetts)? Not something you might find at Air Force Lodging! The Coast Guard facilities are located on both coasts, as well as at the Great Lakes.

In most cases, reservations are taken 90 days in advance for PCS and 60 days in advance for recreational visitors. However, each location may have its own twist, so be sure to check. For example, the lighthouse keeper's house is so popular that anyone interested in staying there must enter into a lottery to see who get the prized spots.

Leave it to the Coasties to keep simple what should be a simple thing! The local command typically handles reservations for these facilities. The address and instructions are listed along with a description of the property online at www.uscg.mil/mwr/Cottages/RecreationalLodging.htm.

Air Force Inn

Temporary lodging can be a big business—even if it is just something offered as a convenience for personnel. The chain of Air Force Inns totals to 32,229 beds, making it one of the top 25 lodging operations. You can locate Air Force Inns through www.dodlodging.net, or if you know where you want to go, you can call that hotel directly. You can also call 1-888-AF-LODGE (1-888-235-6343) to make reservations.

> **For Your Benefits**
>
> Pets may be lodged in Temporary Lodging Facilities (TLFs) with their owners, if approved by the base commander. Always ask the reservations agent if pets are permitted before confirming your reservation.

As with the other services, duty personnel on orders have top priority. How far in advance space-available reservations can be made is based on that facility's historical occupancy rate.

Marines

Back in the old Corps, a GP Medium tent without holes was considered luxurious temporary lodging. The modern Corps has replaced all of that with a series of temporary lodging facilities at all of the major bases. Each is equipped with a coffeemaker, a microwave, a refrigerator, and free cable TV. Some facilities also offer equipped kitchenettes.

Eligibility, in priority sequence, is as follows:

◆ Military personnel and their families who are without housing due to permanent change of station orders

◆ Military members, Ready Reservists, and DoD civilian personnel on TDY

◆ All military personnel in a nonduty status, including Ready Reservists, retirees, and DoD civilian personnel, their families, and their bona fide guests

> **Attention!**
>
> Pets are not permitted in Marine Corps Temporary Lodging Facilities.

Reservations should be made as far in advance as possible. Every Marine Corps Temporary Lodging Facility has its own rules for when reservations will be accepted. Typically, the highest-priority group can reserve any time and the lowest-priority group might not be able to reserve a room until just a short time before traveling. Check out www.usmc-mccs.org/lodging/index.cfm.

Marines Offer Additional Recreational Lodging

The Corps always seems to know how to make a good thing better. At major facilities, they have created a set of recreational facilities that are a real bargain. Tired of fighting your way through the beach crowds to the ocean? How about a "private" beach with a bargain-priced cottage or house trailer? Actually, the beach is not private, but it will seem like it, since it is on-base and the civilian crowds cannot enter!

Recreational Lodging is available at several Marine Corps Installations. These facilities might be beach houses or mountain chalets. This program offers Marines and other authorized patrons the opportunity to relax and enjoy their vacation at a premier location, while enjoying significant savings.

Camp Pendleton Beach Cottages

MCB Camp Pendleton offers lodging on Del Mar Beach and San Onofre Beach. Cottages and campsites with electrical hookups are available to rent at both beaches. The cottages have one to three bedrooms, all have kitchens and TVs, and many have fire rings. Each beach has a bath house, and lifeguards are on duty year-round.

For online information, check out www.mccscp.com/lodging/index.cfm. Del Mar Beach cottage rates are $70 per night for a one-bedroom cottage. Make a reservation at 760-725-2134.

San Onofre Beach Cottages nightly rates are $55 for a one-bedroom, $65 for a two-bedroom, and $75 for a three-bedroom. Make your reservation at 760-763-SURF (760-763-7873) or 760-763-SAND (760-763-7263).

Big Bear Mountain Cottages

Move out to the high country. What a relief from the desert below! Miramar Marine Corps Air Station manages the Big Bear Recreational Facility, with eight cabins that are available year-round.

Each cabin has a bedroom downstairs with a queen-size bed, and two full-size beds in the upstairs loft. Each cabin is fully furnished and equipped with a refrigerator, gas range/oven, microwave oven, and coffeemaker. Cooking items such as pots and pans are provided, as are dishes and flatware for six. The Main Lodge has a limited supply of high chairs and playpens available.

The maximum occupancy of a cabin is six people (adults, children, and infants). At no time must the "floor load" limit of six occupants be exceeded.

Authorized patrons include active duty, Reserve, and retired military, as well as DoD employees and family members. Cabins are rented to these authorized patrons on a priority system.

◆ First Priority goes to active duty military personnel stationed on Marine Corps installations. Reservations may be made the first business day of the month for the month after next (for the following 60 days).

◆ Second Priority is for all other active duty personnel. Reservations may be made on the second business day of the month for the month after next (for the following 60 days).

◆ Third Priority is for all other authorized patrons. Reservations may be made on the third business day of the month for the month after next (for the following 60 days).

Cabin reservations are accepted in person at the Entertainment Ticket Office, Bldg. 2524, MCAS Miramar, or by calling 858-577-4126/4141 between 9 A.M. and 5 P.M., Monday to Friday. Reservations must be paid in full four weeks before the reservation date.

Beachside campsites are open year-round, weather permitting. There are five RV sites with hook-ups and five tent sites. Tent camping is permitted only in specified campsite areas. The maximum total occupancy of an RV/campsite is eight people (adults, children, and infants).

Cottages at Kaneohe Bay

Enjoy the serenity and beauty of Kaneohe Bay and the Pacific Ocean from a beach cottage. Kaneohe Bay is the breeding ground for the endangered Hawaiian monk seal and sea turtle. Those lucky enough may catch a glimpse of these graceful creatures from their cottage.

All units have a full kitchen, two bedrooms, living and dining areas, cable TV, and daily maid service. Kaneohe Bay Cottages are the perfect getaway for the whole family and out-of-town guests. However, only the Marines would force you to drive across an active runway to access these beautiful cottages. Pedestrians are at a speed disadvantage and are not permitted.

Reservations are accepted for these cottages according to this priority system:

◆ Active military stationed at Kaneohe Bay or Camp Smith can reserve their lodging 60 days in advance.

◆ Active military stationed at other bases have 45 days in advance to make a reservation.

◆ Retired military, Reservists, and DOD employees can reserve their spot 30 days out.

To reserve your relaxing spot, contact Kaneohe Bay Building 3038 at 808-254-2806 from Monday to Sunday any time of the day. You can also e-mail your request to thelodgeatkbay@usmc-mccs.org.

Camp Butler

Okinawa is a tropical paradise well known to many Marines. For a quiet getaway, consider a stay at The Cottages at Oura Wan Beach on Camp Schwab. Ten private cottages with Ryukyun-inspired interiors have queen-sized beds, a full kitchen, and a dining room. Unwind on your private patio with a spectacular beachside view of the ocean. Guests can also rent kayaks, sailboats, and windsurfs, or charter a boat through Oura Wan Boating. The Cottages at Oura Wan Beach is also within easy distance of the Beachhead conference facility.

To reserve your piece of oceanfront quiet, phone 011-81-611-725-5005. Check it out online at www.mccsokinawa.com/mccs.asp?id=124.

Camp Lejeune

Why pay the high prices at Myrtle Beach or the Outer Banks when there are beach houses and campsites available at Onslow Beach at Camp Lejeune, North Carolina? Facilities include cabanas, house trailers, and special quarters for E-9 and lieutenant colonel and colonel ranks. All are furnished and sleep four or six.

Active duty personnel stationed at Camp Lejeune, Cherry Point, and MCAS New River can make their reservations 20 weeks in advance. All other military and spouses with a valid military ID, or DoD employees from Camp Lejeune, Cherry Point, and MCAS New River can make their reservations eight weeks in advance. Payment is due in full within 14 days of the booking date.

Lodging is broken into three categories: Enlisted, Staff NCO (SNCO), and Officer. Prices are based on packages of nights and the type of facility rented. Enlisted packages range from three nights in a Cabana for $75, to seven nights in a lodge for $189. Staff NCO quarters range from $114 for a two-bedroom trailer for three nights, to $329 for seven nights in the E9 House. Officer packages range from $114 for a three-night package in a two-bedroom trailer, to $350 for a week in the O5/O6 house.

The Onslow Beach RV park has 37 RV sites and 6 tent sites with water, electric, sewage, and cable hookups. There are also five dry camping sites available for $8 per night.

Additional information is available online at www.mccslejeune.com/beach/index.html.

Reservations can be called in from 8 A.M. to 6 P.M. (Eastern Standard Time) to 910-450-7502. Reservations can also be made in the Main Exchange's lobby at the Onslow Beach reservation booth from Monday through Friday.

Private Military Hotels

Over time, veterans have recognized the need for a place to stay in the midst of expensive cities. Each of these hotels is its own charity and has its own rules. Be sure to check eligibility requirements before making a reservation. However, if in doubt, call them directly: their goal is to serve the military community and they will patiently answer any of your questions.

New York City–SSMAC

There is no place quite like the Soldiers', Sailors', Marines', and Airmen's Club (SSMAC) located in the heart of New York City. The Club provides convenient, safe, affordable accommodations in midtown Manhattan, within walking distance of transportation (Penn Station, Grand Central Station, and Port Authority Bus Terminal) and popular attractions such as the Empire State Building and the Theater District.

The SSMAC is available to all members of the uniformed services and the Merchant Marine. It also opens its doors to the New York Police Department, Fire Department, and Emergency Medical Service. Additional information about SSMAC is available online at www.ssmaclub.org/, or you can request additional information by e-mail from info@ssmaclub.org.

To minimize rates, the Club, unlike other hotels, rents individual beds instead of rooms. The Club has 21 rooms with two beds to accommodate couples, six rooms with three beds, one room with four beds, and one room with six beds to accommodate families or groups. The Club consists of five floors, including three sleeping floors. There are separate communal lavatories and showers for men and women on each sleeping floor.

The Club does not have an elevator, as it was originally constructed as a town house. A stair chair is available between the lobby level and the first floor. No meals are served at the Club.

Patrons must prove their eligibility upon check-in by presenting their military ID, dog tags, DD214, and VFW or American Legion ID card. Emergency services must show their ID card. Room rates are based on rank. They range from $30 per day for an E-1 to E-4, ROTC cadet, or service academy cadet; to $60 per day for field-grade officers and above, and veterans. Retirees' rate is $50 per night.

Attention!

Parking garages in the vicinity of the SSMAC charge about $30 per day.

Make your reservations by calling 1-800-678-8443 or mailing your request to:

> Soldiers', Sailors', Marines', and Airmen's Club
> 283 Lexington Ave. (at 37th St.)
> New York, NY 10016-3540

San Francisco'—Marines' Memorial Club and Hotel

Hotels in San Francisco are not cheap, even with a military discount. However, there is one spot where you can bivouac the family at a reasonable price: the Marines' Memorial Club. Founded in 1946, the nonprofit Marines' Memorial Association offers membership to all former and retired members of all branches of the U.S. Armed Forces.

The 138-room/suite facility is located just two blocks from cable cars, Union Square, and the theatre district. The 12-story Beaux-Arts structure's traditional accented furnishings, marble baths, and cherry wood armoires retain the character and elegance of old San Francisco. Additional information about the Marines' Memorial Club and Hotel is available online at www.marineclub.com.

Rates are substantially less if you purchase a membership ($35 for personnel serving in the active and Guard/Reserve forces, and $100 for retirees and veterans). Proof of service is required.

To make a reservation, call 415-673-6672, ext. 250; e-mail lmp@marineclub.com; or send a written request to:

Marines' Memorial Association
The Living Memorial Project
609 Sutter Street
San Francisco, California 94102-1017

Armed Forces Vacation Club

The Armed Forces Vacation Club (AFVC) offers DoD-affiliated personnel affordable condominium vacations at over 3,500 resorts around the world. The AFVC offers several different programs. The first is the space available program, in which condominiums are offered for $329 per unit per week, regardless of unit size, unit occupancy, unit configuration, date, or location. These units are usually opened several weeks before they are available and are rarely available during holidays. If you can make your reservation on short notice, these bargains may be for you.

If you prefer to make your reservations early and lock in where you will be staying, the AFVC High Demand Resort Rentals may work best. This covers the same international set of locations, but you pay a much higher price. Still, your lodging is locked in for the times you want.

AFVC also offers nightly rentals. You must call to check availability for the property you want to rent, as these rooms are on a space-available basis and not all nights may be available.

Eligibility

Eligible participants must be 21 years or older and one of the following:

◆ Member of the U.S. uniformed services (Air Force, Army, Coast Guard, Marine Corps, Navy, NOAA, USPHS; active duty, and both active and inactive Reserve, Auxiliarist, and National Guard) or an adult dependent

- Retired member of the U.S. uniformed services (Air Force, Army, Coast Guard, Marine Corps, Navy, NOAA, USPHS, Reserve, Auxiliarist, and National Guard)

- Spouse or child (21 or older) of an active, Reserve, or retired member of the U.S. uniformed services, and have a current DD Form 1173, United States Uniformed Services Identification and Privilege Card

- Civilian employee of the DoD (appropriated, nonappropriated, or retired)

- Foreign exchange service member on permanent duty with the DoD

- American Red Cross personnel serving overseas with the U.S. military

- DoD dependent school teacher

- Disabled American Veteran rated at 100 percent with a valid U.S. Uniformed Services identification card

- Contractor working on a military installation and in possession of an ID card issued by the installation

Make a Reservation

The first step is to locate where you want to stay. Look at the listing of properties available online at www.afvclub.com/. Remember that the space-available properties may not show availability until just a few weeks before you leave. Also check closely for any additional fees, such as utility fees and club fees. Reservation fees are for seven nights of lodging only.

Next, call the reservation center at 1-800-724-9988 any day of the week from 9:30 A.M. to 6:00 P.M. If this is your first call, tell them you are a "first-time AFVC caller." They will guide you through the free registration process.

Keep in mind these important points:

- Your credit card will be charged at the time of confirmation.

- All rooms have a maximum occupancy. Every person in the room counts, including infants.

- AFVC has strict policies governing cancellation, as explained on their website. Understand what these are if your vacation plans may change.

The Least You Need to Know

◆ Each facility has its own eligibility criteria and pricing structures.

◆ The term "space available" for free military means literally that.

◆ Many low-cost vacation lodgings are available for active duty personnel, Reserve members, retirees, and, in some cases, DoD civilians.

◆ Unless you are active duty military, you must re-enter the United States through a commercial airport so that you can clear Customs and Immigration.

Part 4

Go to School

Many young people exit high school with little idea of what they want to do with their life. Furthermore, they lack the money to attend college. Both active duty and Guard/Reserve service can provide an opportunity to explore the world, job training, and money for further schooling. Regardless of financial background, through service, veterans have earned financial support for attending college—if they will take advantage of it.

The military can make something as simple as money for college into something complex. Various programs exist for active duty, Guard, and Reserve, all based on when you enlisted or reenlisted. These benefits have a time limit, so drain them before the clock runs out. Some states reward National Guard service by providing free tuition to any state college. When combined with federal benefits, a student may complete a degree with little or no debt.

Chapter

14

Money for College While Still Serving

In This Chapter

- ◆ Going to college for free
- ◆ Testing for credit
- ◆ Forgiving your loans
- ◆ Obtaining school money for your honey

You don't have to wait until you have finished your term of service to go to school. Whether it is finishing high school or taking college classes to get a degree, you can achieve it in your off-duty time. What's that, you say? School is the last thing you want to do in your free time? You remember how awful and boring high school was? Well, as helpful as it is in television commercials to have a military background when you are job hunting, a college degree is just as helpful, if not more so.

Even if you realize just how important a college degree is today, you may think it is just out of your price range, and the cost is climbing each year! There are ways to go to school and pay little or nothing while still in the military. Sure, there are ways to get things paid for when you are out, but in most cases, you are paying into an account that will pay out more for you later. If you are still serving, it seems that the government is a little more inclined to bear more of the financial burden.

Military Tuition Assistance (TA)

Tuition Assistance (TA) is a great benefit, a partial repayment for college class expenses. In some cases, with careful planning, it can cover the costs completely! TA provides money for classes taken during off-duty time. It funds 100 percent of tuition costs for high school completion and college-level courses, up to a maximum of $4,500 per fiscal year. For college classes, this money can be used for tuition; instructional, lab, and computer fees; and mandatory enrollment fees combined, but unfortunately not textbooks. Money gets cut off at $250 per semester hour (or equivalent), and the $4,500 cap per fiscal year includes all levels of education being completed during that time period.

The Montgomery GI Bill's Top-Up is compatible with Tuition Assistance.

Each service branch has its own criteria for eligibility, service requirements, application processes, and restrictions.

> **For Your Benefits**
>
> You can use Tuition Assistance while you're still serving and save your GI Bill for when you get out!

◆ Air Force active duty service members and Reservists are eligible. The 100 percent tuition and fees maximum payout is $250 per semester hour, $166 per quarter-hour, and $4,500 overall per fiscal year. TA covers tuition, lab, enrollment, computer, and *special fees*. Airmen fill out Form AF1227 to apply.

◆ Army active duty service members and Reservists, as well as Army National Guard and Army Reserve members who are on active duty, are eligible. The 100 percent tuition and fees maximum payout is $250 per semester hour, $166 per quarter-hour, and $4,500 overall per fiscal year. TA covers tuition, lab, enrollment, computer, and special fees. Soldiers fill out DA Form 2171 E to apply.

> **def•i•ni•tion**
>
> **Special fees** are considered to be everything else the school charges you for, above the cost of tuition, before they will let you into the class. Colleges love their fees. They have fees for using the parking lot, for student clubs, and for the computer network. These fees vary widely between schools but are added onto your tuition bill like taxes you cannot avoid.

◆ Coast Guard service members who are on active duty or in the Selective Reserve qualify for tuition assistance. The Coast Guard even lets its civilian employees take advantage of this benefit. The 100 percent tuition and fees maximum payout is $250 per semester hour, $166 per quarter-hour, and $4,500 per fiscal year. TA covers tuition and lab fees. Coast Guard members need to fill out Form CG-4147 to apply.

◆ Marines on active duty only qualify for Tuition Assistance. The 100 percent tuition and fees maximum payout is $250 per semester hour, $166 per quarter-hour, and $4,500 per fiscal year. TA covers tuition, lab, enrollment, computer, and special fees. Marines need to fill out Form NETPDTC 1560 to apply.

◆ Navy active duty service members and Navy Reservists who are currently on active duty status are eligible for Tuition Assistance. The 100 percent tuition and fees maximum payout is $250 per semester hour and $166 per quarter-hour, with a maximum of 12 semester hours per fiscal year. TA covers tuition, lab, enrollment, computer, and special fees. Sailors need to fill out Form NETPDTC 1560 to apply.

DANTES

The mission of Defense Activity for Non-Traditional Education Support (DANTES) is "to support the off-duty, voluntary education programs of the Department of Defense and to conduct special projects and development activities in support of education-related functions of the Department"—or, in layman's terms, to help you get the training you need for what you want to do. DANTES offers a wide range of programs, materials, and tests for service members and their families.

The basis for DANTES began back in 1941, when the War Department authorized the creation of the Army Institute, which expanded to become the United States Armed Forces Institute (USAFI) in 1941. Located in Madison, Wisconsin, USAFI was responsible for the education of the United States military during the World War II era. Wisconsin was only a command base for the program, which had over 300,000 students enrolled in almost 50 colleges and universities, and offered more than 6,000 correspondence courses. In 1964, however, Congress stopped funding USAFI due to budget cuts. That same year, the Department of Defense and Military Services proposed a more streamlined version of the previous one, and DANTES was officially established on July 31, 1974.

DANTES with ACE and SOCs

DANTES works with the American Council on Education and the Servicemembers Opportunity Colleges to attribute credit where it has been earned by service members.

ACE is responsible for the Military Evaluation Program and the Military Installation Voluntary Education Review (MIVER) Program, and the American Association of State Colleges and Universities (AASCU), which conducts the Servicemembers Opportunity Colleges (SOC) programs.

The Military Evaluation Program provides for the evaluation of credit earned through Service School courses, occupations, classifications, and courses taken through respective military branches. Credit can also be earned from simply having been trained or having served. The amount of credit given is determined by the American Council on Education (ACE). The credit can be applied to a college degree or vocational certificate.

The Military Installation Voluntary Education Review (MIVER) program exists to assess the quality of selected on-base voluntary education programs. Each year, the military chooses the programs or schools that it wants to check up on. MIVER visits and makes an assessment of the institution, and then reports and makes suggestions on how to improve the programs or help them meet standards.

The American Association of State Colleges and Universities (AASCU) runs the Servicemember Opportunity Colleges (SOCs). SOC colleges and universities are dedicated to helping service members and their families get college degrees. Military students can take courses in their off-duty hours at or near military installations in the United States, overseas, and on Navy ships. Chapter 16 covers SOCs in more depth.

Attention!

DANTES and several of the national testing programs, such as the College Level Examination Program (CLEP), have been alerted of test prep scams. If you receive information about test preparation materials, beware of …

- Attempts to sell prep services for multiple tests, with payment up front.
- Credit arrangements with a company other than the one selling the prep service.
- Direct sales contact at home.
- Promises of college credit without enrollment.
- Booklists that include dictionaries or encyclopedias.

Before paying for any test prep service, contact your Education Service officer or Navy College Education Specialist. These may be scams. Free information and low-cost study materials are available from your local education center.

Examinations and Aptitude Tests

DANTES sponsors a wide range of examination programs for service members. These tests include the GED, ACT, SAT, GRE, GMAT, PRAXIS, CLEP, DSSTs, and ECEs. Are you unsure of whether any of the tests apply or would be helpful to you? Here is a brief description of each one.

The General Education Development (GED) test is for individuals who have not completed their formal high school education. The official website for the GED is available through ACE at www.acenet.edu/AM/Template.cfm?Section=GEDTS.

The ACT is the ACT Assessment test (the name was an acronym for American College Testing at one point but was shortened to just ACT officially in 1996), which is an admissions requirement at some colleges, mostly in the Midwest and eastern United States. The official website for the ACT is www.act.org. DANTES funds the ACT and SAT only once. This test may require some advance preparation. You can find study materials for this test at most bookstores across the country.

The SAT is the Scholastic Assessment Test. It is used just like the ACT for college admissions and student placement. Most colleges require either ACT or SAT scores to apply because this helps them gauge a student's potential for success at their facility. For more information on the SAT, visit the official website at www.collegeboard.com.

The GRE is the Graduate Record Examination. The GRE General is a computer-based test (CBT) available exclusively through Prometric and selected college and university test centers. This test measures skills not directly related to fields of study. Be careful when you take the test because the military will fund it for you only once. More information is available at the GRE website, www.gre.org.

The GMAT is the Graduate Management Admission Test. It is a computer-adaptive test (CAT) available exclusively through Prometric and selected college and university test centers. More information is available on the GMAT website, www.mba.com/mba.

PRAXIS is a test for those who intend to become licensed teachers. PRAXIS itself has three different levels, Praxis I, Praxis II, and Praxis III. The government covers the costs for one Praxis I test and one Praxis II test. The Praxis I is also known as the Pre-Professional Skills Test. This is a three-part test in reading, math, and writing, and is used as a teacher-licensing test in some states. The Praxis II tests knowledge in a particular subject area and is used to certify a teacher in a certain subject. Praxis II offers tests in over 100 different subject areas. More information on the PRAXIS test can be found on the official website www.ets.org/praxis.

$ **For Your Benefits** _____

Both Praxis exams have two fees: a registration fee and a fee for the test itself. Test takers must pay the registration fee on the day of the test, and that comes out-of-pocket. The military does not cover or reimburse that cost. DANTES covers the test fee, but only if the test is taken at one of its military test centers. Tests taken at national test centers are not paid for.

The CLEP test is the College Level Examination Program. For a service member (or retiree) looking to test out of college classes and just get the credit for them, CLEP certainly gives a lot of options for where to use the credit. Almost 3,000 colleges and universities accept CLEP-granted credit. This test is offered in both electronic and paper format, but some parts of it are offered in only electronic format. For the CLEP test, DANTES covers the test fee but not the registration fee for the testing site. More CLEP information can be found at www.collegeboard.com/clep.

DSSTs are DANTES Subject Standardized Tests. They are designed to be about the same as college undergraduate end-of-term or final exams. This is one of the ways to test out of college classes by proving knowledge of the subject. ACE recommends giving a credit of three semester hours per test. Note that DANTES is tricky about paying for DSSTs. It pays for paper-based testing at its own DANTES testing centers, but not at national testing centers. If a service member wants to take the test at a national testing center, it must be in the Internet-based version. If the test is being taken at a nonmilitary testing center that requires a registration fee, DANTES does not cover that cost. For more information about DSSTs, visit the website www. getcollegecredit.com.

ECEs are Excelsior College Examinations (and used to be known as Regents College Examinations or the ACT Proficiency Examination Program). This test is a credit-by-examination type, and although it is run through Excelsior College (hence the name), the credit is accepted at over 900 colleges and universities. The test has three different styles: ECE Objective Tests (multiple choice), ECE Extended Response (essay), and ECE Mixed Format (both multiple choice and free response). ECEs are available in over 30 different subjects in arts and sciences, business, education, and nursing.

For more information on DANTES, visit the website www.dantes.doded.mil or contact them at their headquarters:

6490 Saufley Field Road
Pensacola, FL 32509
850-452-1111
dantes@voled.doded.mil

For Your Benefits _____

Some colleges or universities offer tuition discounts to service members. This can range anywhere from 0 percent to 25 percent. If you're shopping around for schools, be sure to check for a military discount.

Student Loan Forgiveness

Some service members may find that they are eligible for student loan forgiveness. This can be a great help even if it doesn't seem like instant money in the way that a scholarship or grant can. The military pays off the loan for you! Loan forgiveness keeps the loan you took out from ever coming back to haunt you, and it prevents you from spending years upon years paying it back.

The Air Force, Army, and Navy all offer this option, for varying amounts. Unfortunately, service members who find out about this benefit in retrospect cannot go back and opt for it. This must be part of the agreement when enlisting; when signing up, new service members should talk to their recruiter specifically about this option.

To cover pre-existing student loans, the services pay out up to:

Air Force	$10,000
Army	$65,000
Navy	$65,000

Spouse Assistance

The spouse of a service member can go to school on government money, too. Several programs cater to spouses of military members. Military spouses have the same problems as their mates, in that constant or sudden relocation is a definite factor that must be considered. Then, too, they have to try to afford expensive college classes on military pay, possibly with supplements from a working partner. Through scholarships, military schools, and Veterans Affairs programs, it is possible to achieve a higher education for little or no money.

General Military-Provided Assistance

Service member family members can attend Servicemember Opportunity Colleges for credit. SOCs are a distance-learning program that provides easily transferable credit. Chapter 16 gives more information on SOCs.

Benefits may vary by state. Check with your local Veterans Affairs office for details on local service-related scholarships or benefits.

Spouses and dependants of veterans may be eligible for the Dependant's Educational Assistance program. DEA offers up to 45 months of education benefits, for degree and certificate programs, apprenticeship, on-the-job training, and correspondence courses. Certain remedial, deficiency, and refresher courses may also be approved.

DEA eligibility depends on being the son, daughter, or spouse of ...

- A veteran who died or is permanently and totally disabled as the result of a service-related disability. The disability must arise out of active service in the armed forces.

- A veteran who died from any cause while having such a service-connected disability.

- A service member who is missing in action or was captured in the line of duty.

- A service member who was forcibly detained or interned in the line of duty by a foreign government or power.

- A service member who is hospitalized or is receiving outpatient treatment for a service-related disability. This must be a permanent and total disability that is likely to be grounds for discharge.

Children of veterans who want to receive benefits must be between the ages of 18 and 26. In certain instances, it is possible to begin before 18 and continue after 26. This extension, which is based on time spent on active duty and is determined by Veterans Affairs, generally cannot go beyond the thirty-first birthday of the person receiving the benefits.

Spouses' benefits end 10 years from the date VA declares eligibility or from the date of death of the veteran. For spouses whose service member died on active duty, benefits end 20 years from the date of death.

Aid for Air Force Personnel Spouses

The Air Force Aid Society (AFAS) is the U.S. Air Force's official charity, which seeks to provide aid to airmen and their families in several areas, including education. AFAS offers two programs to help fund higher learning.

The General Henry H. Arnold Education Grant Program provides $2,000 grants to selected children of active duty, retired, retired reserve and deceased Air Force members; spouses (stateside) of active duty members and Title 10 AGR/Reservists; and surviving spouses of deceased personnel for their undergraduate studies. Selections for awards are based on financial need and are administered by ACT Recognition Services. Awarded money can be used for tuition, books, fees, or other curriculum-required materials.

Also offered by AFAS is the General George S. Brown Spouse Tuition Assistance Program, known as STAP. This is for spouses of active duty airmen or officers who accompany their service member to overseas locations and will be attending college programs. STAP provides partial tuition assistance toward the completion of degree or certificate programs. The amount of tuition assistance is 50 percent of unmet tuition charge per course, with a maximum of $1,500 per academic year and a term maximum that is calculated by dividing the annual maximum by the number of terms within the academic year. For example, if there were three terms in the academic year, the maximum assistance per term would be $500. This program considers an "academic year" to be the 12-month period beginning August 1 through July 31 of each year.

Assistance for Army Personnel Spouses

Army Emergency Relief (AER) is an educational assistance program, although it doesn't sound like it.

SEAP is the Stateside Spouse Education Assistance Program, which is a need-based program designed to provide spouses or widow(er)s of Army soldiers with financial assistance for higher education. It applies only to the first undergraduate degree, not a second one or graduate studies. Those who want to participate in the program must live in a stateside residence and be enrolled, be accepted, or have pending acceptance as a full-time student at an institution approved by the U.S. Department of Education. Being a spouse or widow(er) of a service member does not automatically qualify someone for SEAP. If tuition is already covered by the spouse's employer, SEAP money can be used for other fees, supplies, or books relating to classes in which they are enrolled. Financial assistance is given on a need basis, with a $2,700 maximum per academic year. SEAP scholarships are awarded annually for up to four academic years. All students must complete an application and mail all supporting documentation each year.

EAP, another version of SEAP, but without the "stateside" stipulation, provides assistance for spouses of soldiers stationed in Europe, Korea, or Japan. Through EAP, spouses can get up to $350 per term in assistance for costs associated with education.

Contributions for Coast Guard Spouses

Available for Coast Guard families is Coast Guard Mutual Assistance (CGMA). This program provides a Supplemental Educational Grant (SEG) of up to $160 per year for a Coast Guard member or family member pursuing an undergraduate or technical degree. This money can be used for any family member, and more than one person in a family unit can receive it in the same year. SEG cannot be applied to tuition payment. However, the grant can be used to pay for study guides such as ones for the CLEP or the SAT (but not the tests themselves) and other course-required materials. SEG is offered on a first-come, first-served basis, so get your hand out there before everyone else, and it might be better filled. If at first you don't succeed with a SEG, try, try again. Say that the first time you apply, you get only $50. Within that same year, you can apply several times and be granted money, as long as the total granted does not exceed $160 within a calendar year.

CGMA has a Stafford/PLUS Loan Origination Reimbursement Program that offers financial assistance to families of the Coast Guard who fund post-secondary education through the Federal Stafford Loan or Federal Parent Loan for Undergraduate Students (PLUS). This program refunds the mandatory 3 percent loan origination fee that is charged to everyone who borrows the money. The lender ordinarily deducts this fee from the loan disbursement check. After confirming the loan, CGMA reimburses the dollar amount of the loan origination fee to the client.

After the Coast Guard Tuition Assistance (CGTA) program has paid what it will, the Coast Guard will loan eligible clients (that is, Coast Guard members and their families) up to $700 if they demonstrate that further aid is needed.

CGMA loans up to $1,500 to individuals who are pursuing an approved (according to the VA or Department of Education) vocational technical training program, if financial need is demonstrated. This program is designed to help pay for noncollege courses that provide training in knowledge and skills needed to enter a specific career field.

The Coast Guard also offers spouse and federal Coast Guard employees the opportunity to take CLEP, DANTES, and other tests at no cost.

Money for Marine and Navy Spouses

The benefits for Navy and Marine families are the same when it comes to education services by branch. The Navy–Marine Corps Relief Society (NMCRS) is a private nonprofit charitable organization. It is sponsored by the Department of the Navy and operates nearly 250 offices ashore and afloat at Navy and Marine Corps bases throughout the world. NMCRS offers several programs for the families of sailors and marines.

The Admiral Mike Boorda Seaman-to-Admiral Education Assistance Program offers grants and/or interest-free loans of up to $2,000 a year to eligible active duty service members in the Enlisted, Marine Enlisted, or Medical Enlisted Commissioning Programs. It is also open to midshipmen who have been released from active duty and went immediately into the Naval Reserve Officer Training Corps (NROTC) program. To apply for this program, go to the commanding officer of the NROTC unit or contact your local NMCRS headquarters.

The Spouse Tuition Aid Program (STAP) is open to spouses who live with their active duty service member overseas. This program provides a grant of up to 50 percent of tuition for on-base education programs, but only up to a maximum of $300 per undergraduate term or $350 per graduate term. The total of this amount cannot go over $1,500 per undergraduate academic year or $1,750 per graduate academic year. The student does not need to be going to school full-time to be eligible. The amount of money provided is based on financial need. STAP is administered by the local NMCRS office overseas.

The Vice Admiral E. P. Travers Scholarship and Loan Program (also known as VADM EP Travers Scholarship and Loan Program, or just the Travers Program) provides financial assistance for full-time undergraduate students. People eligible for this program are spouses and children of active duty sailors or Marines (including Reservists while on active duty over 30 days), as well as children of sailors or Marines who are retired. The Travers Scholarship can be awarded in any amount between $500 and $2,500 per academic year.

Another part of the Travers Program is the Travers Interest Free Loan. Every student who applies for the scholarship is automatically considered for an interest-free student loan of up to $3,000 per academic year. Service members who take out a loan must repay it within 24 months by pay allotment. The minimum loan is $500, and the minimum monthly payment is $50. The scholarship application is due on the first of March each year, and although late applications are not considered for the scholarship, they are still evaluated for a loan.

The Least You Need to Know

◆ Attending school while serving is the smart way to get a head start on college.

◆ Taking standardized tests through DANTES can save you a pile of money.

◆ Plenty of education benefits are available for family members, too.

15

College Money from Your Rich Uncle

In This Chapter

◆ Converting military skills into college credit

◆ Going to school on the government's dime

◆ Getting an extra boost in the job-skill department

◆ Easily transferring credit around the world

◆ Understanding benefits for September 11–activated service members

For most Americans, it can be said about taxes, "What the good Lord giveth, Uncle Sam taketh away." For them, Uncle Sam is an annoyance who takes and takes, and gives very little back (in an obvious manner). That Uncle Sam is a distant relative. For you, an experienced serviceman (or woman), Uncle Sam is a close family member, one you have become so well acquainted with that he's willing to foot the bill for you to attend college.

College is a way to build on high school education and to prepare for a higher-paying, more interesting job. Advancement through the military ranks is easier with college diplomas, and a diploma also provides a better shot at a well-paying civilian job when you set aside the green (or blue) suit.

Some of these can and should be done while in the service. I went to night school while on active duty and used tuition reimbursement but some of my comrades used GI bill.

AARTS and SMART

Most active duty personnel, veterans, or Reservists in the Army, Navy, or Marine Corps are eligible for free college credit. This is based on your Basic Active-duty Service Date/Basic Pay Entry Dates (BASD/BPED). Credit is awarded through the Army/ACE Registry Transcript System (AARTS) or Sailor/Marine/ACE Registry Transcript (SMART). The credit is determined by the American Council on Education (ACE) based on an official list of military courses, occupations, and college-level exam scores completed during your service. ACE reviews the list and determines credit earned.

Getting Your ACE Credits

More than 2,300 colleges and universities recognize transcripts produced through ACE and award credit accordingly. To request a transcript, send a request to your respective AARTS or SMART operations center. If you are a member of the Air Force or Coast Guard, go to your respective transcript center. The service will send you a copy and also send one to schools you are interested in. As in most things, the different branches of the military do things their own way.

The Air Force Way

As you progress through training, testing, and your military career, the Community College of the Air Force (CCAF) keeps track of eligible college credits for you. All you have to do is request your transcript using the CCAF website at www.maxwell. af.mil/au/ccaf/index.asp.

For more information, check out the Frequently Asked Questions (FAQ) section of the web page, or if you cannot find what you are looking for there, contact the following as it applies to you:

Active duty students can try the Air Force Virtual Education Center under the "Featured Links" section of www.my.af.mil/faf/FAF/fafHome.jsp. If your questions are still not answered, contact your local base education services personnel. They should have the resources to answer any question you can throw at them.

Retired or separated students who cannot get help with answers from the local base education office can go back to the CCAF website and, in the FAQ section, ask a question right there. For a CCAF degree, you must meet certain degree program requirements, and you have only six years after leaving the military to formally apply for your degree.

Air National Guard and Air Force Reserve Command students should visit www.maxwell.af.mil/au/ccaf/ang_info.asp to find appropriate answers or to ask a question.

The Army Does It Differently

As enlisted soldiers complete their training, it is recorded through the Army/ACE Registry Transcript System (AARTS). AARTS is available to enlisted soldiers only. For more information, contact AARTS at:

> AARTS Operations Center
> 415 McPherson Avenue
> Ft. Leavenworth, KS 66027-1373
> Phone: 1-866-297-4427
> Commercial: 913-684-3269
> DSN: 552-3269
> Commercial fax: 913-684-2011 or DSN fax 552-2011
> http://aarts.army.mil

 Hot Scoop

Army officers must report their own training and experience using Form DD 295, "Application for Evaluation of Learning." You can find a copy of the application at http://images.military.com/Resources/Forms/DD_295.pdf.

Coast Guard Institute

To obtain a transcript from the Coast Guard Institute (CGI), you must submit documentation of training and experience (except records for correspondence courses) along with an enrollment form for the university of your choice. You can find more information at:

U.S. Coast Guard Institute
5900 SW 64th Street
Oklahoma City, OK 73169-6990
Executive Officer (phone): 405-954-7232
Command Master Chief (phone): 405-954-7238
Command Master Chief e-mail:
CGI-PF-Resource_Support_Section@oscg.mil
www.uscg.mil/hq/CGI

Navy/Marines ACE Registry

The Navy and Marines have their training and experience automatically recorded by the Sailor/Marine/ACE Registry Transcript (SMART) system, with transcripts available upon request. For more information, contact:

SMART Operations Center
NETPDTC, N2
6490 Saufley Field Road
Pensacola, FL 32509
Phone: 1-877-253-7122
E-mail: ncc@cnet.navy.mil
http://smart.cnet.navy.mil

Veterans

Most veterans can use their former service branch transcript program. Thus, a retired Marine would go to the Marine Corps, a retired airman should go to the Air Force, and so on. If there is a problem getting a transcript, fill out Form DD-295 (same as the Army officers) and provide a copy of your DD-214 Discharge Document to receive a transcript or credit.

> **Hot Scoop**
>
> Some schools consider college credits more than 10 years old as "outdated." In some cases, they will want you to retake the course. Policies vary so check with your school.

GI Bill

President Franklin Roosevelt signed the GI Bill of Rights into action on June 22, 1944. Officially known as the Servicemember's Readjustment Act of 1944, this law gave money to veterans so they could attend college after their term of service.

Many citizens and some in Congress opposed this law. College was considered a privilege for the wealthy, not a right of the common man. Another argument against it was that this handout would discourage vets from looking for work, especially because there is a lot more to the GI Bill than just financial aid—housing loans and unemployment, for example.

It turned out that it was better for the veterans returning from World War II to go into school than it was to enter the workforce, which had adjusted to their absence. Where millions of men would have flooded the workforce, leaving many jobless, they chose to apply to universities. In 1947, they made up 49 percent of college admissions.

The first GI Bill ended on July 25, 1956. Millions had taken advantage of the educational opportunity or job training facility by then.

Over the years, the military has used money for college as a way to entice people to join the military. Every time the law came up for renewal, Congress could not resist tinkering with it here and there—and, in some cases, dropping the college benefit option altogether.

In 1984, the GI Bill got a makeover when Mississippi Congressman Gillespie "Sonny" Montgomery decided to make a few changes to ensure that the benefits of the original bill continued; it has been known as the Montgomery GI Bill ever since.

Eligibility for the Montgomery GI Bill (MGIB)

To qualify for the GI Bill, you must have earned a high school diploma or its equivalent, or you must have completed 12 credit hours toward a college degree. Also your discharge from the service must have been fully honorable. If you were discharged under honorable conditions or with a general discharge, you do not qualify for the MGIB.

Do not put off going to college after you leave the service! Cinderella's college fund expires at midnight 10 years after discharge. If you reentered active duty, were disabled, or had an upgraded discharge, an extension may be granted.

If you entered active duty before completing high school or an equivalent level of education, it is still possible to qualify for the GI Bill. All you have to do is finish high school. Voilà, you now qualify for the benefits. Reapply and use your benefits before they expire 10 years after your discharge from active duty or by November 2, 2010, whichever is later.

The Montgomery GI Bill has four groupings of eligibility to receive the benefits.

Category 1: Service After June 30, 1985

If you entered active duty for the first time after June 30, 1985; did not decline the MGIB in writing; and had your military pay reduced by $100 a month for one year (a total of $1,200 in one year, nonrefundable), this is your category.

You are eligible to apply after two years of continuous service. Also, if you are currently on active duty, enlisted for less than three years, or served for two years of active duty and then signed up for four years in the Selective Reserve (the 2×4 program) and entered the Selective Reserve within one year of discharge, you meet the requirements. Otherwise, you must have completed three continuous years of active duty. If you are a Reservist and have completed the active service requirement, you may pay the $1,200 within one year after completing your active duty service to qualify.

If you received a commission from a service academy or completed an ROTC scholarship, you are not eligible under Category 1 unless you received your commission after becoming eligible for MGIB benefits or after September 30, 1996, and received less than $3,400 during any one year under ROTC scholarship.

If you declined the Montgomery GI Bill because you were receiving repayment of education loans by the military, you are ineligible for Category 1. Additionally, if you did not decline MGIB and still received repayment of loans, the months served to repay the loans are deducted from your entitlement.

If you did not complete the amount of time required in the service but were discharged for one of the following reasons, you may still be eligible for Category 1 :

◆ Discharge due to convenience of the government

◆ Reduction in force

◆ Medical condition diagnosed before joining or one that interfered with your performing of duty (without causing misconduct)

◆ A service-related disability

Category 2: Vietnam Era

Category 2 relates to veterans of the Vietnam era. If you entered active duty before January 1, 1977, and served at least one day between October 19, 1984, and June 30, 1985; and stayed on active duty through June 30, 1988, and as of December 31, 1989, had entitlement left on your Vietnam Era GI Bill, you still have it coming. This also applies to veterans who served three continuous years of active duty beginning on or after July 1, 1985, or two continuous years from the same date, and then followed with four years in the Reserves (joined within one year of leaving active duty).

If you received a commission after December 31, 1976, as a result of graduating from a service academy or completing an ROTC scholarship, you may not use Category 2 unless you received the commission after becoming eligible for the GI Bill or if you received it after September 30, 1996. Also, if the scholarship received was less than $3,400 during any year under an ROTC scholarship, you can still apply for Category 2.

Category 3: Involuntary/Special Separation

Category 3 applies if you did not decline MGIB and paid your full $1,200, but were separated before you completed your service requirement. You must have been on active duty on September 30, 1990, and separated involuntarily after February 2, 1991; or involuntarily separated on or after November 30, 1993; or else voluntarily separated under the Voluntary Separation Incentive (VSI) or Special Separation Benefit (SSB) program.

Category 4: Veterans Educational Assistance Program (VEAP)

Category 4 is for veterans who participated in the Veterans Educational Assistance Program (VEAP) and contributed money to a VEAP account, as well as served on active duty on October 9, 1996, and opted for MGIB by that date and paid the $1,200.

If you participated in VEAP but did not put money into a VEAP account, you may still be eligible if you meet the other requirements and paid $2,700 to MGIB.

Certain National Guard service members may qualify under Category 4 if they served full-time active duty for the first time in the Guard between June 30, 1985, and November 29, 1989. You also must have elected for the MGIB during the nine-month window ending on July 9, 1997, and paid the $1,200.

For Your Benefits

Category 4 gives you the opportunity to double-dip into federal assistance for school. Take advantage of it!

Veterans Benefits Improvement Act of 2000

Two benefits were added to the MGIB in 2000 for active duty service members, Top-Up and Buy-Up.

Top-Up

Top-Up covers the difference between the cost of tuition for a college course and what the military is already paying for through Tuition Assistance. To be eligible for a Top-Up, you must currently be on active duty and must have completed a minimum of two years of service. Of course, you must also meet requirements for the MGIB. To apply for a Top-Up, first complete a Tuition Assistance request form and VA Form 22-1990. Specify Top-Up on the VA application in item 1A under the GI Bill-Active Duty block. Once the Tuition Assistance approval form is received, send it along with VA Form 22-1990 to the address marked on the form, which will be your VA Regional Processing Office.

Buy-Up

Buy-Ups allow active-duty service members to make an additional payment of up to $600 to their GI Bill, which can effectively increase GI Bill payout as much as $5,400. For every additional hundred dollars you put into your account, you get $25 added for you. To be eligible for a Buy-Up, you must have enlisted after August 1985. Fill out DD Form 2366 and contact your personnel support center to submit the form and deposit the money.

Veteran's Educational Assistance Program (VEAP)

The Veteran's Education Assistance Program (VEAP) is available if you choose to use some of your military pay toward it. Deposits are matched on a two-for-one basis, with the military effectively doubling whatever amount you put in. It is also possible to receive monetary contributions in this account from the service for special services rendered. This fund is available to be used toward a degree, certificate, job training program, or vocational flight training program—including study abroad. In certain circumstances, refresher training may also be available. The maximum monthly VEAP payout is $300.

Benefit entitlement runs up to 36 months, depending on the number of monthly contributions you made. As with the GI Bill, this benefit expires 10 years from your release from active duty. If you do not use the money you contributed, it is refunded (but only the money you put in). (The military's two-to-one contribution does not come to you. That was available only if you utilized the service. VEAP was not intended to be a savings account.)

It is possible to get an extension on the 10 years for the amount of time you spent away from active service due to service-related disabilities or prisoner of war status. If this applies, the amount of time you were not actively serving is the amount of time your 10 years is extended by, or 10 years past release from foreign custody. If your discharge was upgraded, you have 10 years from the date of the upgrade. Also, for veterans who re-entered the service on active duty for at least 90 days, the extension is 10 years.

Attention! _____

For fastest action, Veterans should contact their regional VA education office. Locate your region at www.gibill. va.gov/contact/contact.htm.

Eligibility for VEAP

To qualify, you must have entered the service for the first time between January 1, 1977, and June 30, 1985; opened a contribution account before April 1, 1987; and voluntarily contributed something from $25 to $2,700 (this can be done in installments or all at once). You must have served for 181 continuous days and completed your first period of service, unless you were discharged for a service-related disability. If your discharge was dishonorable, you are not eligible.

If you wish to use VEAP while on active duty, you must have at least three months of contributions available. If you want to use your VEAP to complete high school, it takes only one month's contribution. To use VEAP, you must also have completed your first active duty requirement. If your first term lasts more than six years, your benefits may be available after the first six. To finish high school or earlier education, you must be in the last six months of your first enlistment.

Applying for VEAP

The first step is to make sure that the program you want is approved for VA training. Veterans Affairs can tell you whether the school, program, or company you wish to work with meets the requirements.

Next, fill out VA Form 22-1990, "Application for Education Benefits," and send it to the regional office for the state where you will attend your program. For active duty personnel, obtain enrollment approval by your base Education Services Officer or your commanding officer. Other service members need to send a notary certified copy of Copy 4 (Member Copy) of DD Form 214, "Certificate of Release of Discharge from Active Duty."

If you have already started training, take your application and DD Form 214 to your school or employer, and ask them to complete VA Form 22-1999. Send all the forms to Veterans Affairs. You should receive a letter granting eligibility within eight weeks.

Once you are enrolled and attending a school, you must submit a report to Veterans Affairs once a month through the Web Automatic Verification of Enrollment (WAVE). The school must submit VA Form 22-1999 for each new academic term. This can be done online through the VA-Once program. If you are taking a correspondence course, you may have to submit VA Form 22-1999c for each class, to make sure you receive your benefits.

Hot Scoop

VA-Once is an online program for submitting VA forms 22-1999, 22-1999b, and 22-6553c all at once. It is a fast and paperless way to turn in the necessary documentation.

To use VA-Once, your school must complete a Memorandum of Understanding (MOU). Fill out as much information online as possible, print it, get appropriate signatures as called for, and mail it to your Education Liaison Representative (ELR). The MOU is a contract between the school and Veterans Affairs. Investing some time setting up VA-Once will save a lot of time in the future.

Also make sure that you have an up-to-date copy of VA Form 22-8794, "Designation of Certifying Official(s)," submitted to your ELR.

Counseling is available to help service members use VEAP. Advice is provided to decide where to go and how you might accomplish your educational goals.

Veterans Upward Bound

Many veterans did not go to college either because they lacked the desire to spend more years sitting in a classroom or because they felt lacking in academic skills. Once they got out, they had even less incentive to go back because it had been a long time since they'd had to name the capital of Nebraska or multiply fractions. However, the program Veterans Upward Bound (VUB) focuses on helping veterans get a degree even if knowledge of the periodic table has long gone by the wayside. VUB can move you closer to finding your civilian dream job.

VUB is a free program brought to you by the United States Department of Education to help dust off that part of your brain where all book learning is locked away, and aid you in completing a college degree.

To qualify for Veterans Upward Bound, you must be a veteran with 181 or more days of active duty service, and you must have been discharged on or after January 31, 1955, the conditions of which cannot have been dishonorable. You must meet the criteria for low income status according to guidelines published annually by the U.S. Department of Education, and/or be a first-generation potential college graduate. You must demonstrate academic need for VUB according to criteria in the local VUB project's Approved Grant Proposal. Finally, you must meet local eligibility criteria as noted in the local VUB project's Approved Grant Proposal.

Service Member Opportunity Colleges (SOC)

Service Member Opportunity Colleges are not a single place to attend classes. This is a collection of over 1,800 colleges and universities around the world that recognize how difficult it can be for service members to go to school due to frequent moves. SOC allows military students to enroll in programs for associate, bachelor, and graduate degree programs worldwide. Funded by the Department of Defense, SOC— together with the American Association of State Colleges and Universities (AASCU) and the American Association of Community Colleges (AACC), 13 other educational associations, and the United States military—brings together schools that run on the same curriculums and agree to easily transfer credits from one to another.

SOC schools agree to limit the amount of coursework students must take at a single college to no more than 25 percent of degree requirements so that credits transfer smoothly, award credit for military experience through ACE, and give credit for national testing programs.

Each service branch has its own twist on Service Member Opportunity Colleges. The Army has SOCAD, the Coast Guard has SOCCOAST, the Marine Corps has SOCMAR, and the Navy has SOCNAV. The Army National Guard's SOCGuard works more on a local level, helping military students with credits easily transferable in their base area.

Military students enroll in a local college or university that cooperates with SOC. They then take at least six credit hours at that school. From there, they can take classes at any school in that service's degree network. Records of the classes taken and credits earned are sent to the home school.

Students and their family members located in remote areas have the option of taking courses through "distance learning" via the Internet, correspondence, computer, or video. Just try to get a better grade than your kids—or no ice cream this Sunday!

Reserve Educational Assistance Program (REAP)

The Reserve Educational Assistance Program, also known as REAP or Chapter 1607, applies to certain Reservists who were activated for at least 90 days after September 11, 2001.

REAP was signed into law on October 28, 2004, as part of the National Defense Authorization Act. It provides educational assistance to members of the Reserves called to active duty in response to war or national emergency (contingency operation), as declared by the president or Congress.

For Your Benefits

Chapter 1607 benefits cannot be combined with other VA educational benefits. You must choose which benefits you would like to receive. If you are eligible for a Chapter 1606 kicker (remember, Chapter 1606 is the Montgomery GI Bill), you can still be paid that kicker while receiving REAP. REAP pays a bit more than Chapter 1606, but make sure you consider how it would benefit you to use it for future training.

Eligibility

The departments of Defense and Homeland Security determine who is eligible, but the VA executes the program. This benefit is for Reservists who were activated for 90 days or more following September 11, 2001. National Guard members are also eligible if their active duty is under Section 502(f), Title 32 U.S.C., and they served 90 days for a national emergency. As soon as you serve 90 days, you become eligible, regardless of whether you are currently on active duty. Also if you were activated but could not complete your 90 days due to illness or disease incurred or aggravated in the line of duty, you are still eligible.

Unlike the GI Bill, which expires after 10 years, you have as long to use your REAP benefits as you are with your Reserve component. However, if you leave the Reserves or participate in an ROTC, REAP benefits are terminated.

For Your Benefits

Even though REAP was not enacted until 2004, the benefits were theoretically payable from December 9, 2001, 90 days after September 11, for service members who were called into action on that day. As a result of the retroactive nature of REAP, it is possible to get a sort of refund on your college tuition for classes attended after serving but before the creation of Chapter 1607. Reservists attending school will be paid a percentage of the MGIB three-year rate in effect during the time in which they were enrolled.

If you were activated and served, but in the process you became disabled or a previous disability flared up, rendering you unable to continue serving, you are entitled to the level of payment that you qualified for at the time you were released. If you served less than 90 days, you are entitled to the same benefits as those who reached the 90-day mark. However, if you were released for a disability, you have a time limit of 10 years to use your benefits.

Payout

REAP benefits are based on Chapter 30 (the Montgomery GI Bill) in the amounts paid out for a three-year or more enlistment rate ($1,034 as of October 1, 2005) and the amount of active duty served. If you served 90 days or more but less than a year, you receive 40 percent of the three-year rate. If you served more than one year but less than two, you get 60 percent. Serving more than two years on active duty qualifies you for an 80 percent payment.

You receive 36 months of full-time entitlement. Under REAP, you may not use more than 48 months of entitlement under any combination of VA educational programs. So if you have already used some GI Bill benefits, that amount of time will be subtracted from the 48 months allowed.

Attention!

Members on active duty are entitled to be reimbursed for only the actual cost of tuition and fees of the courses taken (not to exceed the amount designated by law).

The Least You Need to Know

◆ Know which programs you qualify for and those programs' limitations.

◆ You can go to school while serving or after separation.

◆ Money is available for you, so ask for it.

◆ It is possible to get college credit without stepping inside a formal classroom.

Part 5

Guard and Reserve

Military forces are expensive. They are expensive to equip, to train, and to pay. All of those military benefits cost the government a lot of money. Active duty military forces are sized according to what is needed to serve the nation's interest. The remainder of its military power resides in its National Guard and Reserve forces. This part-time force's pay and benefits are tuned to its unique needs.

Originally, the Guard and Reserve received few benefits. In recent years, they have gradually acquired many of the benefits that the active forces once exclusively enjoyed, such as use of MWR facilities, unlimited commissary privileges, and, more recently, medical benefits through their own version of TRICARE.

If you are in the National Guard or Reserves—or are considering joining—thumb through these chapters. Due to recent heavy dependence on National Guard and Reserve forces in recent years, a lot has changed.

Moving from Active Duty to the Guard/Reserve

In This Chapter

◆ Checking out the many flavors of the National Guard and Reserve

◆ Joining the Guard/Reserve—cutting the best deal

◆ Learning something new on Uncle Sam's nickel

Sometimes you want to continue serving your country but it is just time to leave active duty behind. Many people find that continuing their service in the National Guard or Reserves fills this need. It provides camaraderie, some excitement, an occasional excursion somewhere, and oh yes, a very nice paycheck for a part time job.

What Is the Guard and Reserve?

Military benefits end when you leave active service. One way to stay on the benefits gravy train is to join a Reserve or National Guard unit. This also continues accumulating time for that no. 1 benefit—a military pension.

People join the Reserves for many reasons—pride of service, as a backup to their civilian employment, as an income supplement, to learn new job skills, and sometimes as an alternative to their humdrum civilian career. It is one way to capitalize on your years of military experience.

Reserves are federal organizations and are under the control of the president. Since only he can call them out, this is rarely done except for wartime. Reserves receive only federal benefits. They are forbidden by law from performing police-type actions by the Posse Comitatus Act.

National Guard units have a dual responsibility to both the president and the governor of their state. That means that either can call out the National Guard, whereas only the president can summon the Reserves.

In a local emergency, a National Guard unit may be activated to assist with a garbage collection strike, prison riot, or natural disaster, whereas the Reserve units cannot. National Guard units under control of the governor are specifically exempt from the Posse Comitatus Act.

For Your Benefits

Did you know that, in most cases, the adjutant general (with the rank of major general) in charge of each state's National Guard is appointed by the governor? The governor can select anyone he or she wants for the job. So polish up your resume and fax it on over!

In appreciation for their local services, most states offer benefits to their National Guard members in addition to those provided by Washington. Examples range from a supplemental pension, to free tuition to state colleges, to free license plates.

It isn't necessary to live in a particular state to be in that state's National Guard. The only requirement is for you to be on time for scheduled drills. So if a nearby state offers significantly better benefits, follow the money!

Reserves: Different Strokes for Different Folks

It just wouldn't be military if something as easy as "active" and "Reserve" was permitted to exist. Not all Guardsmen/Reservists attend weekend drills. Different service categories exist according to the amount of time spent training. Pick the one that fits your situation.

Ready Reserve

This is the category that most people think of when they talk about the Reserves. But once again, this is too simple. The Ready Reserve is made up of yet smaller categories.

The Ready Reserve consists of Reserve and National Guard members, organized in units or as individuals, liable for recall to active duty in time of war or national emergency. The Ready Reserve is broken down into Troop Program Units, Active Guard and Reserve, Individual Ready Reserve, and Individual Mobilization Augmentees.

Troop Program Units (TPUs) are what you typically think of as the "Reserve." Members assigned to a TPU attend weekend drills and deploy as a unit two weeks per year. They muster at their local drill hall and spend quality time together training to maintain *MOS* qualification and preparing for their next annual training deployment.

def•i•ni•tion

Your **Military Occupational Specialty (MOS)** is an alphanumeric code that identifies your unique military job assignment.

Some people want to be less active in attending unit meetings but still remain in the program. This category is known as Individual Mobilization Augmentee (IMA). IMAs are Reservists assigned to active duty units to jobs that are needed only during wartime. For example, an IMA might be assigned as a staff officer or senior NCO in a high-level headquarters. IMAs do not attend drills. Instead, they attend one annual training session augmenting a unit. Many of the IMAs are higher ranking and cannot find a slot in a unit equal to their rank. There can be some very attractive IMA jobs.

Another option is to become a quasicivilian as a full-time Guard/Reserve. AGRs receive full military pay and benefits. They can also retire at 20 years (total active and reserve service). (The Air Force Reserve calls its AGRs Air Reserve Technicians [ARTs]).

Based on available slots, an AGR position allows someone to be in the military full-time while living in their hometown. Guard/Reserve units all have a full-time staff to keep the equipment in tune, to shuffle papers, and to ensure that everything is ready for the next drill. AGRs are a part of their unit and deploy with it.

A variation on the AGR position is a dual-status slot. The service member holds both a civil service position and a specific Reserve slot. In their civilian role, they support their Reserve unit by performing essentially the same tasks as an AGR, but they are Department of Defense civilian government employees. On a drill weekend, they put on a uniform and perform essentially the same job.

Dual-status personnel (generally called "technicians") must maintain both positions. If they lose either one, they lose them both. This can force people to remain at a certain rank longer than they would like to.

The Individual Ready Reserve (IRR) is a category for service members who are on the rolls but who do not attend meetings or training. IRR members do not attend annual training, either. However, they can apply to attend annual training with units that are short of skilled people. Like all classes of Reserve, they can be called to national service.

Service members are assigned to the IRR for a number of reasons. This may be due to a shortage of slots, absence of a local unit, and so on. The IRR is also where drilling Reservists go when they need a break from the one-weekend-a-month grind.

People who are leaving active duty and have fewer than eight years of service are assigned to the IRR. All initial enlistments are for eight years. A portion of that is on active duty, and the rest is in the Individual Ready Reserve (IRR).

The National Guard has its own twist to the IRR. It functions the same as the IRR, but each person is assigned to a unit and must muster with it once per year.

Standby Reserve

Some Reservists have civilian jobs critical to national defense or to their employers, such as a congressman. They are assigned to the Standby Reserve. Standby Reservists can be called up during a full mobilization. Otherwise, they can maintain their Reserve affiliation and are not required to attend training.

Standby Reserve status is sometimes used as a place to hold people with a temporary hardship. Then when the situation is resolved, they are transferred to one of the other Reserve categories.

Retired Reserve

The retired Reserve status is for all Guard and Reserve officers and enlisted personnel who have retired but have not yet hit 60 years of age. Yes, Uncle Sam may call you back, too! On the other hand, if you can still meet the physical requirements and have a skill that is in short supply, you might return to drilling Reserve status.

Different Services ... Different Deals

Those with active duty service in the Air Force, Navy, or Marines often join an Army Reserve or Army National Guard unit. There are just more of them. It may be easier to work with a local unit than a far-off unit that is the same as your active duty service. Many of the Army Guard/Reserve first sergeants and command sergeant majors sport Marine Good Conduct medals.

Those who join a Reserve or Guard unit from the same service may be able to enter at the same rank they held on active duty—if they do so immediately after leaving active duty. If you join a Guard/Reserve unit of a different service, be aware that all have different guidelines for accepting someone trained by a different service. These guidelines change based on how badly they need warm bodies.

Several factors determine what they can offer you. Shop around for the deal that suits you best. Pick a situation that you can live with for years to come.

How Badly They Want Someone Like You

Guard/Reserve units have their own personnel problems. In general, they want someone right off active duty, at the right rank and MOS to match one of their available slots. For this person, they make their best offer.

Good workers are hard to find, and all organizations are short of good workers. Unfortunately, that is not a stated requirement. Likely your most marketable item is MOS qualification. Ideally, you are school trained, have a few years of experience, and your MOS matches an opening in their Table of Organization. Most Guard recruiters will sign up anyone who is eligible and wants to join, wherever they want to join, into whatever slot is available. The unit has many programs that can MOS-qualify the new unit member.

What Rank Would I Have?

Your rank on entry to the Guard/Reserve depends on several factors. Was your active duty with the same service? Likely you'll start with the same rank. However, the longer you are off active duty before joining the Guard/Reserve, the more likely you are to lose a stripe or more. Before signing up, check with each of the other Guard/Reserve services nearby for the best offer.

Just as with active duty, the higher-ranking jobs are "closer to the flagpole." Rank advancements may be easier to find if you are in an aviation wing or division head-quarters rather than in a squadron or company-sized unit.

For Your Benefits

The higher the rank, the harder it is to find a suitable slot. Typically, someone who is a pay grade E-7 or above, or who is an O-4 or above, will stay on active duty to round out a 20-year pension. Good thing, too, because those Reserve slots are hard to find.

Age Can Be a Factor

Each of the services sets its own maximum age for enlistment. A lot of it has to do with the physical demands of training and normal service.

To join the Guard/Reserve, you must complete 20 years of total service (active and Reserve) before turning 60 years old. That means you must be no more than 40 years old when joining, plus the number of years of service creditable toward retirement. So if you had four years of active duty and then waited until you were 44 to join up, you are okay. Just keep in mind that you must be physically fit during your entire Guard/Reserve service, and it can be a bit tough for some of us to run through a PT test with a head full of gray hair.

Is Basic Training Required?

Sometimes a Guard/Reserve component will require that you attend its basic training. For example, the Marine Reserve thinks that a first-name basis with the sand fleas of Parris Island is an essential part of its culture. Others, such as the Air Force Reserve, are likely to not require it. Be sure to ask about this before signing up, as it might influence your choice.

Picking a New Unit

Most people pick a new Guard/Reserve unit based on what is close by. The expense of attending a Guard/Reserve drill is on you. Some armories permit sleeping over in the building. Some units with access to a large facility may also have inexpensive transient quarters available.

Often the available jobs in a unit are different from one of your MOSs, so retraining may be required. Someone can go from radar repairman to clerk typist, or typist to radar repairman! That's the price of convenience!

The key to a unit is its military mission. If it is a civil affairs unit supporting Southwest Asia, that unit may be deployed a lot. If its mobilization mission is to support a Navy base in Japan, then on activation, that is most likely where it will go. However, never doubt that Uncle Sam might send a unit somewhere it is not equipped or trained to go—just to provide some warm bodies to do something.

Reserve units have a mobilization mission that they are staffed and equipped to perform. Typically this is one for the Far East and one for Europe. (However, at this point, most of the destinations somehow seem to be Southwest Asia.) Where possible, Reserve units will spend their annual training at their overseas station or at least visit it once every five years. However, many National Guard units rarely leave the United States for their annual training.

Attention!

Recruiters screen out troublesome people before they can sign up. If you have problems with debts, the police, or drugs—the usual things that are not permitted on active duty—then review each of them with the recruiter to see if a waiver is needed or if something is an outright disqualifier. Also, if you are now a single parent with custody of a child, review this promptly with the recruiter. As always, the mission comes first.

Keep an eye on Guard/Reserve recruiters. They typically recruit for the same few units and try to steer people to the hard-to-fill jobs. Consider contacting the units yourself to see what sort of openings they have before you contact the recruiter.

◆ Contact every unit within a two-hour drive of your home. This casts the net wide to find a good fit. You may look farther from home for a perfect fit.

◆ Select a unit that fits your prior service experience or that offers vocational training. This will put you back in uniform during training, but it is a great way to pick up a free tech school that will improve your civilian income.

◆ Find a slot in that unit that fits your MOS or that agrees to train you to fill it. (Being MOS qualified is a critical requirement to retaining a slot and being promoted.)

◆ Contact the recruiter to fill in the paperwork.

What's My Job?

U.S. military units use a Table of Organization to identify the number of people with a certain job skill needed for a specific unit. In the Guard/Reserve world, this is called a slot. When you join a Guard/Reserve unit, you are enlisting into a specific slot.

Each slot has a rank or rank range associated with it. It might be E-4 to E-6 or O-1 to O-3. The higher the rank, the more likely only one rank can fill it, such as an E-8 filling a first sergeant slot.

> **Attention!**
>
> At times, the Guard/Reserve units are allowed to double-slot some jobs, but when a force reduction arrives, the extra person may be pushed out of the unit.

When it comes time for promotion, you must be promoted from your slot into the higher-ranking slot. The higher an open slot's rank, the more people are competing for it. In some cases, the person selected for it is a "done deal." This is one reason the Guard has corporals with grey hair.

Some people join the Reserves to do the same thing they do in their civilian jobs. Examples of this are policemen, bulldozer operators, truck drivers, lawyers, and nurses. Their Reserve drills are primarily a matter of changing uniforms and places of work.

Others join to learn how to do something different. They might want to learn small arms repair as a hobby or sideline, learn about heavy equipment operation, or even fulfill their fantasy as a warrior one week end out of the month. They want to do something very different from their day-to-day grind.

Training is based on service needs, but there are many technical jobs out there if you try to dig them out. In fact, because some technical schools are so long, units occasionally have difficulties finding someone to fill them. This is a great place for someone who wants to retrain into a technical skill (and let someone else pay for it).

Officer Material

Life being as it is, not all of us had a shot at being an officer when we joined. By using the GI Bill (and maybe free state tuition from the Guard) to obtain a college degree, it may be time to move on up.

The Guard and Reserve offer many opportunities to obtain a commission. Many of the National Guard officers came from the enlisted ranks. (This can do wonders for your retirement pay.) Most states operate a National Guard Officers Candidate Course for training enlisted service members to become officers. The Air National Guard uses one officer academy in Tennessee.

If you're attending college, consider joining an ROTC unit. This will provide a commission at the same time you're receiving a college degree. Guard/Reserve can also apply for direct commissions or warrant officer school. In general, it is much easier to move from enlisted to officer status in the Guard/Reserve than it is when on active duty—if you are willing to work for it.

Pride and Yes, Just Enough of the Old Times

Marines drill instructors like to remind recruits, "If home was such a great place, why did you leave it?" The same can be true for the military. If you liked active duty so much, why did you get out? There are as many answers as there are people. Whatever the difficult times, there were also good times—camaraderie, the military way of getting things done, the perks of going different places, and, of course, the pride of belonging to the nation's finest.

Participating in a Guard/Reserve unit can be frustrating, as the best weather always falls on a drill weekend. The most interesting things in life seem to be scheduled for Saturday mornings on a drill weekend. Aside from these distractions, you will get out of the Guard and Reserves what you put into it. If you are inclined to do as little as possible, then it will seem a bore and drudgery. If you dig in, learn about what is going on, and maintain mastery of military and MOS skills, it will be a rather fun time.

The Least You Need to Know

- ◆ Do your homework about a Guard/Reserve unit before signing up.
- ◆ For a stay-at-home military job, consider full-time active Guard/Reserve or dual-status positions.
- ◆ Cast your net wide when looking for the best match between you and the Reserves.
- ◆ Negotiate your best overall deal in terms of rank, MOS training, and slot.

17

Unique Benefits for Guard and Reserves

In This Chapter

- ◆ Working the angles of the Reserve pay system
- ◆ Earning a retirement from your part-time job
- ◆ Racking up those retirement points
- ◆ Requesting a retirement check

Over the last several decades, the Guard/Reserve has been awarded more of the benefits once found exclusively in the active duty forces. Part of this is due to the force drawdown in the 1990s. As bases sought to maintain nonappropriated financing for their recreations facilities with fewer active duty personnel, the commissary and other faculties have been opened to the point that most of the Morale, Welfare, and Recreation (MWR) activities are available to personnel with Guard/Reserve ID cards.

Some of the many benefits open to Guard/Reserve (as described in earlier chapters) include the following:

- Commissary, a reduced-price grocery store, typically saving shoppers 20 percent off their food bills.

- Serviceman's Group Life Insurance (SGLI)—up to $400,000 of term life insurance for a low monthly cost

- Use of military recreation areas, vacation cabins, and gyms—based on availability

- Space-available travel for the Guardsman/Reservist (but not their families)

- Home loans guaranteed by the VA

Pay and Allowances

Some people seem to find all of the big-money civilian jobs—and then there are the rest of us. We can apply for a minimum-wage weekend job at the local discount store or make the most of our military years. Service in the Guard and Reserve can be a tidy family income supplement.

Guard and Reserve personnel serve one weekend per month and two weeks of annual training (unless they are packing to visit Southwest Asia). These two weeks may be at any time of the year but are often during the summer.

Hot Scoop

The website for Guard/ Reserve current drill pay is www. dod.mil/dfas/militarypay.html.

Each weekend is considered to be four drills: two on Saturday and two on Sunday. Each participant is paid one day's base pay (no housing or food allowances) and is awarded one retirement point per drill. So if someone misses Saturday morning drill but is present for the remainder of the weekend, he or she can still be paid for three of the drills and earn three retirement points.

So what can this amount to? In 2007 an E-4 petty officer third class with four years of service (usually from active duty time) is paid $263.80 for what is essentially 16 hours of work. Yes, Uncle Sam will twist this into two long days or even a weekend sleeping in the field, but this pays way more than a weekend flipping burgers, and it comes with benefits.

And there is more! Each day during a drill weekend, enlisted members are provided with a free lunch (no promises about quality).

Special Incentive Pay

Just like their active duty counterparts, Guard/Reserve can receive hazardous duty and special service pay prorated to their number of days of monthly service. Essentially, this is $\frac{1}{30}$ of the hazardous duty pay per drill or per day of active duty for training.

These special pay categories are the same as for active duty. They include aviation, parachute, diving, medical, nuclear, and so on.

Bonuses

Bonuses are a personnel-management tool for encouraging people to do something: enlist, reenlist, stay in the service (such as for pilots or doctors), and so on. Bonuses come and go based on how full a particular category is. They often have a time frame (from-to dates). Always check the bonuses and their specific requirements before re-enlisting or making a MOS change.

Not all bonuses are for enlisted personnel, and not all are cash. Some include student loan forgiveness or a college fund increase. At this time, all services provide a significant bonus for enlisting in their Reserve (or Guard) components straight off active duty.

Check online for bonuses at these websites:

- www.1800goguard.com
- www.uscg.mil/hq/reserve/pay_benefits/bonus.htm
- www.goarmy.com/reserve/ps/money.jsp
- navyreserve.navy.mil/Public/Staff/Centers/Forces+Command/WelcomeAboard/Enlisted+Bonuses.htm
- www.manpower.usmc.mil/portal/page?_pageid=278,1956240&_dad=portal&_schema=PORTAL
- www.afrc.af.mil/news/story.asp?id=123014152

Tax Breaks

Participating in the Guard/Reserve is like any other second job. If you meet the criteria set by the Internal Revenue Service (and these rules may change from year to year), you might be able to deduct specific expenses created by participation in the

Guard/Reserve. For example, in 2006, the IRS allowed travel deductions for attending drills if they were more than 100 miles from home and included an overnight stay. Given the price of gas, a deduction for mileage might add up to a chunk of change over a year.

For Your Benefits

Many employers support participation in the Guard/Reserve by making up the difference between annual training's base pay and the employee's 40-hour pay. This can lessen the financial impact of missing two weeks of work. During active duty for training, Guard/Reserve members receive Basic Allowance for Housing (BAH) and Basic Allowance for Subsistence (BAS). Most employers' calculations do not include these amounts, since they are considered reimbursements.

Some people schedule their annual training as vacation time to keep checks from both sources. After all, what could be more relaxing than chipping paint on a ship, mopping out a barracks, and standing guard all night?

Servicemembers Civil Relief Act

In 2003 the Soldiers and Sailors Civil Relief Act (SSCRA) was rewritten and renamed the Servicemembers Civil Relief Act. This law protects National Guard and Reserve service members called to active duty from some of the financial hardships created by their call to active service.

Protection under this law begins on the first day of active duty and includes attending basic and MOS training. National Guard members called to state service by the president, such as to guard critical areas from terrorists or to serve during a major natural disaster, may also be covered by this act.

High points of this law address residential leases, car leases, installment contracts, and interest rate caps.

Residential Leases

SSCRA permits the breaking of a residential lease with no penalty. The lease of the service member's residence or the residence of the service member's dependents is covered under this law, if the lease was made before going onto active duty. This also applies to service members who receive permanent change of station orders.

To break the lease, the service member must make a formal written request notifying the land owner (always keep a copy for your own records). Attach a copy of your orders to it, and hand-deliver it or send it registered mail with a return receipt.

After properly delivering the notice, the service member is responsible for the rest of that month's rent (be it one day or almost a whole month) and all of the next month's rent. It is possible that the landlord may agree to let you off the hook early if someone else wants in.

Car Leases

Who wants to make big lease payments on an ordinary car when Uncle Sam provides a HUMVEE to tool around the desert? If the service member has signed an automobile lease (for personal use by the service member or his or her dependents) before going on active duty, the service member may request to end the lease when active service begins.

Submit the request to end the lease to the leaseholder along with a copy of your orders. As with any important legal document, either hand-deliver it or send it by certified mail (return receipt). Return the vehicle within 15 days of submitting the notice.

This is not a free ride; it relieves the service member of the early termination fee. However, all other charges and fees may apply, including excessive mileage and wear and tear. These are due when the vehicle is turned in.

Installment Contracts

Income suddenly reduced by converting from civilian to military pay may make it difficult to meet payments for installment contracts. This law protects you against repossession if the agreement was made before active duty and at least one payment was made. The creditor is also prohibited from terminating the contract without a court order.

Interest Rate Caps

Debts made by the service member or dependents before active duty, such as a home mortgage or credit card, can have their interest rate capped at 6 percent. This applies only if the active service makes it difficult for you to pay your debts. However, it is up to the lender to prove otherwise. The 6 percent rate lasts as long as the military obligation.

Temporary Military Jobs

Life is full of ups and downs. Sometimes the civilian job market is bleak. Based on availability, temporary full-time work could be available through the Guard/Reserve units.

"Man Days"

Guard/Reserve units sometimes have a pool of extra days they can pay unit members to come in and help around the armory. This might be to prepare for an inspection or to clean up some equipment. These days are sparsely handed to units (but somehow the higher headquarters always seem to have plenty of them). They provide one day of base pay (no allowances are paid) and one retirement point.

Temporary Duty

The Guard/Reserve sometimes needs extra hands for an extended period of time to assist with work surges. Often these are supplementary staffing for a Reserve training facility. For example, if a base is to host an ROTC summer camp, a Reserve unit retraining, or a major field exercise, it will need extra people.

> **Attention!**
>
> In the Guard/Reserve, the closer you are to the flagpole (high headquarters), the more discretionary money there is to pay members for extra training, extra man days, and so on.

To fill these assignments, open jobs are posted with the various units. These jobs require a specific MOS and rank range. They state when the work begins and ends. They also say how to apply.

Don't be shy about asking when these assignments will come out. As soon as a qualified candidate is accepted, the job goes away. Units rarely wait until every possible person has applied. Allow adequate time for paperwork to flow through the process.

If you're selected for one of these assignments (which may range from a few weeks to many months), you'll be given temporary active duty orders. Full pay is provided just as with any other activation, and one retirement point is provided per day of service.

Extra School

Everyone likes to get promoted. The pay is better, there are more people to do your work for you, and so on. In general, the Guard and Reserve attend the same career-advancement schools as active duty personnel to be eligible for promotion. Depending on funding available, you may be able to attend both a service school and annual training with your unit within the same year. The key is to apply to attend school early in the fiscal year before funds are cut off.

State Benefits

Each of the states provides its own incentives for joining its National Guard. A state may provide a wide range of benefits, including free license plates, an annual cash bonus, or whatever else it feels can reel in new recruits.

The most popular benefit for young people right out of high school is the college assistance program (each state has its own version of this). For example, in Ohio, the National Guard provides (for members working toward their first four-year degree) four years of free tuition to any state university. This is in addition to any federal school assistance from the GI Bill or other sources.

Other states also offer a limited amount of student loan forgiveness for members who have already earned a four-year degree. Always check the details before signing the paper; a better deal could be waiting just across the state line.

Uniformed Services Employment and Re-employment Rights Act (USERRA)

Service in the National Guard or Reserves is a part-time job. The employment that pays the bills and supports the family is the one you work at during the weekdays. Without that income, the family likely won't be able to pay its bills. An important concern of Guard/Reserve members is to ensure that the weekend job does not detract from the primary one.

USERRA guarantees that if you are called to active service for annual training or for an extended period, your employment is guaranteed. USERRA applies only if you were discharged from active service with an honorable or general discharge.

It may not be possible to return to the exact same job, but employers are required to provide a comparable position at the same pay, seniority, and benefits, as if you never left. The law further requires that employers provide refresher training necessary to qualify you for reemployment. Also, reinstatement to employment may not be immediate, but it must be within a reasonable amount of time.

USERRA covers only federal service. National Guard activations by governors for state service are not covered under this law. However, many states have enacted a similar law to cover Guard call-ups.

USERRA protects Guard/Reserve members by prohibiting employers from requiring you to use vacation time to cover military absences. However, you may do so if you wish. Also if the employer allows employees on nonmilitary leave to earn vacation while they are away, then USERRA requires that this benefit also apply to military leave.

In times past, if someone volunteered to be activated, employers took this to mean that you wanted the military job in place of your civilian position. USERRA treats voluntary and involuntary military service absences the same way.

If your active service is for less than 31 days, maintain your civilian health-care plan as before. If your service is for more than 30 days, you have the option of maintaining your employer-sponsored health care, but you are responsible for paying up to 102 percent (the employer's share plus a 2% administration fee) of health-care premium expense.

Hot Scoop

For more information on the Uniformed Services Employment and Reemployment Rights Act (USERRA), see www.dol.gov/ vets/programs/userra/userra_ fs.htm.

USERRA protects your civilian pension plan coverage. Your active military service time is not to be considered a break in service for calculating the pension.

Employers are required to provide notice of the rights, benefits, and obligations of covered persons and employers under USERRA.

Employers may choose to post the poster "Your Rights Under USERRA" where employee notices are customarily placed. If they want, they may also notify employees by handing or mailing out the notice, or distributing the notice via e-mail.

Your Responsibilities Under USERRA

You must inform your employer of your upcoming military deployment as far in advance as possible. Employers can be informed verbally, but you are better protected by providing written notice. If possible, provide a copy of your orders to active duty. For Guard/Reserve annual training, usually plenty of advance warning is given. If your unit is mobilized for service (national or state), there may not be much warning.

As soon as the active duty service is completed, you must report back to your place of employment:

◆ If you were gone for 31 days or less, you must report the next regularly scheduled workday (after allowing time for safe travel home and an eight-hour rest period).

◆ For service longer than 30 days and less than 180 days, you have 14 days to submit an application for re-employment.

◆ For service longer than 180 days, you have 90 days to submit an application for re-employment.

◆ If you are recovering from injuries received during service, you have up to two years to apply for reemployment.

USERRA is not intended to act as a placeholder for someone who wants to bounce on and off active duty. It has a cumulative five-year limit on the amount of military leave an employer must provide. Inactive duty for training, annual training, involuntary active duty extensions, and recalls due to a war or national emergency are not counted in the five-year cumulative total.

Disabled Veterans and USERRA

Veterans returning to their place of employment with a disability are also covered under this act. Employers are required to make reasonable efforts to accommodate the disability.

Filing a Complaint Under USERRA

If you feel that your employer has not complied with this law, contact the Department of Labor through the Veterans' Employment and Training Service. Complaints filed under this act are investigated at no cost to you. (In many cases, just a polite conversation between your employer and the Department of Labor attorney is enough to ensure full compliance with the law.)

If the employer still cannot see the light, the case is referred to the Department of Justice for consideration by a district court. Again, there is no cost to you.

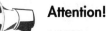

Attention!

USERRA applies only to service of less than five years. If your active service was for five consecutive years or more, this law does not apply to you.

Employer Support for the Guard and Reserve (ESGR)

Sometimes disagreements between Guard/Reserve members and their employers is a matter of misunderstanding of what is required of each under USERRA. To assist in the resolution of conflicts, the Department of Defense created the Employer Support for the Guard and Reserve (ESGR).

ESGR's mission is to gain and maintain active support from all public and private employers for their employees' participation in the National Guard and Reserve. To accomplish this, ESGR depends on a network of hundreds of volunteers.

ESGR's role is as follows:

◆ To operate a proactive program to increase appreciation of the role of the National Guard and Reserve in the nation's armed forces

◆ To encourage voluntary compliance with federal and state laws governing rights of Reserve component members

◆ To educate Guard/Reserve members on their responsibilities to employers

◆ To provide informal mediation for problems and misunderstandings that result from National Guard or Reserve membership, training, or duty requirements

The primary means of assistance is through a nationwide ombudsman program. Ombudsmen receive extensive training on USERRA and dispute-resolution techniques. They serve as informal mediators between the employer and employee to inform and educate them on what the law requires, and assist in finding a mutually agreeable solution. ESGR ombudsmen can be reached via e-mail at ESGRMailbox@ navy.mil or by phone at 1-800-336-4590.

Hot Scoop

Not every employer is a problem. Many will go far beyond what the law requires to support their serving employees. Nominate your employer for the ESGR Patriot's Award recognizing their support for the Guard/Reserve programs. Anyone in the Guard/Reserve can nominate their employer at esgr.org/resources.asp?p=awards.

Guard/Reserve Retirement

Ask any Guardsman or Reservist what their number one benefit is, and they are very likely to say their retirement package. Few civilian employers offer pensions. The savings plans they have substituted for pensions will cost you more and pay far less than the retirement checks they replaced. Aside from the military, the other big employers paying a pension are the civilian government agencies.

Not only does the Guard/Reserve provide a pension, but the retirement money is for a part-time job. This retirement package offers many other benefits, such as medical care for retirees and survivor benefits. Other chapters discuss these. Here we focus on the Guard/Reserve retirement pay.

Active duty retirements begin paying as soon as the service member retires. (Chapter 6 describes active duty pensions.) Not so for a Reserve pension. Money does not begin to flow until the service member's sixtieth birthday.

Military retired pay is not a pension or annuity, nor is it awarded as a vested interest or contractual right. It is "reduced compensation for reduced services." That means keep your uniforms in good shape. If the good of the service calls for your return, you may get a letter.

Retirement Eligibility

The primary qualification for a reserve pension is 20 "good" years of service (combined active and reserve). A good year is considered to be one in which the service member earned at least 50 retirement points. Points earned in a year with less than 50 points can still be added into the total points for calculating retirement pay, but that year does not count toward the 20 years required for retirement entitlement.

The big event in the life of a Guard/Reserve person is the receipt of the "20-year letter." Public Law 89-652 requires the service secretaries to provide a "Notification of Eligibility for Retired Pay at Age 60" letter. Often you must wait up to one year to receive the letter after it has been earned.

National Guard members receive their 20-year letter from their state headquarters. Reservists' letters are issued by their service component's Personnel Management Office.

This letter cannot be revoked unless it can be proved that you provided false information to qualify for it. Mistakes by the services cannot be used to revoke the letter. (The logic is that if someone is officially told they have qualified for a retirement and they stop participating, they cannot be later denied retirement cash due to a paperwork foul-up.)

Once you receive the letter, take time to check all your records to ensure that every retirement point earned is reflected in the official records. Although the letter cannot be taken back, retirement points can be recalculated at any time. Always keep all receipts, copies of orders, and training certificates in a safe place to justify retirement point credit.

Count Those Points

Active duty pensions are based on 20 years of service. That is a lot of days, a lot of inspections, a lot of nights spent at sea, and a lot of horrible food.

Guard/Reserve pensions are likewise based on 20 years of service, but sleeping in your own bed is not the same thing as snoozing away a frosty night in the back of a 5-ton truck. So to determine the comparable number of days of service between the active duty and Reserve components, a points system is used.

- One point is awarded for each day of active duty service. This includes basic training, annual training, active duty service prior to the Guard/Reserve, and so on.

- One point is awarded for each drill. A typical weekend has four drills.

- Points can be awarded for correspondence courses, for drills for no pay (points-only drills), or for other reasons.

- Fifteen membership points are awarded annually just for being in the Guard/Reserve during that year.

- The maximum number of points a member can receive for Guard/Reserve inactive participation is 60 for retirement years ending before September 23, 1996. Retirement years ending after that day and through October 30, 2000, may earn a maximum of 75 inactive duty points. After that the maximum is 90 points per year. To this maximum is added 1 point for each active duty day served, including annual training.

For example, let's calculate the points for a 22 year Reservist with 4 years of active duty.

Active duty is 1 point per day. 4 × 365 = 1460 points (plus 1 point for leap year)

18 years of service in the reserves at 15 membership points per year = 18 × 15 = 270

18 years if 15 day annual training, 1 point per day of training = 270 point

18 years of 48 drills per year (4 drills per weekend, 1 weekend per month, times 12 months—assuming this person attended them all) = 864 points

Assuming that the maximum number of points was never exceeded in a year, this person has 2,864 points

To this would be added correspondence courses, extra days of active duty, etc.

Calculating Retirement Pay

Calculating retirement pay is a four-step process. Online calculators can assist with this. Of course, you can wade through these calculations, but the rest of us will use the free online service (Guard/Reserve retirement pay is figured the same for all services).

1. Determine your retirement plan and base pay amount.

    a. If your first day of military service (the day ink hit the enlistment contract) was before September 8, 1980, you are under the base pay system. Start with the base pay for your rank and number of years of service.

    b. Otherwise, you are under the High-3 system. Start with an average of your highest three years of pay. Use the active duty pay chart for your rank and years of service. Chapter 6 explains the High-3 retirement pay calculation method.

 **Hot Scoop** _____

Your can find a quick retirement pay calculator at www.hrc.army.mil/site/reserve/soldierservices/retirement/retirementcalc.asp.

Attention! _____

When you leave the military for retirement, the key is to transfer to the Retired Reserve. If you request a discharge, your final pay rate will be based on you last day of service—or your High-3 base pay for retirement is based on your last three years of service. Otherwise, they are based on when you turn sixty years of age.

2. Determine your equivalent number of years of service. Do this by dividing your total points by 360. For example, someone who was in the Guard/Reserve for only 20 years (no active duty time) might retire at 20 years with 2,000 points. Dividing this by 360 shows an equivalent of 5.5 years of active service.

3. Multiply the number of equivalent service years by 2.5 percent.

4. Multiply the active duty monthly base pay amount (step 1) by the number in step 3.

Here is an actual example.

1. Choose either a or b:

    a. If your DIEM date is prior to September 8, 1980, then find the pay chart and look up the base pay for your rank and number of years of service on the pay scale for the first day that you will draw retirement pay. In 2008 the base pay for an E-8 over 22 years is $4,478.

    b. If your DIEM date is on or after September 8, 1980, then you must find the pay chart that shows the three years of your highest base pay (usually the last three years) prior to drawing retirement pay—the years you were 57, 58 and 59 years old. Average these 36 months to determine the base pay amount to use. In 2008, the High-3.

2. Divide your total number of points by 360 to find the number of equivalent years. Using the previous example, that would be 2864/360 = 7.95 years.

3. Multiply 7.95 × 2.5 percent = 19.87 percent.

4. Multiply 19.87 percent times the number in step one to arrive at the final pay. So if the base pay for this per was $4,470 × 19.87 percent = $888.19 per month.

For Your Benefits

If you are a Guard/Reserve member in "pay status," you may qualify to participate in the Thrift Savings Plan (TSP) tax-deferred savings account. This retirement supplement (similar to an employer-sponsored retirement savings plan) is subject to IRS limits.

Challenging the Point Count

If the official records do not reflect all your service, the number of points can be changed if supported by the proper documentation. Keep all receipts, copies of orders, and training certificates in a safe place to justify retirement credit.

Acceptable proof includes the following:

- ◆ DD Form 214 (proof of active duty service)

- ◆ DA Form 1383 (proof of Army Reserve duty)

- ◆ ARPC Form 249-2-E, DARC Form 249, or AGUZ Form 115 (proof of Army Reserve duty)

- ◆ NGB Form 23, or a detailed statement of service from the state adjutant general (proof of National Guard duty)

- ◆ AF Form 526 (proof of Air Force or Air Force Reserve duty)

- ◆ NAVPERS Form 1070-611 (proof of Naval Reserve duty)

- ◆ NAVMC Form 768 (proof of Marine Corps Reserve duty)

- ◆ CG HQ Form 4973 (proof of Coast Guard Reserve duty)

- ◆ Any document proving inactive duty training (IDT), such as DA Form 1380 or DA Form 1379

- ◆ Correspondence or extension school courses completion notices

- ◆ Any appointment or enlistment documents or notices to prove membership

- ◆ Military pay vouchers, travel vouchers, and performance evaluations to substantiate periods of active duty for training (ADT)

Attention!

Once someone in the Guard/Reserve retires, that person is classified as a "grey area" retired person. This is a sort of limbo land between where you are today and a paid retirement at age sixty. "Grey area" retired have the same benefits as Guard/Reserve participants in a Troop Program Unit, but they do not receive retirement pay.

Fully Retired At Last

Becoming "fully" retired brings several additional benefits. You receive full military retirement benefits, such as space-available travel for your spouse and dependent children. Your dependents also receive medical coverage (which may be more financially valuable than the retirement income).

Send Me a Check!

Retirement pay does not begin by itself; you must formally request it. For a smooth transition, submit the paperwork six months before you turn 60. If you forget to apply for it, up to six years of retroactive retirement pay can be made.

To request retirement checks, submit DD Form 108. Include DD Form 2656 ("Data for Payment"), SF 1199A ("Direct Deposit"), and DD Form 1883 ("Survivor Benefit Plan Election"), as appropriate. (Ah, you knew the military could not function without its endless supply of forms.)

Check Out the New Credentials

Time to exchange that pink ID card for a blue one! Find a local facility that can issue new ID cards for yourself and eligible dependents. Military bases can do this. Some Guard/Reserve units (such as State National Guard Headquarters units) can do this, but call ahead to ensure that they have the blank retiree ID cards.

The Least You Need to Know

- ◆ You are not officially retired from the Guard/Reserves without a 20-year letter.
- ◆ See if your Guard/Reserve participation qualifies for income tax deductions.
- ◆ Keep every document that can support a claim for retirement points.
- ◆ Always check for bonuses before re-enlisting.

Full-Time Health Insurance for Part-Time Warriors

In This Chapter

- ◆ How to apply for TRICARE Reserve Select
- ◆ Dental insurance for Guard and Reserve members
- ◆ Survivor benefits for TRICARE Reserve Select and the TRICARE Dental Program
- ◆ Transitioning medical coverage from active duty back to the Reserve program

TRICARE is the uniformed services' medical insurance program. Members of the Reserves and the National Guard who are called to active duty receive the same benefits as the active duty forces. This includes the TRICARE medical insurance program.

TRICARE Reserve Select (TRS) is a benefit provided to the Selected Reserve for both National Guard and Reserves who are not on active duty, or covered under the Transitional Assistance Management Program [TAMP]. It is similar to TRICARE Standard and TRICARE Extra (as described in Chapter 9). It also includes the TRICARE Dental Program for Guard and Reserve members. All members of the Selected Reserve are eligible for TRICARE Reserve Select and the TRICARE Dental Program.

TRICARE Reserve Select Premiums

The price for TRICARE Reserve Select is set annually and takes effect on January 1. The price for coverage in 2008 is $81 per month for member-only coverage, and $253 per month for family coverage. This program provides the same TRICARE services as provided to the active duty forces. TRS members pay the same TRICARE Standard deductibles and cost shares as active duty service members. See Chapter 9 for more information.

TRICARE does not require you to live near a military base to receive services. In many cases, you can retain your family physician.

Three things to remember:

- Participation in TRICARE Reserve Select requires membership in the Selected Reserve for the entire period. Coverage ends as soon as you leave the Selected Reserve.

- All monthly premiums are due prior to the beginning of the month that they apply to.

- You are not eligible for this program if you or your spouse are eligible for coverage under the Federal Employees Health Benefits program.

Hot Scoop

For current TRICARE Reserve Select information, visit www.tricare.osd.mil/reserve/reserveselect.

Signing Up for TRICARE Reserve Select

To purchase TRICARE Reserve Select, submit a DD Form 2896, "TRICARE Reserve Select Request," along with the first month's premium payment to your regional contractor. Select whether coverage will begin on the first of the next month, or the first day of the following month. TRS uses the date on the postmark of your application along with your choice to set your first day of coverage.

The regional TRS contractor will bill you on the 10th of every month, for coverage of the following month. If payment is not received by the end of the month, then coverage may be cancelled for the following month and you may be locked out of the TRS program for 12 months.

Payments can be made by:

◆ Direct billing

◆ Automatically charged to a credit card or debit card

◆ Automatic Bank Withdrawal

To enroll, log on to the Guard and Reserve Web Portal at www.dmdc.osd.mil/appj/trs/index.jsp. You will need your myPay PIN number. Next select the "Purchase Coverage" option. You must identify which family members will be enrolled along with a coverage start date. Print the request form (DD Form 2896. Sign in and submit it with the initial payment to the regional TRICARE office identified by your unit administrator.

Tricare Service Centers

Tricare Reserve Select is provided through three regional service centers. These centers can provide information about accessing health care in your area. Northern Region

Health Net Federal Services, Inc.
TRICARE Reserve Select
Enrollment
PO Box 870162
Surfside Beach, SC 29587-9762
1-800-555-2605
www.healthnetfederalservices.com

Southern Region and TRICARE Overseas

Humana Military
Healthcare Services, Inc.
PO Box 105389
Atlanta, GA 30348-5389
1-800-444-5445
www.humana-military.com

For Your Benefits _____

New participants receive a TRICARE Reserve Select Handbook detailing covered services, how to get care, and how to request assistance.

Western Region

TriWest Healthcare Alliance
PO Box 42048
Phoenix, AZ 85080-2048
1-888-TRIWEST
(1-888-874-9378)
www.triwest.com

Pre-Activation Eligibility

If you have received orders to active duty in support of a contingency operation, such as Operation Enduring Freedom or Noble Eagle, you and your family are legible for early TRICARE coverage such as medical, pharmacy and dental coverage. Your orders will indicate if you service is for a contingency operation.

Pre-activation Tricare coverage is for up to 90 days. Coverage will continue on after reporting to active duty. Eligibility begins on the date of the orders (if less than 90 days before activation), or when you are within 90 days of call-up.

Qualifying Life Events

Whenever a qualifying event adds to or subtracts from your family, you might need to update your coverage. The first step is always to update the DEERS database through your personnel office. Examples of qualifying life events include these:

◆ Marriage

◆ Birth or adoption of a child

◆ Legal separation

◆ Divorce or annulment

◆ Death of a spouse or family member

Some qualifying events may suspend your coverage. For example, if you become eligible for TRICARE For Life due to retirement, your coverage must be transferred to that program. You also lose coverage if you become covered by Medicaid or other government-sponsored coverage.

TRICARE Reserve Select Survivor Benefits

Family members covered on the day of the member's death, surviving family members may purchase TRS coverage for an additional six months from the date of death. If there is only one surviving TRS-enrolled member, the survivor pays for coverage at the member-only rate. If there are two or more surviving TRS-enrolled family members, member-and-family rates apply. Surviving family members must submit a TRS request form to request survivor coverage no later than 60 days after the member's death. If the application is not submitted in the proper timeframe, it will be returned. If the TRS-covered member was recalled to active duty and dies while on active duty, surviving family members are eligible for active duty survivor benefits.

Voluntarily Terminating TRS Coverage

If you decide to end your Tricare Reserve Select coverage, you must formally request it. Stopping premium payments will also end your coverage but you may be subject to collection fees and additional premiums.

To disenroll, log into the Guard and Reserve website at www.dmdc.osd.mil/appj/trs. Complete the TRS request form and print it. Sign it and mail to your regional TRS contract support center. Voluntary disenrollment locks you out of the TRS program for 12 months.

For Your Benefits

If you leave the Selected Reserve or lose eligibility for any other reason, your TRS coverage is lost. You may re-apply again when you qualify for coverage.

TRICARE Dental Program

The TRICARE Dental Program (TDP) is provided by United Concordia Companies, Inc., through the TRICARE Management Activity. TRICARE Dental is available for members of the Selected Reserve, members of the Individual Ready Reserve, and their eligible family members. United Concordia verifies member eligibility in the TDP using the Defense Enrollment Eligibility Reporting System (DEERS). If DEERS is not up-to-date, enrollment may be denied.

Eligible family members include spouses and unmarried children under the age of 21. Unmarried children are eligible up to the end of the month in which they turn 21. Family members over age 21 may be eligible for TDP benefits through the end of the month in which they turn age 23 if they are enrolled full-time at an accredited college or are more than 50 percent financially dependent on the sponsor.

TDP Services

TDP offers comprehensive dental coverage:

- Diagnostic and preventive services (exams, cleanings, fluorides, sealants, and x-rays)

- Basic restorative services (fillings)

- Endodontics (root canals)

- Periodontics (gum surgery)

- Oral surgery (extractions)

- Prosthodontics (crowns, dentures)

- Orthodontics (braces)

TDP Premiums

The government pays 60 percent of the Selected Reserve member's monthly premium. Family members and IRR participants in a category other than the Special Mobilization category pay the full monthly premium. Premium charges are updated every February 1. National Guard/Selected Reserve monthly premiums from February 2008 to January 2009 are as follows:

- Sponsor only: $11.58

- One family member, excluding sponsor: $28.95

- More than one family member, excluding sponsor: $72.37

- Monthly sponsor and family: $83.95

IRR members can also participate in the TRICARE Dental Program—but at a different price. IRR monthly premiums for February 2008 to January 2009 are as follows:

- Sponsor only: $28.95

- One family member, excluding sponsor: $28.95

- More than one family member, excluding sponsor: $72.37

- Monthly sponsor and family: $101.32

Under the TDP family enrollment, all eligible National Guard/Reserve family members must be enrolled. However, children under the age of 4 may be excluded from enrollment at the discretion of the sponsor if only one member of the family age 4 or older is enrolled (single coverage). If the sponsor chooses to enroll one child under the age of 4, all children under the age of 4 automatically are enrolled. This may change the sponsor's status (and expense) from single to family coverage. Children are automatically enrolled on the first day of the month following the month in which they reach age 4.

Enrollment Rules

All new enrollments to the TRICARE Dental Program are for at least 12 months. After the initial 12-month period, enrollment is month to month until cancelled. Disenrollment during the initial 12-month period is permitted only under specific circumstances, such as retirement, a call to active duty, a transfer to the Standby Reserve, or loss of eligibility due to death, divorce, age limit of a child, or marriage.

Premiums must be paid every month. Partial payment is never accepted. If you miss a premium payment during the 12-month enrollment period, the government will not pay any portion of the premium for the remaining months. United Concordia will collect the full amount—government and member portions of any remaining premium due for the 12-month enrollment period—from you. Failure to pay the required premiums may result in referral of the account to a collection agency.

What Happens If You Are Called to Active Duty?

National Guard/Reserve members (and their dependents) ordered to active duty for more than 30 consecutive days are disenrolled from the TDP and receive the same dental coverage as active duty service members. Upon deactivation, National Guard/Reserve service members are automatically reenrolled in TDP.

Survivor Benefits

TDP survivor benefits are available to surviving family members currently enrolled in the TDP, as well as previously enrolled surviving family members:

◆ This survivor benefit also applies to enrolled family members of the Selected Reserve (National Guard/Reserve) and IRR (Special Mobilization only), regardless of whether the sponsor was on active duty orders or was enrolled in TDP at the time of death.

◆ Eligible surviving family members enrolled at the time of their sponsor's death are disenrolled from their current TDP coverage plan and reenrolled in a TDP survivor benefit plan.

The government pays 100 percent of the TDP survivor benefit premium for three years from the month following the sponsor's death. However, family members are still responsible for any applicable cost-shares. Before the three-year period ends, surviving family members will be notified of coverage termination.

Attention!

TRICARE policies and benefits are changed as public law is amended. For the most recent information, contact your TRICARE regional contractor.

Once the three-year TDP survivor benefit period ends, surviving family members are eligible for the TRICARE Retiree Dental Program (TRDP). The TRDP may also be available to surviving family members who do not qualify for the TDP survivor benefit. For more information about the TRDP, visit www.tricaredentalprogram.com/tdptws/enrollees/benefits/survivor_benefits.jsp

Transition Assistance Management Program (TAMP)

The Transition Assistance Management Program (TAMP) provides health-care coverage for you and your family during your transition to civilian life. TAMP coverage begins on your separation date. You may choose from TRICARE Prime, TRICARE Standard, and TRICARE Extra.

Guard/Reserve members separated after active service in support of a contingency operation for an active duty period of more than 30 days and their family members are eligible for transition assistance through the Transition Assistance Management Program (TAMP). Guard and Reserve members returning from active duty may be eligible for 180 days of TRICARE coverage.

Even if you had TRICARE Prime while on active duty, you must submit an enrollment form for yourself and each family member. The transition from active duty coverage to coverage under TAMP will be smoother if you submit these forms before separation. If this is your first enrollment for TRICARE Prime, coverage begins at the start of the next month if enrollment is received by the twentieth of the month. An important part of your enrollment is to ensure that information about yourself and every family member contained in the DEERS database is correct.

Under TAMP, former activated Reservists and family members are not eligible to enroll or re-enroll in TRICARE Prime Remote or in TRICARE Prime Remote for Active Duty Family Members because both programs require the sponsor to be on active duty. Under TAMP, the sponsor is no longer on active duty and is treated as an active duty family member for benefits and cost-sharing purposes.

The Least You Need to Know

- How you can determine your cost for TRICARE Reserve Select and the TRICARE Dental Program.

- How you apply for the dental and health insurance programs.

- What the survivor benefits are for the Guard/Reserve medical plans.

- The way that TAMP provides active duty cost TRICARE coverage after returning from a contingency operation.

Part 6

Leaving the Service

A valuable government benefit is preferential hiring for government jobs. Although some people may be reluctant to jump from one government job to another, this may be the best deal around. Just as in the military, government civilian workers are among the few who are still awarded a retirement pension. Some states also provide veteran hiring preferences—if you know how to apply.

After you leave military service, the benefits keep right on rolling. If you served on active duty, the National Guard, or the Reserves, you have likely earned some of the veterans benefits. The Veterans Administration provides hospitals and outpatient clinics support for service-related injuries. It also provides nursing homes to those in financial need.

At some point, we all pass from this life. The Veterans Administration can arrange military honors at the funeral and provide cemetery plots and markers dedicated to your service. Of course, the people arranging things after you are gone must know about all of this.

Chapter 19

Am I a Vet?

In This Chapter

- Determining whether you are legally a "veteran"
- Understanding the different categories of veterans
- Proving entitlement to benefits
- Appealing a VA decision

Providing cash and support benefits to its veterans is just one of the ways that a grateful nation rewards those who stepped forward to protect it. In the early days of our nation, military service was considered a duty—and a good idea, to protect your own property from invading armies. It was something that you did and then went home. With luck, some sort of pay went with it. Modern veterans are rewarded with a long list of benefits promised to them before they even sign on.

The basic question is, what makes someone a "veteran"? Typically, it means someone who is experienced in something, like a veteran baseball pitcher or veteran policeman. More often it reflects someone who is successful in a high-pressure job. However, common usage in the United States is to indicate a person who has served in the armed forces.

The federal government spends a lot of money to support veterans, so it is keen to determine who is eligible to receive what. It generally defines a veteran as someone who served at least 180 days of active service before September 7, 1980. After that, someone must have completed two years of active duty. These time periods are waived if the person was medically discharged or received a service-connected disability stipend. Guard/Reserve active duty for training does not count toward this requirement.

States set their own legal definition of what a veteran is for eligibility for state-provided benefits (in addition to federal benefits). Their definitions may differ significantly based on what their legislatures want to pay for.

How Many Vets Are There?

As of September 2006, the estimated veteran population was 24 million. Every day, more people join the armed forces, and every day, more of the older veterans die. The typical World War II veteran today is in his or her 80s.

The largest group of veterans today is the eight million from the Vietnam era. Gulf War–era veterans now comprise the second-largest component, numbering 4.5 million. There are about three million World War II veterans and a similar number of Korean War veterans. World War I veterans are too few to estimate reliably. In addition, six million veterans have served only in peacetime.

Another group eligible for benefits is made up of parents, widows, and dependent children of veterans. They may survive long after the veteran has died. For example, in the 1930s, some Civil War veterans in their 80s married young women who then inherited their Civil War pensions. The last Union Army soldier died in 1956, and the last Union Army widow died in 2003! (Then again, the last child from the Revolutionary War whom the VA recognized died in 1911.)

For Your Benefits

Abraham Lincoln's second inaugural address included the phrase "to care for him who shall have borne the battle and for his widow, and his orphan." The VA uses this small but powerful phrase as the guiding principle for its many programs.

A Short History of Veteran Benefits

It is easier to understand the benefits offered today if you look back in history to see what was offered before and why. Benefits today are based on experience providing services to veterans from previous conflicts.

A natural question of anyone marching off to a violent confrontation is, "What will happen to me if I return disabled? What will happen to my children and widow if I die?" The United States has a long history of caring for veterans, stretching back to the Pilgrims, who passed a law providing for the support of anyone disabled fighting the natives.

After the Revolutionary War and through the Mexican War, veterans were provided "Bounty Land" as partial reward for their service. After the Revolution, these lands were in Virginia, Kentucky, and Ohio. Each bounty had the thinly disguised act of expanding westward and of forcing off the existing inhabitants. Land bounties were discontinued in 1862 when the Homestead Act opened federal lands to anyone.

After the Revolutionary War, the federal government provided small pensions for disabled veterans and impoverished widows. An 1862 law established disability pensions for injuries suffered in the line of duty. Later pensions provided for widows and dependents. By 1906, pensions were offered to any Union veteran who had served honorably. (Confederate pensions were provided by the individual Southern states.)

In 1851, Congress established the Soldier's Home in Washington, D.C. It was financed with the $150,000 ransom that Mexico City paid to avoid being sacked during the war. The facility survives today as the Armed Forces Retirement Home.

The Civil War created a large number of seriously wounded veterans. Existing facilities were used for the benefit of regular soldiers and sailors. However, most of the soldiers and sailors were volunteers provided by the individual states. Initially, their home states carried the burden of caring for them. Also most veterans worked on farms. This hard work was more difficult with an empty sleeve or trouser leg. To help these shattered bodies heal and to provide some support to those no longer able to work, Congress approved the creation of the first three National Soldiers' Homes in 1865.

Meanwhile, the states began to build veteran hospitals to assist Civil War veterans. In some cases, these hospitals faded with the veterans. In others, they continue on today, supporting veterans of later conflicts.

Who Is Eligible?

This question has no easy answer. In general, benefits are intended as a reward for honorable service. Each benefit is created by a law passed by Congress or a state legislature. Therefore, each benefit may have its own unique eligibility requirements that are looser or tighter than with previous benefits. Sometimes benefits are targeted to a specific group or conflict.

The simplest criterion is that veterans benefits are a reward for honorable service to the nation. Therefore, the best ticket is an honorable discharge from active duty. Active duty means full-time service in one of the seven uniformed services: Air Force, Coast Guard, Navy, Army, Marines, Public Health Service, or National Oceanic and Atmospheric Administration (or its predecessor, the Coast and Geodetic Survey).

This also includes members of the Guard/Reserve called to active duty. If this active duty was for the full term of the call-up or was for more than 90 days, a DD214 is issued to characterize the service as honorable or otherwise.

Honorable Service

The primary document for proving eligibility for veterans benefits is the Department of Defense Form 214, commonly referred to as a DD214. On it is a place that indicates the type of separation from military service, such as "Honorable."

To be considered a "veteran" eligible for most Department of Veterans Affairs (VA) health-care benefits, a former service member must have been discharged "under conditions other than dishonorable." The VA views qualifying administrative discharges to be those characterized by the issuing armed services as honorable or general under honorable conditions. Punitive discharges such as dishonorable and bad conduct are disqualifying.

In a few cases, discharges of other than honorable and punitive bad conduct discharges issued by a special court-martial may still qualify. When in doubt about your entitlements, let the VA decide. If you apply for VA health-care benefits with an other than honorable or bad conduct discharge, you can be registered in a Pending Verification status. Submit a request for an administrative decision regarding the character of service with the local VA Regional Office using VA Form 7131, "Exchange of Beneficiary Information and Request for Administrative and Adjudicative Action."

Dishonorable and bad conduct discharges issued by a general court-martial may bar someone from VA benefits. VA benefits will not be provided to any veteran or dependent wanted for an outstanding felony warrant.

Length of Service

The length of active duty service is another important eligibility requirement. There's a 180-day service requirement for enlisted persons who started their active duty before September 8, 1980, or officers who first entered active duty before October 17, 1981.

All other veterans must have 24 months of continuous active duty military service. Exceptions to this are as follows:

- ◆ Guard/Reserve who were called to active duty and who completed the term for which they were called, and who were granted an other than dishonorable discharge

- ◆ Members who were discharged or released from active duty for a hardship or service-connected medical condition

Periods

Certain veterans benefits require wartime service. Under the law, the VA recognizes these war periods:

- ◆ World War II: December 7, 1941, through December 31, 1946

- ◆ Korean War: June 27, 1950, through January 31, 1955

- ◆ Vietnam War: August 5, 1964 (February 28, 1961, for veterans who served "in country" before August 5, 1964), through May 7, 1975

- ◆ Gulf War: August 2, 1990, through a date to be set by law or presidential proclamation

For Your Benefits

The government has awarded veterans benefits to many special groups from the World War II era. These are typically civilian organizations or local native forces that provided direct support to the armed forces.

How the Veterans Administration Is Organized

The Veterans Administration is the second-largest federal department, with more than 235,000 employees. As advocates for veterans and their families, the VA is committed to providing the best services with an attitude of caring and courtesy. Services and benefits are provided through a nationwide network of hospitals, clinics, nursing homes, regional offices, and national cemeteries.

The VA is divided into three major organizations: Veterans Health Administration (VHA), Veterans Benefits Administration (VBA), and National Cemetery Administration (NCA). If you go searching for something, it is important to look for it in the right place.

Don't let the size and complexity of the Veterans Administration intimidate you. Federal and state veterans' affairs counselors are available to help you navigate the VA departments.

Veterans Health Administration

The Veterans Health Administration (VHA) operates the United States' largest integrated health system. It administers a nationwide network of medical centers, ambulatory care clinics, nursing homes, readjustment counseling centers, and comprehensive home-care programs. Its 200,000 employees annually treat 1.1 million inpatients and have an average daily inpatient census of 87,504.

For Your Benefits

The VA provides combat veterans free medical care for any illness possibly associated with service during a period of hostility for two years from the veteran's release from active duty.

The VHA has a comprehensive array of services for disabled veterans. It also provides the largest network of homeless assistance programs in the country.

Veterans Benefits Administration

The Veterans Benefits Administration (VBA) is responsible for administering the department's programs that provide financial and other forms of assistance to veterans, their dependents, and survivors. Major benefits include veterans' compensation, veterans' pension, survivors' benefits, rehabilitation and employment assistance, education assistance, home loan guaranties, and life insurance coverage.

National Cemetery Administration

The National Cemetery Administration (NCA) operates 125 national cemeteries in the United States and territories, together with oversight and management of 33 soldiers' lots, Confederate cemeteries, and monument sites. It honors our nation's veterans with a carefully maintained final resting place and commemorates their service to our nation.

The NCA coordinates burial honors for veterans' funerals. It also provides headstones and markers for veterans' graves located outside of federal and state veterans' cemeteries.

Special Veteran Groups

The nation's veterans' population is a reflection of the society it draws from; no single group characterizes it. The VA works to identify their unique needs and meet them.

Women Veterans

In the beginning, veterans were all men. An occasional woman might have assisted in battle, or nurses assisted in the medical service, but in comparison with the number of men involved, their numbers were few. Therefore, the facilities and treatments have all been focused on men. Single-sex facilities can be large, simple, and inexpensive.

Since World War II, women have served in the armed forces in large numbers. Once found mainly in the rear battle areas, they are moving more into the line of fire. For example, many military nurses became POWs when the Japanese captured the Philippines and endured the same cruel treatment as the male prisoners.

In recent times, the military services have increased the number of women in the ranks. The Veterans Administration estimates that, by 2010, 10 percent of the nation's veterans will be women, so it has adjusted its services and facilities accordingly. Women veterans receive gender-specific services, including breast and pelvic examinations and other reproductive health-care services.

In 1994, public law established a Center for Women Veterans to oversee VA programs for women veterans. It ensures that women veterans receive benefits and services on par with those of male veterans. It also ensures that VA programs address the gender-specific needs of women veterans. The center identifies policies, practices, programs, and related activities that may be unresponsive or insensitive to the needs of women veterans, and recommends changes, revisions, or new initiatives to address the identified deficiencies.

Veterans Overseas

Veterans living or traveling overseas can still use some of their benefits while overseas. The VA pays for medical services to treat service-connected disabilities and related conditions, or for medical services needed as part of a vocational rehabilitation program for veterans living or traveling outside the United States.

VA monetary benefits, including disability compensation, pension, and educational and burial allowances, generally are payable overseas. Some programs are restricted.

For example, home loan guaranties are available only in the United States and selected U.S. territories and possessions. Educational benefits are limited to approved degree-granting programs in institutions of higher learning.

Beneficiaries living in foreign countries should contact the nearest American embassy or consulate for help. In Canada, contact an office of Veterans Affairs Canada. For more information, visit www.vba.va.gov/bln/21/foreign/index.htm.

Special Groups

World War–II era Filipino veterans are eligible for certain VA benefits. Generally, Old Philippine Scouts are eligible for VA benefits in the same manner as U.S. veterans. Commonwealth Army veterans, including certain organized Filipino guerrilla forces and New Philippine Scouts residing in the United States who are citizens or lawfully admitted for permanent residence, are also eligible for VA health care in the United States on the same basis as U.S. veterans. Eligibility and the rates of benefits vary based on the recipient's citizenship and place of residence. Call 1-800-827-1000 to determine eligibility. Certain Merchant Marine seamen who served in World War II may qualify for veterans benefits. When applying for medical care, seamen must present their discharge certificate from the Department of Defense. Call 1-800-827-1000 for assistance in obtaining a certificate.

Parents, Widows (or Widowers), and Children

In some cases, widows and dependent children are eligible for VA benefits based on the deceased veteran's service. To demonstrate eligibility for these benefits, you need the following:

◆ A copy of the veteran's DD214 showing that the service was other than dishonorable

◆ Veteran's marriage certificate for claims of a surviving spouse or children

◆ Veteran's death certificate if the veteran did not die in a VA health-care facility

◆ Children's birth certificates or adoption papers to determine children's benefits

◆ Veteran's birth certificate to determine parents' benefits

Incarcerated Veterans

Benefits for veterans who have been convicted of a felony (an offense punishable by death or more than one year in prison) and were imprisoned for more than 60 days may be reduced. Disability or death pensions paid to incarcerated beneficiaries are stopped. Disability compensation paid to incarcerated veterans rated 20 percent or more disabled are limited to the 10 percent rate. Veterans with a 10 percent disability are paid at the 5 percent rate. For a surviving spouse, child, or dependent parent receiving Dependency and Indemnity Compensation (DIC), or a veteran whose disability rating is 10 percent, the payment is reduced to half the rate payable to a veteran evaluated as 10 percent disabled.

Failure to notify the VA of a veteran's incarceration can result in overpayment of benefits and the subsequent loss of all VA financial benefits until the overpayment is recovered. VA benefits are not provided to any veteran or dependent who is wanted for an outstanding felony warrant.

Any amounts not paid to the vet may be apportioned to eligible dependents. Payments are not reduced for participants who are in work-release programs, who reside in halfway houses, or who are under community control. Veterans benefits resume on the first day of release, but not automatically. Veterans must notify the VA of their new status. However, the VA must be informed within one year of the release to ensure that you receive all of your benefits.

Incarcerated veterans rejoining a community are at risk for homelessness and a wide range of mental and physical illnesses. To assist veterans leaving prison, the VA's Healthcare for Re-Entry Veterans program provides counseling and assistance. It provides outreach and prerelease assessments services. It also provides referrals to medical, psychiatric, and social services, including employment services.

Attention!

Veterans convicted of a federal or state capital crime are barred from receiving VA burial benefits.

The VA's Priority Rating System

VA services are limited by the amount of funds Congress provides. The demand for medical services is hard to predict, so to ensure that limited resources are applied to the places with the greatest need, the VA uses a medical services priority system. Enrolling veterans are assigned to a priority of service group. The lower the priority number, the faster the service.

Group 1 includes veterans with service-connected disabilities rated 50 percent or more, or veterans the VA determines to be unemployable due to service-connected conditions. This group receives priority in scheduling hospital or outpatient medical appointments.

Group 2 consists of veterans with service-connected disabilities rated 30 or 40 percent.

Group 3 members are veterans with service-connected disabilities rated 10 and 20 percent, veterans who are former prisoners of war (POW) or who were awarded a Purple Heart, veterans awarded special eligibility for disabilities incurred in treatment or participation in a VA Vocational Rehabilitation program, and veterans whose discharge was for a disability incurred or aggravated in the line of duty.

Group 4 priority includes veterans receiving aid and attendance, or housebound benefits, and veterans the VA determines to be catastrophically disabled.

Group 5 veterans include non-service-connected veterans and noncompensable, 0 percent service-connected veterans whose annual income and net worth are below the established VA means thresholds.

Group 6 is for veterans of the Mexican border period or World War I; veterans seeking care solely for certain conditions associated with exposure to radiation or exposure to herbicides while serving in Vietnam; veterans who have any illness associated with combat service in a war after the Gulf War or during a period of hostility after November 11, 1998; veterans who have any illness associated with participation in tests conducted by the Defense Department as part of Project 112/Project SHAD; and veterans with 0 percent service-connected disabilities who are receiving disability compensation benefits.

Group 7 includes veterans with disabilities that are not connected with their military service who meet certain financial need thresholds.

Group 8 is for all other veterans with disabilities that are not connected with their military service who agree to pay co-payments. (Effective January 17, 2003, the VA no longer enrolls new veterans in this group.)

Appealing a VA Decision

An appeal is a request for the VA to reconsider a decision it has made. The decision may involve a person's eligibility for a specific benefit, the amount of disability stipend awarded, or essentially anything that the VA decides.

The appeal process must begin within one year of the date that the local VA office mailed you the denial to your claim. You must write a statement to the local VA office saying that you disagree with the denial of your claim. This is known as a Notice of Disagreement. It does not have a standard format, but be sure to clearly reference the denied claim number. Include as much detail about your case as possible and provide copies of documents supporting your claim. Note your claim number on anything sent to the VA.

For Your Benefits

You do not have to struggle through this alone. You can obtain help with the appeal process from Veterans Service Organizations, such as the American Legion or the Disabled American Veterans. You may also obtain legal advice from an attorney specializing in veterans' claims.

Next, request that a Decision Review Officer (DRO) review your documents. This person will examine all documents and arrange for a personal interview with you. Bring supporting documents with you to this meeting to support your reasons for why the decision was incorrect.

The DRO will send you a document called a Statement of Case. This explains the evidence used to review the case, along with references to the laws used to make the decision. If your appeal is denied, the letter from the DRO will also include a VA Form 9, Substantive Appeal Form. This form is your next level of appeal.

You must mail VA Form 9 back to the local VA office within 60 days of the mailing date of the Statement of Case. You can request a personal hearing at the local VA office or with a member of the Board of Veterans' Appeals.

The Board of Veterans' Appeals reviews benefit claim determinations made by local VA offices and issues decisions on appeals. Board members are attorneys experienced in veterans' law. They review benefit claims and are the only ones who can issue board decisions. Staff attorneys, also trained in veterans' law, review the facts of each appeal and assist the board members.

If this appeal was denied, you can continue on to the U.S. Court of Appeals for Veterans Claims or file a motion for the board to reconsider because there is a clear error in the board's decision.

The Least You Need to Know

◆ Documented honorable service in time of war is the surest ticket to VA benefits.

◆ Incarcerated veterans must contact the VA or risk problems from overpayments.

◆ If you have doubts about eligibility, apply anyway and let the VA determine your status.

◆ If the VA makes a mistake, file your appeal within one year.

Chapter 20

Veterans Benefits

In This Chapter

- ◆ VA-guaranteed home loans
- ◆ Insurance for disabled veterans
- ◆ VA disabled compensation
- ◆ Dependent indemnity compensation

In the uniformed services, as in the world of civilians, employees are provided a "total compensation" package of pay and benefits. Unlike a civilian job, some of your military benefits linger long after leaving the job. The key to using these benefits is to understand what is available and who is eligible, as well as know their limitations and how to apply for them. This chapter will explain some of the more important benefits and how to apply for them.

The Veterans Benefits Administration (VBA) section of the Department of Veterans Affairs (VA) administers programs that provide financial and other forms of assistance to veterans, their dependents, and survivors. Major benefits include veterans' compensation, veterans' pensions, survivors' benefits, rehabilitation and employment assistance, education assistance, home loan guaranties, and life insurance coverage. (Chapter 15 addressed education assistance.)

Home Loan Guaranty Program

The VA offers home loan services to eligible veterans, active duty military personnel, and certain surviving spouses. A "VA home loan" is one way to finance a new home. Actually, it is not a loan and, hopefully, the VA will never put up any money. Instead, it is a form of mortgage insurance in which the government promises to pay off a portion of the loan if the veteran defaults on payments. By removing some of the risk from the loan, the lender can offer a lower rate. This may also result in a reduced (or zero) down payment (which is another way a lender protects against default). Since the VA is protecting the loan, private mortgage insurance (PMI) is not required for your mortgage (because the VA guarantee provides that function).

Attention!

A VA home loan guarantee is useful only if your credit otherwise qualifies you for the loan.

The VA guarantees the lesser of either 25 percent of the loan amount or $104,000. You must occupy the property as your home. (These loans are not made for investment properties.)

Program Details

The maximum coverage for a VA loan is $104,250 for a maximum loan amount of $417,000. The exact amount of a veteran's entitlement is shown on the Certificate of Eligibility (see below). Veterans can use their entitlement to purchase, build, alter, improve, refinance, or repair a home. There is no requirement that the entitlement must be used within a certain period of time. VA home loan eligibility does not have an expiration date. However, each veteran is provided a set amount of coverage (currently $417,000). When that coverage is used by a loan, no further coverage is available until that loan is paid off.

VA loans offer the following important features:

♦ The buyer is informed of the reasonable value of the property.

♦ No down payment is required (unless the lender requires it, the purchase price is more than the VA property valuation estimate, or the loan is made with graduated payment features).

♦ The VA places limits on closing costs to reduce the chance of lenders from piling charges onto a veteran's loan.

◆ The buyer has the right to prepay without penalty.

◆ Forbearance (delays on debt collection) is extended to VA homeowners experiencing temporary financial difficulty, such as a natural disaster.

For Your Benefits

If you have a VA-guaranteed mortgage, the VA can help you refinance your loan at a lower interest rate. You may also use a VA loan to refinance a non-VA loan.

Closing Costs

Purchasing real estate can be complex, as the lender requires inspections to ensure that the title is clear and the property is sound. These costs and pending property taxes are all a part of "closing" the purchase of a house. However, mortgage companies you see advertising heavily also add in additional "fees" that can drive closing costs into thousands of dollars (and put more of your money into their pockets). The VA regulates the closing costs that a veteran may be charged in connection with closing a VA loan. This saves you money and drives off some of the more serious abuses. If a lender refuses to handle a VA loan, it may be due to excessive closing costs.

Although some additional costs are unique to certain localities, VA-approved closing costs generally include VA appraisal, a credit report, a survey, title evidence, recording fees, a 1 percent loan origination fee, and discount points. The closing costs and origination charge may not be included in the loan, except in VA refinancing loans. Veterans may choose to negotiate the payment of discount points and other closing costs with the seller.

VA Loan Guarantee Funding Fee

The VA loan funding fee is required by law to help finance this program. The applicant must pay it for all VA-backed loans. However, it is waived for veterans in receipt of disability compensation, and for surviving spouses of veterans who died in service or from service-connected disabilities. The fee can range from 0.5 percent to 3.3 percent, based on the type of loan and the amount of down payment.

Eligibility

Eligibility for this program depends upon meeting two criteria. The first is the type of discharge you were awarded. It must have been under conditions other than dishonorable. The VA makes an individual determination of eligibility for all other types of discharges.

The second criterion is when and how long the veteran served. The length of service required varies according to when it occurred. In general, the service can be less than the requirement if the veteran was discharged due to a compensable service-connected disability.

To qualify for this program, service must have been during one of these time periods:

◆ You served at least 90 days of active duty service during World War II (September 16, 1940, to July 25, 1947), the Korean War (June 27, 1950, to January 31, 1955), or the Vietnam War (August 5, 1964, to May 7, 1975)

◆ If your active duty service was during peacetime prior to September 8, 1980 (enlisted), and October 16, 1981 (officer), and you did not qualify for one of the wartime periods, then you must have served 181 days of continuous active duty.

If your active service was after September 7, 1980 (enlisted), or October 16, 1981 (officer), to August 1, 1990, one of the following must be true:

◆ You completed 24 months of continuous active duty or the full period (at least 181 days) for which you were ordered to active duty.

◆ You completed at least 181 days of active duty and were discharged under the specific authority of Title 10 USC 1173 (Hardship) or Title 10 USC 1171 (Early out), or you have been determined to have a compensable service-connected disability.

◆ You were discharged with less than 181 days of service for a service-connected disability. Individuals may also be eligible if they were released from active duty due to an involuntary reduction in force, certain medical conditions, or, in some instances, for the convenience of the government.

For active duty service after August 2, 1990 (to the present), one of the following must be true:

◆ You completed 24 months of continuous active duty or the full period (at least 90 days) for which you were ordered to active duty.

◆ You completed at least 90 days of active duty and were discharged under the specific authority of Title 10 USC 1173 (Hardship) or Title 10 USC 1173 (Early out), or you have been determined to have a compensable service-connected disability.

◆ You were discharged with less than 90 days of service for a service-connected disability, or were released from active duty due to an involuntary reduction in force, due to certain medical conditions, or, in some instances, for the convenience of the government.

Guard/Reserves are eligible if they have served six continuous years in the Selected Reserves. (Of course, if they were called to active duty, they may qualify under the previous active duty categories.)

The spouse of a veteran who died in service or from a service-connected disability is also eligible for the VA Home Loan Program. The spouse of any member of the Armed Forces serving on active duty who is listed as missing in action or who is a prisoner of war for more than 90 days is also eligible.

Obtaining a Certificate of Eligibility

Your mortgage lender will need a Certificate of Eligibility from the VA with your name on it. They submit this with their paperwork for the VA Loan Guarantee. Some of the larger lenders have a connection into the VA Loan databases and can obtain a certificate for you. Otherwise, request a certificate using VA Form 26-1880, "Request for a Certificate of Eligibility for VA Home Loan Benefits."

You must attach to your VA Form 26-1880 proof of your eligibility. Submit a copy of page 4 of your DD214 (which shows the type of discharge). In both cases, the form also indicates the years of service, which addresses the second eligibility criteria. Allow at least two weeks for processing.

If you served in the Selected Reserve, you must establish that you served a minimum of six years with points earned for weekend drills or active duty for training, and received an honorable discharge. Since the Selected Reserve does not issue anything like a DD214, a number of different documents may be accepted. For example, a Retirement Points Statement that shows years of service and the number of points earned each year might be acceptable. If you served in the National Guard and were discharged after six years of service, your NGB Form 22 may be sufficient.

If you are now on active duty and have not been previously discharged from active duty service, you must submit a statement of service that includes the name of the issuing authority (base or command) and is signed by or at the direction of an appropriate official. The statement must include your date of entry on active duty and the duration of any time lost.

The spouse of a veteran who died in service or from a service-connected disability, and the spouse of missing or POWs can apply using VA Form 26-1817, "Request for Determination of Loan Guaranty Eligibility—Unmarried Surviving Spouse."

Restoring Your VA Eligibility

If you have used all or part of your entitlement, you can get that entitlement back to purchase another home if the following conditions for "restoration" are met:

◆ The property has been sold and the loan has been paid in full.

◆ A qualified veteran agrees to assume the outstanding mortgage.

◆ If you have repaid the previous VA loan in full but have not disposed of the property securing that loan, the entitlement you used in connection with that loan may be restored. However, this is a one-time allowance.

◆ Any loss suffered by the VA to guarantee a loan for you (such as a loan that went into foreclosure) must be repaid in full before the entitlement used on the loan can be restored.

Restoration of entitlement is not automatic. Apply for it using VA Form 26-1880, "Request for a Certificate of Eligibility." You can obtain this form from any VA office or at www.va.gov/vaforms.

Hot Scoop

For more information about a VA-guaranteed home loan, visit www.homeloans.va.gov.

When seeking restoration of previously used benefits, include evidence of payment in full of your previous loan (such as a copy of HUD-1, "Settlement Statement"). The VA determines your eligibility and will issue you a certificate of eligibility if you are qualified.

Special Situations

Certain disabled veterans and military personnel can receive grants to adapt or acquire housing suitable for their needs.

◆ Specially adapted housing grants are available to veterans with service-connected disabilities, for constructing or modifying a home to meet the veterans' needs. The VA's goal is to provide a barrier-free living environment that affords the veterans a level of independent living. Eligible veterans temporarily residing in a home owned by a family member may also receive a grant to assist the veteran in adapting the family member's home.

◆ Direct home loans from the VA are available to eligible Native American veterans to purchase or construct a home on trust lands.

◆ Servicing assistance provides help for borrowers having difficulty making their loan payments, such as after a natural disaster. The goal is to keep the veterans in the property and avoid foreclosure.

Disability Compensation

Disability compensation is money paid to veterans disabled by an injury or disease that was incurred or aggravated during active military service. The amount of compensation varies with the degree of the veteran's disability on a scale from 0 percent to 100 percent (in increments of 10 percent), and the number of the veteran's dependents. Veterans with severe disabilities may be eligible for additional monthly compensation. These benefits are not subject to federal or state income tax.

To be eligible, the veteran's service must have been terminated through separation or discharge under conditions other than dishonorable. The basic monthly compensation for 2007 ranges from $115 per month for a 10 percent disability to $2,471 per month for a 100 percent disability. Veterans with disability ratings of at least 30 percent are eligible for additional allowances for eligible dependents. The additional amount depends on the disability rating and the number of dependents.

Applying for Compensation

The first step is to apply at your regional office using VA Form 21-526, "Veterans Application for Compensation or Pension." Based on your condition (and the paperwork submitted), you will then get a "Ratings Decision." Be sure to attach documentation of the disability to the form, such as the following:

◆ List of disabilities you are claiming, supported by hospital reports and doctors' statements that describe the disability

◆ Dependency records, such as a marriage certificate and birth certificates of dependent children

◆ Copy of your DD214 showing the character of service (honorable, general, and so on)

A veteran may receive a 0 percent noncompensable rating. This means that the VA has determined that the veteran's condition can be classified as service connected. However, it is not severe enough to qualify for monetary compensation on the basis of the medical criteria specified in the schedule. Some veterans with a 0 percent rating may receive special monthly compensation under the VA disability program. On the basis of 1994 data, VA estimated there were about 1.2 million 0 percent–rated veterans.

> **For Your Benefits**
>
> A 0 percent rating can be increased to a compensable rating of 10 percent or more if the veteran's condition worsens.

The first step is to medically evaluate the veteran's condition to determine its severity. Then the VA compares the evaluation results with the medical criteria in the schedule for that condition to determine a disability rating. The veteran will receive the amount Congress has set for that disability rating. Where a veteran has more than one disability, the percentages are not simply added together to produce a new rating. Instead, a formula described in federal regulations calculates the overall rating.

Although the primary purpose of the VA's disability compensation program is compensation for impairment in future earnings, the program provides additional compensation for loss of "physical integrity." This is defined as tissue loss, loss of body parts, or any disease or injury that makes an individual less functionally whole.

VA regulations also allow veterans to receive "extra-schedular" awards when the VA determines that the severity of a veteran's condition is not adequately captured by the rating that the schedule assigns to it. In a case of unemployability, for example, if the criteria in the schedule indicate that a veteran's condition warrants at least a 60 percent disability rating but the VA determines that the veteran is unable to obtain and sustain gainful employment, the VA can raise the compensation to a rating of 100 percent.

> **For Your Benefits**
>
> The largest category of service-connected disabilities is for musculoskeletal problems, accounting for about 40 percent of all disabilities. This includes such problems as impairment of the knee and arthritis due to trauma.

You can wade through the criteria for rating the severity of various disabilities online at www.access.gpo.gov/nara/cfr/waisidx_04/38cfr4_04.html. As medical knowledge, laws, and procedures change, the VA publishes proposed changes to these criteria in the Federal Register for public comment before a final regulation is adopted.

A cost of living increase is included in the president's annual budget. However, the actual percentage increase is set through a separate bill debated by Congress and usually signed into law the following fall. Legislators historically have mirrored the percentage given to Social Security recipients. The Social Security increase, in turn, is based on a Bureau of Labor Statistics calculation of the rise in the Consumer Price Index for urban wage earners and clerical workers (CPI-W). Cost of living adjustments become effective December 1 each year and are reflected in the payment received by veterans on or about the first day of the new year.

Presumptive Conditions

Certain veterans are eligible for disability compensation based on the presumption that their disability is service connected.

- ◆ Prisoners of war (POWs) who were imprisoned for any length of time. Disabilities are presumed to be service connected if they are rated at least 10 percent disabling anytime after military service.

- ◆ Veterans exposed to Agent Orange and other herbicides. A veteran who served in Vietnam between January 9, 1962, and May 7, 1975, is presumed to have been exposed to Agent Orange and other herbicides used in support of military operations.

- ◆ Veterans exposed to radiation as defined in VA regulations while on active duty.

- ◆ Gulf War veterans may receive disability compensation for chronic disabilities resulting from undiagnosed illnesses or medically unexplained chronic multi-symptom illnesses defined by a cluster of signs or symptoms. A disability is considered chronic if it has existed for at least six months. The undiagnosed illnesses must have appeared either during active service in the Southwest Asia theater of operations during the Gulf War or to a degree of at least 10 percent at any time since then through December 31, 2011.

Combat-Related Special Compensation (CRSC) for Retired Veterans

Combat-Related Special Compensation (CRSC) provides tax-free monthly payments to eligible retired veterans with combat-related injuries. With CRSC, veterans can receive both their full military retirement pay and their VA disability compensation if the injury is combat related.

Retired veterans with combat-related injuries must meet all of the following criteria to apply for CRSC:

- Are active, Reserve, or medically retired with 20 years of creditable service

- Receive military retired pay

- Have a 10 percent or greater VA-rated injury

Other VA Compensation and Pension

Compensation and pension programs provide direct payments to veterans, dependents, and survivors as a result of the veteran's service-connected disability or because of financial need. Pension programs are designed to provide income support to veterans with wartime service and their families for a non-service-connected disability or death. These programs are for low-income veterans and survivors.

Dependency and Indemnity Compensation for Surviving Spouse and Children

Dependency and Indemnity Compensation (DIC) benefits provide financial support for survivors of service members who died while on active duty or survivors of veterans who died from their service-connected disabilities. It is a needs-based program paid to spouses, dependent children, or parents.

The surviving spouse eligibility includes any of the following:

- Was validly married to the veteran before January 1, 1957

- Was married to a service member who died on active duty

- Married the veteran within 15 years of discharge from the period of military service in which the disease or injury that caused the veteran's death began or was aggravated

- Was married to the veteran for at least one year

- Had a child with the veteran, cohabited with the veteran continuously until the veteran's death, or, if separated, was not at fault for the separation, and is not currently remarried

Surviving children, are eligible in these situations:

◆ They are not included on the surviving spouse's DIC benefits claim.

◆ They are unmarried, under age 18, or between the ages of 18 and 23 and attending school.

◆ In some cases, helpless adult children are entitled to DIC. Each case is reviewed separately. Check with the VA for eligibility requirements and the application process.

The basic monthly rate of DIC is $1,067 for an eligible surviving spouse. This increases for each dependent child, and if the surviving spouse is housebound or in need of Aid and Attendance. The VA also adds a transitional benefit of $250 per family if there are children under age 18.

Request DIC for a surviving spouse and dependent children using VA Form 21-534, "Application for Dependency and Indemnity Compensation, Death Pension and Accrued Benefits by a Surviving Spouse or Child." Submit the completed form along with the veteran's DD Form 1300, "Report of Casualty." Fax these documents to 215-381-3084, or mail them to:

Department of Veterans Affairs
Regional Office and Insurance Center
PO Box 8079
Philadelphia, PA 19101

Most states employ a network of county veterans' service officers to assist veterans, their dependents and survivors with the completion of VA claims applications. This service also provides the veteran or the family member with someone to answer questions about their claim.

For Your Benefits

A surviving spouse age 57 years old or older who remarries after December 15, 2003, is entitled to continue to receive benefits.

Dependency and Indemnity Compensation for Surviving Parents

The surviving parent(s) of a deceased veteran may be eligible for assistance, based on their financial need. A "parent" includes biological, adoptive, and foster parents. A foster parent is a person who stood in the relationship of a parent to the veteran for at least one year before the veteran's last entry into active duty.

Eligible parents must report all sources of income to VA. The spouse's income is included if both parents live together. A spouse may be the other parent of the deceased veteran, or the other parent from remarriage. In December 2006, a sole surviving parent living with a spouse must have an adjusted annual income of less than $16,710 to be eligible for this program.

Apply using VA Form 21-535, "Application for Dependency and Indemnity Compensation by Parent(s)." This 10-page form delves into the background of the veteran and parents, and also includes a disclosure of all income (but does not ask about assets). Attach a copy of the veteran's death certificate unless the death occurred on active duty.

Benefit rates are adjusted annually. In December 1, 2006, sole surviving parent would receive an annual benefit of up to $6,288. They are also eligible for Aid and Attendance (A&A) allowance if they qualify for that. VA Form 21-535 includes information for determining A&A qualification.

Death Pension

A VA death pension is paid to an unremarried surviving spouse or an unmarried child of a deceased wartime veteran. This benefit is based on financial need. You must meet all of these conditions:

- ◆ The deceased veteran was discharged from service under conditions other than dishonorable.

- ◆ The deceased veteran served at least 90 days of active military service, 1 day of which was during a wartime period. (Service from August 2, 1990, to present is considered to be a period of war.) If the veteran entered active duty after September 7, 1980, at least 24 months of active duty service are required, or the full period for which a Guard/Reserve member was ordered to active duty.

- ◆ You are the surviving spouse or unmarried child of the deceased veteran.

- ◆ Your countable income is below a yearly limit set by law.

If you are unsure about your eligibility, file an application and let the VA determine your eligibility. If the VA denies your application, you may reapply when your financial situation changes.

Service-Connected Birth Defects

Spina Bifida Monthly Allowance under Title 38 U.S.C. 1805 is provided for children born with spina bifida who are children of individuals who served in Vietnam or served in or near the demilitarization zone in Korea during the period September 1, 1967, through August 31, 1971. Payment is made at one of three levels and is based on degree of the child's disability.

The Children of Women Vietnam Veterans Born with Certain Defects program provides a monetary allowance, health care, and vocational training benefits to eligible children born to women who served in Vietnam from February 28, 1961, to May 7, 1975, if they suffer from certain covered birth defects. The VA identifies the birth defects as those that are associated with the service of the mother in Vietnam and result in permanent physical or mental disability.

Assisted Living VA Style

The VA offers two programs to veterans, surviving parents, spouses, or children who need assistance in their daily living. The claimant must already receive a VA disability pension. Claimants may not receive both Aid and Attendance benefits and Housebound benefits at the same time.

Aid and Attendance is a benefit paid in addition to monthly pension. Claimants are eligible if they …

◆ Require the aid of another person to perform everyday personal functions, such as bathing, feeding, dressing, attending to the wants of nature, adjusting prosthetic devices, or require protection from the hazards of daily environment.

◆ Are bedridden.

◆ Are a patient in a nursing home due to mental or physical incapacity.

◆ Have corrected visual acuity of 5/200 or less in both eyes, or concentric contraction of the visual field to 5 degrees or less.

Housebound benefits are paid to a claimant when the veteran is substantially confined to the immediate premises because of permanent disability.

Apply for Aid and Attendance or Housebound benefits by writing to the local VA Regional Office. Include copies of any evidence, such as a report from an attending physician validating the need for Aid and Attendance or Housebound type care. This report should be in sufficient detail to determine whether there is disease or injury producing physical or mental impairment, loss of coordination, or conditions affecting the ability to dress and undress, to feed oneself, to attend to sanitary needs, and to keep oneself ordinarily clean and presentable.

In addition, it is necessary to determine whether the claimant is confined to the home or immediate premises. The report should indicate how well the individual gets around, where the individual goes, and what the claimant is able to do during a typical day.

Insurance

The VBA offers several insurance programs to service the needs of disabled veterans. CHAMPVA provides medical insurance for the dependents of disabled veterans. Service-Disabled Veterans Insurance (SDVI) offers life insurance for disabled veterans if they cannot obtain it from other sources. Veterans Mortgage Life Insurance provides life insurance to pay off a mortgage on a property specially modified to meet a disabled veteran's needs.

CHAMPVA

The Civilian Health and Medical Program of the Department of Veterans Affairs (CHAMPVA) is a comprehensive health-care program in which the VA shares the cost of covered health-care services and supplies with eligible beneficiaries. The program is administered by Health Administration Center, and offices are located in Denver, Colorado.

Due to the similarity between CHAMPVA and the Department of Defense's (DoD) TRICARE program, the two are often mistaken for each other. They are distinctly different programs, each with its own rules and eligibility. To be eligible for CHAMPVA, you cannot be eligible for TRICARE and you must fulfill one of these requirements:

- ◆ You are the spouse or child of a veteran who is rated permanently and totally disabled from a service-connected disability.

- ◆ You are the surviving spouse or child of a veteran who died from a VA-rated service connected disability.

- ◆ You are the surviving spouse or child of a military member who died in the line of duty, not due to misconduct (if the veteran is not eligible for TRICARE).

An eligible CHAMPVA sponsor must be entitled to medical care through the VA health-care system. If the eligible CHAMPVA sponsor is the spouse of another eligible CHAMPVA sponsor, both may use CHAMPVA benefits.

In general, CHAMPVA covers most health-care services and supplies that are medically and psychologically necessary. Upon confirmation of eligibility, you receive a CHAMPVA handbook describing covered services and supplies. Most TRICARE- and Medicare-authorized medical service providers will also accept the CHAMPVA program. They agree to accept what CHAMPVA will pay for their services and do not bill you any additional amounts. They also submit their bills to CHAMPVA so that you do not need to file a claim for reimbursement.

The outpatient deductible (per calendar year) is $50 per beneficiary or a maximum of $100 per family per year. The annual deductible must be paid before CHAMPVA pays 75 percent of the allowable amount. As claims are processed for covered services, charges are automatically credited to individual and cumulative family deductible requirements for each calendar year. There is no deductible for inpatient services, ambulatory surgery facility services, partial psychiatric day programs, hospice services, or services provided by VA medical facilities (called the CITI program) or for the Meds By Mail program.

A cost share, or co-payment, is required for care (unless provided by a VA facility). For covered outpatient services, CHAMPVA pays up to 75 percent of the allowable amount after the deductible is met. Your share of the cost for inpatient services varies.

CHAMPVA provides a catastrophic cap of $3,000 per family, per calendar year. Once this cap amount is reached, CHAMPVA pays 100 percent of the covered services for the remainder of the calendar year.

CHAMPVA is always the secondary payer to Medicare. For benefits to extend past age 65, you must meet these conditions:

◆ If you were 65 or older prior to June 5, 2001, and are otherwise eligible for CHAMPVA, and are entitled to Medicare Part A coverage, then you are eligible for CHAMPVA without Medicare Part B coverage.

◆ If you turned 65 on or before June 5, 2001, and have Medicare Parts A and B, you must keep both parts to be eligible.

◆ If you turned 65 on or after June 5, 2001, you must be enrolled in Medicare Parts A and B to be eligible.

Attention!

You are not required to enroll in Medicare Part D for CHAMPVA eligibility.

If the former spouse of a veteran remarries, that person's eligibility for CHAMPVA ends at midnight on the date of the remarriage, if it occurs before age 55. If the remarriage occurs after the former spouse's fifty-fifth birthday, CHAMPVA benefits remain.

If you are a widow(er) of a qualifying sponsor and you remarry, and the remarriage is later terminated by death, divorce, or annulment, you may reestablish CHAMPVA eligibility. The beginning date of your re-eligibility is the first day of the month after termination of the remarriage or December 1, 1999, whichever date is later. To re-establish CHAMPVA eligibility, you must provide copies of the marriage certificate and death, divorce, or annulment documents (as appropriate).

If you have a general question, need information on payment, or need to reprocess a denied claim, contact:

> VA Health Administration Center
> CHAMPVA
> PO Box 65023
> Denver CO 80206-9023

Application for CHAMPVA requires that you provide supporting documents along with your application. If packet is complete, processing takes about three to six weeks. To apply for CHAMPVA benefits, you must submit the following documents:

◆ VA Form 10-10d, "Application for CHAMPVA Benefits."

◆ VA Form 10-7959c, "Other Health Insurance (OHI) Certification."

◆ For individuals who are eligible for Medicare (normally those age 65 and older), a copy of your Medicare card.

◆ If you are age 65 or older and are not entitled to Medicare, documentation from the Social Security Administration that confirms that you are not entitled to Medicare benefits under someone else's Social Security number.

◆ Veteran and spouse marriage license.

◆ Birth certificate/adoption papers for dependent children.

◆ The page from the VBA rating decision that shows the veteran has a service-connected disability, or grants Chapter 35 benefits and/or dependents educational assistance, and the effective date it was granted.

◆ If you are a remarried widow/widower and are no longer married, a copy of the legal documentation that terminated the remarriage. The legal documentation of termination of a remarriage may be a divorce decree, death certificate, or annulment decree.

◆ School certification of full-time enrollment for dependent children between the ages of 18 and 23.

Send the complete package to:

CHAMPVA—Eligibility
PO Box 469028
Denver, CO 80246-9028

Service-Disabled Veterans Insurance

Service-Disabled Veterans Insurance (SDVI) provides life insurance for a veteran with a VA service-connected disability but who is otherwise in good health. A policy is available for up to $10,000 for applications made within two years of the date of VA notification of the service-connected status. SDVI is available in a variety of permanent plans as well as term insurance.

Policies are issued for a maximum face amount of $10,000. The insurance premium is based on age, type of plan (term or permanent), and amount of coverage desired. The basic SDVI policy provides for a waiver of premiums in case of total disability. Use VA Form 29-357, "Claim for Disability Insurance Benefits," to apply for this premiums waiver.

To be eligible for basic SDVI, a veteran must have been released from active duty under conditions other than dishonorable on or after April 25, 1951; must have received a rating for a service-connected disability; and must be in good health except for any service-connected conditions.

Veterans who are granted service connection for a disability receive VA Form 29-4364, "Application for Service-Disabled Veterans Life Insurance," along with a copy of their Notice of Disability Rating. They must submit the application along with the first month's premium.

For Your Benefits

If a disabled veteran has access to other insurance programs through an employer or other source, they may be a better value than SDVI.

If the veteran is totally disabled, he or she may apply for an additional $20,000 of coverage under the Supplemental SDVI program. Policyholders who carry the basic SDVI coverage and who become eligible for a waiver of premiums due to total disability can apply for and be granted additional Supplemental SDVI of up to $20,000. The insured has up to one year after being notified of eligibility for waiver on the basic policy to apply for the Supplemental SDVI. No waiver of premiums due to total disability can be granted on Supplemental SDVI coverage.

Veterans Mortgage Life Insurance (VMLI)

VMLI is life insurance protection for up to $90,000 to pay off an outstanding mortgage after a veteran's death. It is available to severely disabled veterans who receive a Specially Adapted Housing Grant for building, remodeling, or purchasing an adapted home. The veteran must have the title to the home and a mortgage on it. VMLI premiums must be paid by deduction from the veteran's monthly compensation.

VMLI covers up to $90,000 on a new mortgage, an existing mortgage, a refinanced mortgage, or a second mortgage. It is decreasing term insurance that reduces as the amount of the mortgage is reduced. VMLI has no loan or cash values and pays no dividends. The insurance pays out only to the mortgage holder, not to the family members.

VMLI premiums are determined by a combination of the following:

- ◆ The age of the veteran
- ◆ The outstanding balance of the mortgage
- ◆ The remaining time on the mortgage

Eligible veterans must apply for the coverage before their 70th birthday. Submit VA Form 29-8636, "Veterans Mortgage Life Insurance Statement," to the Department of Veterans Affairs Regional Office and Insurance Center in Philadelphia. Veterans can contact the Insurance Center for an application or visit the website to obtain an application and learn more information about the VMLI program.

Vocational Rehabilitation

The VA's Vocational Rehabilitation and Employment Program provides vocational rehabilitation services for veterans who have a service-connected disability. The goal is to prepare veterans for suitable employment that is consistent with their aptitudes and interests, or to help them achieve independence in their daily living.

To be eligible, a veteran must have a VA service-connected disability rated at least 20 percent with an employment handicap, or rated 10 percent with a serious employment handicap, and be discharged or released from military service under conditions other than dishonorable. Service members pending medical separation from active duty may also apply if their disabilities are reasonably expected to be rated at least 20 percent following their discharge. Veterans must complete their vocational rehabilitation program within 12 years of their separation from military service or within 12 years of the date VA notifies them that they have a compensable service-connected disability.

Vocational and Educational Counseling

Vocational and Educational Counseling (VR&E) provides vocational and educational counseling services to service members still on active duty, as well as veterans and dependents who are eligible for one of the VA's educational benefit programs. These services help an individual choose a vocational direction and determine the training needed to achieve the chosen goal. VR&E counselors assist veterans with service-connected disabilities prepare for, find, and keep suitable jobs. Assistance includes the following:

◆ Interest and aptitude testing

◆ Occupational exploration

◆ Occupational goal setting

◆ Help in locating the right type of training program

VR&E offers veterans with disabilities services help in improving their independent living. Generally, a veteran must complete a program of rehabilitation services within 12 years of the date of VA notification of entitlement to compensation. This period may be deferred or extended if a medical condition prevents the veteran from pursuing rehabilitation services for a period of time, or if the veteran has a serious employment handicap.

Veteran Entrepreneurship

The VA, in partnership with the Small Business Administration and the Association of Small Business Development Centers, provides entrepreneurial assistance to service-connected disabled veterans participating in a VR&E program. It supports veterans who are exploring business ownership, expanding a business, or moving into the federal marketplace. The program seeks to achieve rehabilitation through self-employment. Counselors assist the veteran in applying for loans through the Small Business Administration.

For some disabled veterans, self-employment is the most realistic and viable option for suitable employment. Guidance is provided as program participants research the economic viability of their proposed business, develop a business plan, and demonstrate the financial feasibility of their plan.

Veterans Industries/Compensated Work Therapy (VI/CWT)

Veterans Industries/Compensated Work Therapy training prepares veterans for competitive employment opportunities. It provides industry support in temporary and permanent staffing for information technology, manufacturing, warehousing, construction, office support, retail, and the services delivery industry. The program identifies veteran strengths and matches those skills and abilities to industries' job requirements. These services include the following:

- Supported employment and follow-along services

- Ongoing situational assessment

- Vocational assistance

- Counseling and case management

- Transitional work experience (temporary to permanent staffing)

- Sheltered work therapy (not available at all program locations)

- CWT/transitional residence (residential rehabilitation program)

Homeless Veterans

The VA provides comprehensive medical, psychological, and rehabilitation treatment for eligible homeless veterans, and conducts homeless outreach such as community-based "stand-downs" to help homeless veterans. Many VA benefits, including disability compensation, pensions, and education, can help at-risk veterans avoid homelessness.

Other programs for homeless veterans include residential rehabilitation services at VA domiciliaries, therapeutic group homes, special day centers, and comprehensive homeless centers. For assistance, contact the nearest VA medical facility or visit www.va.gov/homeless.

The VA also gives funds to community agencies that provide services to homeless veterans. The grant program pays up to 65 percent of the cost of construction, renovation, or acquisition of a building for use as a service center or transitional housing for homeless veterans, or for the purchase of vans for the transportation of homeless veterans. The per-diem program provides funding for operational costs. Call toll-free 1-877-332-0334 or visit the website listed earlier for information.

The Department of Labor provides employment and training services, as well as grants, to community organizations that provide counseling, job search and placement assistance, remedial education, and on-the-job training for homeless veterans. For information, call 202-693-4700 or visit www.dol.gov/vets/welcome.html.

The VA Homeless programs also address disadvantaged, at-risk, and homeless veterans who live in community-based supervised group homes while working for pay in Veterans Industries. The average stay is 174 days. The VA contracts with private industry and the public sector for work done by these veterans, who learn new job skills, relearn successful work habits, and regain a sense of self-esteem and self-worth.

The Least You Need to Know

- ◆ VA-guaranteed loans have built-in safeguards to protect veterans buying a home.

- ◆ Pensions are available to veterans and dependents, based on financial need.

- ◆ Disabled veterans can apply for grants to modify their home to remove barriers.

- ◆ Additional funds are available to provide help with day-to-day living tasks.

Chapter 21

Gaining a Government Job

In This Chapter

- ◆ The veteran's edge to getting a government job
- ◆ Dependents, spouses, widows, and parents may also qualify
- ◆ Special preferences for disabled vets
- ◆ Where to search for local federal government jobs

The military provided us many things—travel, "food," and a paycheck. Moving from predictable military life to the unorganized world of civilians means that veterans must find a paycheck to keep the groceries flowing. Many veterans have found careers as workers for the federal government.

Working for the government feels familiar. The Department of Defense (just one of many government agencies) employs military personnel alongside civilian workers. Many military positions have a government civilian counterpart with similar or the same duties. If you were an admin clerk and worked in a warehouse or repaired equipment, it is not usual to leave on Friday as a discharged sailor, airman, or solider, and return on Monday as a civilian worker right into the same position.

As a further reward for honorable military service, the federal government (and most state and local governments) provides a hiring preference for veterans. The amount of preference is based on service during wartime, service-connected disability, and so on. However, this preference applies only if you are otherwise qualified for that position.

Another important reason to consider joining the federal workforce is that few companies offer pensions anymore. Years of military service are counted as years of government service for retirement, vacation, and promotion. So instead of walking in with no seniority, you can wring one more benefit out of those green (or blue)–suited years.

Government Civilian Pay Scales

Before applying for a job, it helps to understand how the compensation system is organized. Government jobs are divided into three main types: General Schedule (GS), Federal Wage System (FWS), and Senior Executive Service (SES). GS roughly equates to a white-collar (office) worker. FWS includes the blue-collar jobs of trade, craft, labor, and so on. SES is the executives of the government workers.

Attention!

Advancing from a GS rating to a SES classification is highly competitive. Open SES positions must be posted government wide and on the www.USAJOBS.gov website. If you see an SES appointment in your future, download the SES Qualifications Guide from www.opm.gov/ses/qualify.asp.

GS pay is a salary-based amount and a series of "steps" within that same pay bracket. You advance through the steps based on how long you have held that GS level. GS pay is also adjusted according to the cost of living in that area. For example, a GS-11 in San Francisco is paid a different amount than someone in the same grade in Maine. Fifteen GS grades exist, each with 10 steps. Beyond the GS ranks are the SES.

The Federal Wage System is broken into three categories: Wage Grade (WG), Wage Leader (WL), and Wage Supervisor (WS). These positions are paid by the hour. The WG and WL pay rates each have 15 grades with five steps in each, and the WS has 19 grades with five steps. Pay is based on a survey of local wages for similar work.

The Senior Executive Service does not recognize a veteran-hiring preference. The president appoints these individuals to these high-paying positions.

Government Hiring Process

In years past, applicants were given a civil service examination. Those who passed were listed on a standing register of eligible candidates. If you were on the list, you could then submit an SF-171 Standard Federal to apply for a specific position. This is no longer done. Few positions still require a written test.

The federal government now breaks its workforce into two classes of jobs:

◆ Excepted service agencies, such as the FBI and CIA, set their own qualification requirements. They are not subject to the appointment, pay, and classification rules in Title 5 of United States Code. However, they do provide a veterans' preference.

◆ Competitive service positions are controlled by the Office of Personnel Management (OPM). They are governed by civil service laws that ensure that everyone receives equal treatment during the hiring process. Hiring officials may look at various sources of applicants before selecting the best-qualified person. A basic requirement is that anyone appointed to a job must meet all of that position's basic requirements.

Agencies filling competitive service jobs choose from three groups of applicants:

◆ A competitive list of applicants, ranked by their scores, who meet all of the basic qualifications

◆ A list of eligible persons with civil service status who can move into a job based on promotion, reassignment, transfer, or reinstatement

◆ Applicants using a special noncompetitive appointment, such as the Veterans' Readjustment Appointment (VRA), or the special authority for veterans 30 percent or more disabled

Competitive service agencies are legally required to post vacancies with OPM whenever they are seeking external candidates for positions lasting more than 120 days. These vacancies are posted online at USAJOBS and HireVetsFirst. Excepted agencies are not required to post their job announcements in USAJOBS. To learn about their job opportunities, you must go to their individual websites.

The area of consideration, listed on the vacancy announcement, is the source from which the agency will consider candidates. This might be internal candidates only, people whose federal jobs have been eliminated through restructuring, or the general public. Only applicants from that area will be considered.

Veterans' Preferences

Since the Civil War, the federal government has recognized the sacrifice veterans made by giving them preference when filling federal jobs. Disabled veterans or those who served on active duty during specified time periods or in military campaigns are given preference over nonveterans both in federal hiring and in retention during reductions in force (RIF). Of course, a federal job is not an automatic veteran's benefit. Veterans' preference applies only if the veteran also meets all of the basic requirements of the position.

When the government evaluates candidates for a position, it tries to arrange the evaluation to be as fair as possible to everyone. Before speaking to the first applicant, the hiring manager assigns a score to each of the job requirements (for example, if the candidate is an expert FORTRAN programmer, he or she receives a maximum of 10 points). When candidates are evaluated, they are assigned points based on how closely they meet that requirement. In this example, if the candidate was only slightly familiar with FORTRAN, he may be assigned 3 of the possible 10 points. After scoring a candidate against all requirements, the numbers are added, to result in a score for this position. The candidates are ranked according to their scores, from high to low. Veterans with preference appear ahead of other candidates on a referral list with the same score, and they must be selected before considering candidates without a veterans' preference.

Typical job criteria are related education, experience, special skills, and awards. For a skills-based position, a written test may be required. The maximum points anyone can accumulate is 100. A minimal acceptable score to be considered for a position is 70 points. As a reward for service, the government adds 5 or 10 points to the veteran's score. Veterans' preference does not apply to promotion, reassignment, movement to a lower grade, transfer, or reinstatement.

Hiring preference in civil service examinations is awarded regardless of scores. Qualified veterans with a compensable service-connected disability of 10 percent or more are placed at the top of most civil service examination registers, except for scientific and professional jobs at GS-9 or higher.

Military Retirees Do Not Get a Hiring Preference

Retired members of the armed forces do not receive a veterans' hiring preference for a federal job unless retirement is based on disability that either resulted from injury or disease received in the line of duty as a direct result of armed conflict, or was caused by an instrumentality of war. Veterans retired from the military may not be appointed to a civilian position in the DoD (including a nonappropriated fund position) within 180 days of retirement.

Reservists who are retired from the Reserves but are not receiving retired pay are not considered "retired military" for purposes of veterans' preference. They have not completed 20 years of active service and do not receive retirement pay until they turn 60 years old.

Five-Point Preference

A five-point preference is awarded to those veterans who separated from the service with an honorable or general discharge, and who served on active duty in the armed forces. This does not include Guard/Reserve active duty for training.

Qualifying periods are these:

◆ December 7, 1941, to July 1, 1955

◆ More than 180 consecutive days, any part of which occurred after January 31, 1955, and before October 15, 1976

◆ Gulf War from August 2, 1990, through January 2, 1992

Veterans are also eligible for a five-point preference if they were awarded a campaign medal for armed operations in El Salvador, Grenada, Haiti, Lebanon, Panama, Somalia, Southwest Asia, or Bosnia.

Veterans with a campaign medal; Gulf War veterans who enlisted after September 7, 1980; or those who entered on active duty on or after October 14, 1982, must have served continuously for 24 months or the full period of active duty. This service requirement does not apply to veterans with compensable service-connected disabilities, or to veterans separated for disability in the line of duty or for hardship.

Attention!

Effective on October 1, 1980, military retirees ranked major (lieutenant commander) or above are not entitled to preference unless they qualify as disabled veterans.

Ten-Point Preference

The highest veteran preference available is 10 points. Claims to a 10-point preference must be documented on a Standard Form 15 (SF-15), "Application for 10-Point

Veteran Preference." It is awarded to honorably discharged active duty veterans or their dependents who meet one of these criteria:

◆ A veterans who was awarded a Purple Heart.

◆ A veteran who served at any time and who has a present service-connected disability or is receiving compensation, disability retirement benefits, or a disability pension from the military or the Department of Veterans Affairs.

◆ The spouse of an unemployed veteran who is unable to work because of a 100 percent service-connected disability.

◆ The unmarried widows or widowers of certain deceased veterans, provided that the veteran served during a war; or during the period April 28, 1952, through July 1, 1955; or in a campaign or expedition for which a campaign medal has been authorized. The preference is also authorized if the veteran died while on active duty that included service just described under conditions that would not have been the basis for other than an honorable or general discharge.

◆ The mother of a veteran who died in service or of a veteran that is permanently and totally disabled, if the veteran was separated with an honorable or general discharge from active duty, including training service in the Reserves or National Guard.

Noncompetitive Hiring Through Veterans Recruitment Appointments (VRAs)

A VRA allows agencies to appoint an eligible veteran to a position without the normal competition. However, the veteran must still meet the basic qualifications for that job. Agencies can use the VRA authority to fill positions up through GS-11 and equivalent jobs under other pay systems.

If the veteran satisfactorily performs the job for two years, the veteran is converted to a career-conditional appointment in the competitive service. However, when accepting a VRA, the candidate must understand that some positions are temporary and do not lead to career jobs.

VRAs are available to veterans who served 180 days of active duty and received other than a dishonorable discharge and are …

◆ Disabled veterans.

◆ Veterans who served on active duty in the armed forces during a war declared by Congress (the last one was World War II), or in a campaign or expedition for which a campaign badge has been authorized.

◆ Veterans who served in a military operation for which the Armed Forces Service Medal was awarded.

◆ Veterans separated from active duty within the past three years. (Active duty for training does not count toward this requirement.)

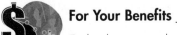

For Your Benefits

Federal agencies have the legal authority to give non-competitive appointments to any veteran who has a service-connected disability of 30 percent or more.

Appealing a Denied Preference

If you believe that an agency has violated your rights under any statute or regulation relating to veterans' preference, you should promptly file a complaint with the Secretary of Labor, The Veterans Employment and Training Service Agency (VETS). Complaints must be filed within 60 days after the date of the alleged violation. Not earlier than 61 days after filing a complaint with VETS, you may appeal your case to the Merit Systems Protection Board (MSPB).

Veterans who believe that they have not been accorded the preference to which they are entitled may file a complaint under a U.S. Department of Labor and U.S. Office of Personnel Management memorandum of understanding (refer to Federal Employment Info Line Sheet EI-44, "Special Complaint Procedures for Veterans").

Finding the Ideal Job

Federal agencies now fill open positions in the same way private industry does. Instead of contacting a central point, applicants now directly contact government agencies for job information. The trick is to know what jobs are open and where so you can apply for them.

Most government websites offer candidates advice on how to format a resumé for easy comparison to federal hiring practices. They also provide information on the process by which veterans can claim their hiring preference points.

USAJOBS

Finding the right government job for you can be time consuming. The federal government has employees in every county in the country. You can locate jobs and apply to them directly using the USAJOBS website.

USAJOBS is run by the Office of Personnel Management. It is the federal government's official one-stop source for federal jobs and employment information. You can find it at www.usajobs.com.

Hire Vets First

The Department of Labor runs the website Hire Vets First. It provides a range of services, such as resumé-writing tips, interviewing skills, career counseling, and, of course, job listings. It can be found at www.HireVetsFirst.gov.

CareerOneStop

CareerOneStop is a Department of Labor site to help individuals make informed decisions about their employment options. In addition to job listings, it provides occupation and industry information, salary data, education resources, and self-assessment tools.

An interesting option of the CareerOneStop website (www.careerinfonet.org) is a tab called Military Transitions, which matches military experience to civilian occupations. However, these "civilian equivalents" are just ideas to get you thinking. It is difficult to match the complexities and many responsibilities and experiences of military life to civilian occupation.

Base Postings

Military bases are frequently the largest local employer. Their civilian positions are broken into civil service and nonappropriated funds. Although USAJOBS is the primary site, bases often post jobs on their own websites. This is important because if you have decided where you are going to live, jobs in other places are just so much noise. The local base's website focuses your search.

When checking base job sites, there are different categories to check into. One is the DoD civilian positions. nonappropriated funds jobs on the base also are posted only for that base's website.

- Worldwide listing of jobs at a commissary: www.commissaries.com/inside_deca/HR/index.cfm

- Worldwide listing of jobs at the Army Air Force Exchange Service (AAFES): http://odin.aafes.com/employment/default.asp

- Air Force Personnel Center: https://ww2.afpc.randolph.af.mil/resweb

- Army: http://acpol.army.mil/employment

- Defense Finance and Accounting Service (DFAS): www.dfas.mil/careers/search. html

- Navy: www.donhr.navy.mil

State Hiring Preferences

Most (if not all) states provide hiring preference to veterans. This is usually true for city and county jobs. The key is to check in advance about this, as it may not be clearly spelled out on the open job postings web pages.

The first stop should be your state office of Veterans Affairs (the names used by states may vary). They will have information on your state's veteran hiring preferences and what you must do to claim the preference. Some of the state agencies, such as Corrections or Law Enforcement, may offer even more veteran benefits than others. Many states credit your years of active duty service toward the number of years of service required for state retirement eligibility. However, you must have been honorably discharged from your most recent military service.

Most state veterans' offices also offer special programs for placing disabled veterans into a state job that they are qualified to perform. Contacting one of these specially trained counselors can make the hiring process easier.

The Least You Need to Know

- Veteran hiring preference can increase your chance of selection for a government job.

- State and local governments also offer veteran hiring preferences.

- In some cases, a widow, widower, or dependent may also qualify for hiring preference.

- Use the online tools such as USAJOBS to find out which jobs are available locally.

Chapter 22

Veterans Medical Benefits

In This Chapter

- ◆ The VA medical services system
- ◆ Who is eligible to use a VA hospital?
- ◆ Special medical services

For many people, the concept of "veterans' benefits" is the medical support provided to old soldiers. But as you will see in this chapter, it is much more than that. Today's VA provides veterans with a wide range of medical services, including medicine, surgical, and rehabilitative care to old and young veterans alike.

What Is the VHA?

The Veterans Health Administration (VHA) is one of the three major components of the Department of Veterans Affairs (VA). The VHA is the largest integrated health-care system in the United States, operating outpatient clinics, hospitals, medical centers, and long-term health-care facilities across the United States and its territories.

Throughout our nation's earliest history, the government has provided care for the wounded veterans of its battles. In early times, this care was provided by the family, who might receive some sort of assistance from the government. However, the large numbers of wounded and maimed veterans from the Civil War called for much more. A series of National Asylums for Disabled Volunteer Soldiers and Sailors was established. More commonly referred to as "old soldiers' homes" or "national military homes," these facilities provided food, shelter, and care for Union veterans. (Confederate veterans were cared for by their respective states.)

Following World War II, this system was greatly expanded to support the needs of returning veterans and for the aging World War I veteran population. Specialized services were provided to the more than one million soldiers, sailors, airmen, and Marines returning with physical and emotional trauma. This called for an expanded care system and new services.

During the 1980s and early 1990s, the VA medical services suffered from a tarnished reputation of bureaucracy, inefficiency, and mediocre care. In 1995, the VA began reinventing itself as a model system providing patient-centered, high-quality, high-value health care.

Today the VHA operates 172 medical centers, more than 800 ambulatory care clinics, 137 nursing homes, 43 domiciliaries, 200 readjustment counseling centers, and 73 comprehensive home-care programs. Its 200,000 employees annually treat 1.1 million inpatients and have an average daily inpatient census of 87,500. In addition, VHA has the largest network of homeless assistance programs in the country.

VA Medical Benefits

VA health-care professionals provide counseling and treatment to help veterans overcome physical and psychological issues occurred while serving on active duty, or active duty for training. Appropriate services are provided for any injury, illness, or psychological condition resulting from such trauma.

Women Veterans' Program Managers are available in a private setting at all VA facilities to help women veterans seeking treatment and benefits. For information online, look up www.va.gov/womenvet.

The VA's medical benefits package provides the following health-care services to all enrolled veterans:

 ◆ Immunizations

 ◆ Physical examinations

- Health-care assessments

- Screening tests

- Ambulatory (outpatient) diagnostic and treatment services

- Emergency care in VA facilities

- Surgical care (including reconstructive/plastic surgery as a result of disease or trauma)

- Chiropractic care

- Bereavement counseling

- Substance abuse

- Medications

- Medical and surgical supplies

Attention!

Prescriptions are honored only if prescribed by a VA provider and are available under the VA's national formulary system.

Outpatient Pharmacy

A part of any modern medical care is the use of medicines. This can be a significant cost for the chronically ill. Eight categories of veterans receive free outpatient pharmacy services:

- Veterans with a service-connected disability of 50 percent or more

- Veterans receiving medication for service-connected conditions

- Veterans whose annual income does not exceed the maximum annual rate of the VA pension

- Veterans enrolled in priority group 6 who receive medication for service-connected conditions

- Veterans receiving medication for conditions related to sexual trauma while serving on active duty

- Certain veterans receiving medication for treatment of cancer of the head or neck

- Veterans receiving medication for a VA-approved research project

- Former prisoners of war

All other veterans are charged a co-pay of $8 for each 30-day or less supply of medication. For veterans enrolled in priority groups 2 through 6, the maximum co-pay amount for calendar year 2006 is $960. (This amount typically increases every year). Once the maximum co-pay amount has been reached, no further co-pays are required for that calendar year.

Co-pays apply to prescription and over-the-counter medications, such as aspirin, cough syrup, or vitamins, dispensed by a VA pharmacy. However, veterans may prefer to purchase over-the-counter drugs, such as aspirin or vitamins, at a local pharmacy rather than making the co-pay. Co-pays are not charged for medications injected during the course of treatment or for medical supplies such as syringes or alcohol wipes.

Outpatient Dental Services

VA outpatient dental treatment includes the full spectrum of diagnostic, surgical, restorative, and preventive procedures. Some veterans may be required to provide co-payments for dental services if they exceed the means test limits.

The following veterans are eligible to receive dental care:

- Veterans with service-connected, compensable dental conditions
- Former prisoners of war imprisoned 90 days or more
- Veterans with service-connected, noncompensable dental conditions as a result of combat wounds or service injuries
- Veterans with service-connected conditions rated permanently and totally disabling or 100 percent by reason of unemployability
- Veterans in a VA vocational rehabilitation program
- Certain enrolled homeless veterans
- Veterans with non-service-connected dental conditions that received dental treatment while an inpatient in a VA facility
- Veterans requiring treatment for dental conditions clinically determined to be complicating a medical condition currently under treatment

Recently discharged veterans who served on active duty 90 days or more, and who apply for VA dental care within 90 days of separation from active duty, may receive one-time dental treatment if their certificate of discharge does not indicate that they received necessary dental care within a 90-day period before discharge.

VA's Prosthetics and Sensory Aids

A valuable VA service is assisting veterans disabled during their military service. These disabilities might be the loss of one or more limbs, hearing, eyesight, or other critical physical or mental functions. One of the VA's four strategic goals is to restore the capabilities of disabled veterans to the greatest extent possible.

The VA provides medically prescribed prosthetic and sensory aids, devices, assistive aids, repairs, and services to disabled veterans. This is organized to provide a seamless service from prescription through procurement, delivery, training, replacement, and repair.

These products and services include wheelchairs and scooters, braces, shoes and orthotics, oxygen and respiratory equipment, other medical equipment and supplies (beds, lifts, computer equipment, telehealth products), and surgical implants (pacemakers, cardiac defibrillators, stents, dental devices). The VA provides items ranging from simple $2 foam shoe inserts to $30,000 stair-climbing wheelchairs to allow disabled veterans to live independently. The VA also provides home improvements and structural changes, and adaptive equipment for automobiles, to veterans with service-connected disabilities.

VA currently has 58 orthotic-prosthetic labs staffed by 185 employees called prosthetists and orthotists. Prosthetists and medical specialists in various disciplines form amputee clinic teams who see the veteran regularly after fitting to ensure that the artificial limb functions well. These specialists evaluate a veteran's lifestyle and medical condition to recommend which type of prosthetic limb or brace to provide. An orthotist designs and fabricates custom braces, and fits these to a patient's extremities or spine. A prosthetist designs custom prostheses and fabricates custom sockets, orders components, assembles the prosthesis, and fits it to the veteran's residual limb.

> **For Your Benefits**
>
> Most service related injuries get worse over the years. Be sure to keep all of your military injury documentation for possible use later.

Eligibility

All veterans are potentially eligible for at least some of the VA's medical services. Each program has its own requirements. When in doubt about eligibility, ask your local VA office benefits counselor. In general, eligibility is based on active military service in the Army, Navy, Air Force, Marines, or Coast Guard (or Merchant Marines during World War II), and discharge under conditions other than dishonorable.

Reservists and National Guard members called to active duty by a federal executive order may qualify for VA health-care benefits. Service members returning from duty in a theater of combat operations, including Guard/Reserve members, have special benefits eligibility for two years following their discharge from active duty.

Enroll for veterans benefits by completing VA Form 10-10EZ, "Application for Health Benefits." You can obtain this from any VA office or at www.va.gov/1010EZ. htm.

You can get help filling in this form from a VA counselor or from a local Veterans Service organization. You can also ask questions about filling in the form by calling the VA at 1-877-222-8387 or visiting its website, www.va.gov. Select the "Contact the VA" tab.

Some of the information you must provide on your enrollment form includes the following:

◆ Any existing health insurance policies.

◆ Proof of military service, preferably a copy of your DD214 that includes the type of discharge (honorable, general, and so on). This also verifies other eligibility categories, such as a Purple Heart or POW status.

◆ Financial disclosure to determine whether you qualify for free health care for nonservice-connected conditions, or if you will be charged co-pays.

Submit the completed form to a nearby VA office. You can also use the www.va.gov website to find the address of the nearest office. Indicate on your application that you want an appointment with a VA counselor. This person will review your application and explain which benefits you are eligible to receive.

For Your Benefits

Your local VA health-care facility schedules a primary care appointment for you as soon as one becomes available. The full range of VA health benefits package is coordinated by the comprehensive primary care program.

VA provides priority access to veterans who …

◆ Need care for a service-connected disability.

◆ Are 50 percent service-connected or higher and need care for any condition.

In these cases, the VA will schedule a primary care evaluation within 30 days. All other veterans will be scheduled for a primary care appointment as soon as one becomes available.

Once you are enrolled in the VA health care system, you are issued a VA ID card. This is not an insurance card. Rather, it is a ticket to all of the VA facilities. It enables traveling veterans to obtain care at any VA health-care facility across the country without having to reapply.

The VA's Priority Rating System

VA services are limited by the amount of funds Congress provides. The demand for medical services is hard to predict. So to ensure that limited resources are applied to the places with the greatest need, the VA uses a medical services priority system. Enrolling veterans are assigned to a priority of service group. The lower the priority number, the faster the service.

Group 1 includes veterans with service-connected disabilities rated 50 percent or more, or veterans the VA has determined to be unemployable due to service-connected conditions. This group receives priority in scheduling hospital or outpatient medical appointments.

Group 2 is for veterans with service-connected disabilities rated 30 or 40 percent.

Group 3 members are veterans with service-connected disabilities rated 10 and 20 percent, veterans who are former prisoners of war (POW), veterans who were awarded a Purple Heart, veterans awarded special eligibility for disabilities incurred in treatment or participation in a VA vocational rehabilitation program, and veterans whose discharge was for a disability incurred or aggravated in the line of duty.

Group 4 priority includes veterans receiving Aid and Attendance, or Housebound benefits, or veterans determined by VA to be catastrophically disabled.

Group 5 veterans include nonservice-connected veterans and noncompensable, 0 percent service-connected veterans whose annual income and net worth are below the established VA means thresholds.

Group 6 is for veterans of the Mexican border period or World War I; veterans seeking care solely for certain conditions associated with exposure to radiation or exposure to herbicides while serving in Vietnam; for any illness associated with combat service in a war after the Gulf War or during a period of hostility after November 11, 1998; for any illness associated with participation in tests conducted by the Department of Defense as part of Project 112/Project SHAD; and veterans with 0 percent service-connected disabilities who are receiving disability compensation benefits.

Group 7 includes veterans with disabilities not connected with their military service that meet certain financial need thresholds, and who enrolled prior to January 16, 2003, and have remained enrolled since that date. Veterans who meet this criterion are placed in specific subgroups and may or may not be eligible for care.

Group 8 is for all other veterans with disabilities not connected with their military service who agree to pay co-payments, and who enrolled before January 16, 2003, and have remained enrolled since that date. Veterans who meet this criterion are placed in specific subgroups and may or may not receive care. Non-service-connected veterans who enroll after January 16, 2003, will most likely not be eligible for care.

The demand for VA health care has seen a dramatic increase in the past several years. Because of the rapid growth in demand, the VA has been unable to give all enrolled veterans timely access to quality health care. The growth also has resulted in veterans being placed on waiting lists for appointments to see a medical care provider.

Effective January 17, 2003, the VA suspended new enrollment of veterans assigned to priority group 8. Changes in the VA's available resources may affect the number of priority groups the VA can enroll in a given year. If that occurs, the VA will publicize the enrollment changes and notify affected enrollees.

Cost for VA Medical Services

Your cost for VA services depends on the nature of your military service and whether you have any service-connected disabilities. For example, free services are available if you are a former prisoner of war or a Purple Heart medal recipient, or if you have low income. If you are otherwise qualified, you may be required to share the cost of your care through co-payments. For some veterans, existing health-care policies may cover these co-pays.

Means Test

To determine who may make co-payments, two "means tests" are used. These compare your income and assets contained in the VA enrollment form to a local and a national level published annually. If you fall below both of these tests, you qualify for free services. If you exceed the local level but fall below the national level, you are required to make co-payments for services. If you exceed both thresholds, you qualify only for priority 8 services.

Up to 2003, the VA was enrolling veterans who exceeded the net worth levels into priority 7. This group is billed co-pays for services. New enrollments into this category ended due to demands for services and funding limitations. Veterans already in this category remain eligible for the full range of VA health-care benefits enrolled, but veterans who enrolled after January 16, 2003, are placed in priority 8 and have the lowest service priority.

The means test includes all of a veteran's income, including Social Security, military retirement, unemployment insurance, interest and dividends, and so on. The VA may compare the veteran's statements with information from the Social Security Administration and the Internal Revenue Service.

The Geographic Means Test income tables are organized by state and county. Different counties within a state have different values. Always check the current VA rate tables to verify eligibility. You can view the current means data on the Internet at www.va.gov/healtheligibility/library/pubs/GMTIncomeThresholds.

The National Means Test income threshold table for the financial Tests for 2007 is as follows:

- A veteran with no dependents was awarded free health care, prescriptions, and travel benefits if income was no more than $10,929 per year, and total net worth was less than $80,000. A veteran with one dependent was allowed a $14,313 income.

- A veteran with no dependents was awarded free health care if income was no more than $27,790 per year, or $33,350 with one dependent. Again, the maximum net worth was $80,000.

 For Your Benefits

If you refuse to provide financial information, you will be placed in priority group 8 which may not be eligible for care.

The latest version of the National Means Test income threshold table is available at www.va.gov/healtheligibility/DOCS/VAIncomeThresholds.

Some Co-Pays Are Waived for Everyone

These are some of the services exempt from co-pays:

- Special registry examinations offered by the VA to evaluate possible health risks associated with military service

♦ Counseling and care for military sexual trauma

♦ Compensation and pension examination requested by the VA's Veterans Benefit Administration

♦ Care related to a VA-rated service-connected disability

♦ Readjustment counseling and related mental health services for post-traumatic stress disorder (PTSD)

♦ Care for cancer of the head or neck caused from nose or throat radium treatments given while in the military

♦ Publicly announced VA public health initiatives (health fairs)

♦ Care related to service for veterans who served in combat or against a hostile force during a period of hostilities after November 11, 1998

♦ Laboratory services such as flat film radiology services and electrocardiograms

♦ Preventive screenings (hypertension, hepatitis C, tobacco, alcohol, colorectal cancer, and so on)

♦ Immunizations such as flu shots

Co-Pay for Services

Veterans who do not qualify for priority groups 1 through 6 are billed co-pays for services. If veterans refuses to make these payments, they will not be provided services.

Inpatient co-pay has two rates, full and reduced. The full rate is for veterans in priority group 8. The reduced inpatient co-pay rate is 80 percent of the full inpatient rate. This applies to veterans who meet specific income requirements, as discussed in the earlier section on the Geographic Means Test (GMT).

The full 2007 co-pay rate is calculated by adding $10 to each day of hospitalization. This is in addition to $992 for the first 90 days of hospitalization. An additional $496 is added for each additional 90 days of hospitalization beyond this. These rates are updated annually.

Upon enrollment, you must provide information about any health-care policies you have. Based on your coverage and the services provided, these policies may reduce a co-pay. The VA will also bill your private health insurance company for medical services not connected to a military service condition.

Can't Pay Your Co-Pay?

If you cannot afford to make the co-payments, the VA can help. The Financial Means Test (described earlier) is based on the previous year. Your financial situation may have changed since then. Application for co-pay waivers is based on your financial situation today. The VA offers three types of waivers.

The first waiver is for relief from a balance of co-payments that you currently owe the VA. To get this relief, you must provide the Revenue Coordinator at your local VA facility proof of your financial hardship. Contact the Revenue Coordinator at your local VA facility for additional details. Approval of this waiver may take several months.

The second type of waiver is a request for a hardship determination. This waiver relieves you of all future co-pays. In essence, this moves you to a lower-numbered priority group assignment. To obtain this waiver, you must submit current financial information. Be sure to carefully document your situation. The VA's decision is based on the information provided. Contact the Enrollment Coordinator at your local VA office for additional waiver application information.

The third option is to request that a partial payment be accepted as full satisfaction of your debt to the VA. You will need to submit specific financial information about your current-year income. Most compromise offers are lump-sum payments payable in full 30 days from the date of acceptance of the offer. Contact the Enrollment Coordinator at your local VA for more information.

Long-Term Care

A historical part of the VA's services is as a long-term care facility or "Old Soldier's Home." This is still an important part of the VA health system. These services are based on the priority ranking system, with the highest priority given to those with severe service-related disabilities. The availability of long-term care services from the VA is also subject to funding limitations and may vary by geographic area. The VA provides these services through payments to state-supported veterans' homes. Approximately 65,000 veterans receive inpatient long-term care annually through programs of the VA or state veterans' homes.

Most VA medical centers provide home- and community-based outpatient long-term care programs. This allows patients to live at home for as long as possible. They may receive home-based primary care, contract home health care, adult day health care, homemaker and home health aide services, home respite care, home hospice care, and community residential care.

The need for long-term care help might be due to a terminal condition, a disability, illness, an injury, or the infirmity of old age. The need for long-term care may last for only a few weeks or months, or it may go on for years. It all depends on the underlying reasons for needing care.

Temporary long-term care (need for care for only weeks or months):

- ◆ Rehabilitation from a hospital stay, such as for surgery
- ◆ Recovery from illness or injury
- ◆ Terminal medical condition

For Your Benefits

Many states support their own long term care facilities for veterans.

Ongoing long-term care (need for care for many months or years):

- ◆ Chronic medical conditions or severe pain
- ◆ Permanent disabilities
- ◆ Dementia
- ◆ Ongoing need for help with activities of daily living

Long-term care services may be provided in any of the following settings:

- ◆ In the home of the recipient, or a family member or friend of the recipient
- ◆ At an adult day services location for health maintenance and rehabilitative services during daytime hours
- ◆ In an assisted living facility or board-and-care home
- ◆ In a hospice facility
- ◆ In a nursing home

Other VA programs (that may not be offered in all areas) include these:

- ◆ The Homemaker and Home Health Aide Program offers health-related services for service-connected veterans who need nursing home care.

◆ The community residential care program provides room, board, limited personal care, and supervision to veterans who do not require hospital or nursing home care, but are not able to live independently. The veteran pays for the cost of this living arrangement. The VA's contribution is limited to the cost of administration and clinical services. Medical care is provided on an outpatient basis at VA facilities.

◆ Respite care temporarily relieves the spouse or other caregiver from the burden of caring for a chronically ill or disabled veteran at home. Respite care is usually limited to 30 days per year.

◆ Home hospice care provides comfort-oriented and supportive services in the home for persons in the advanced stages of incurable disease.

◆ Domiciliary care is a residential rehabilitation program that provides short-term rehabilitation and long-term health maintenance to veterans who require minimal medical care as they recover from medical, psychiatric, or psychosocial problems. Most domiciliary patients return to the community after a period of rehabilitation.

◆ Psychiatric residential rehabilitation programs include ones for veterans coping with post-traumatic stress disorder and substance abuse, and compensated work therapy or transitional residences for homeless chronically mentally ill veterans and veterans recovering from substance abuse.

Nursing Home Care

The VA's nursing home programs include VA-operated nursing home care units, contract community nursing homes, and state homes. The VA contracts with approximately 2,500 community nursing homes. The community nursing home program has the advantage of being offered in many local communities where veterans can receive care near their homes and families.

The following is a list of who is eligible for nursing home care:

◆ Any veteran with a service-connected disability rating of 70 percent or more

◆ A veteran who is rated 60 percent service connected and is unemployable, or has an official rating of "permanent and total disabled"

◆ A veteran whose service-connected disability is clinically determined to require nursing home care

- ◆ Nonservice-connected veterans and those officially referred to as "0 percent, noncompensable, service-connected" veterans who require nursing home care for any nonservice-connected disability and who meet income and asset criteria

- ◆ If space and resources are available, other veterans on a case-by-case basis, with priority given to service-connected veterans and those who need care for post-acute rehabilitation, respite, hospice, geriatric evaluation and management, or spinal cord injury

National PTSD Center

The VA's National Center for Post-Traumatic Stress Disorder promotes research into the causes and diagnosis of the disorder, to train health-care and related personnel in diagnosis and treatment, and to serve as an information resource for professionals.

Post-traumatic stress disorder (PTSD) is an ailment that results from exposure to an experience involving direct or indirect threat of serious injury or death. The trauma an be something that happened to you or that you witnessed happening to others. It may be experienced alone, as in rape or assault, or in the company of others, as in combat. The events that can cause PTSD are called stressors.

After the event, you may feel scared, confused, and angry. If these feelings don't go away or get worse, you may have PTSD. PTSD may disrupt your life, making it hard to continue with daily activities. Symptoms include recurrent thoughts of a traumatic event, reduced involvement in work or outside interests, hyperalertness, anxiety, and irritability. The disorder apparently is more severe and longer lasting when the stress is of human design.

If you think you may have PTSD, do something about it. Contact the local VA facility located in your telephone book. You can also call the VA Health Benefits Service Center toll-free at 1-877-222-VETS (1-877-222-8387). Online help is available at the MyHealtheVet and Seamless Transition websites.

To begin the treatment process, submit a VA Form 10 (available from any VA facility). The first step is a "social history" interview (a review of family, work, and educational experiences before, during, and after military service), followed by a "psychiatric status" interview (a review of past and current psychological symptoms, and of traumatic experiences during military service).

The process of applying for a VA disability for PTSD can take several months, and can be both complicated and quite stressful. The Veteran's Service Organizations

(VSOs) provide "Service Officers" at no cost to help veterans and family members pursue VA disability claims. Service Officers are familiar with every step in the application and interview process, and can provide both technical guidance and moral support. In addition, some Service Officers particularly specialize in assisting veterans with PTSD disability claims. To find someone to help with your claim, directly contact the local office of any Veterans Service Organization, ask for recommendations from other veterans who have applied for VA disability, or ask a PTSD specialist at a VA PTSD clinic.

Veteran Health Registries

Certain veterans can participate in a VA health registry and receive free medical examinations, including laboratory and other diagnostic tests deemed necessary by an examining clinician. VA maintains health registries to provide special health examinations and health-related information:

- **Gulf War Registry**—This registry is for veterans who served in the Gulf War and Operation Iraqi Freedom. It includes veterans who may have been exposed to smoke or Leishmaniasis, who experienced problems due to their immunizations, or who were exposed to chemical or biological agents. Eligible veterans served on active military duty in Southwest Asia during the Gulf War, which began in 1990 and continues to the present, including Operation Iraqi Freedom.

For Your Benefits

All veterans who can prove that they meet the criteria of a health registry are eligible for its services. The type of discharge is not relevant.

- **Two Depleted Uranium Registries**—The first is for veterans who served in the Gulf War, including Operation Iraqi Freedom. The second is for veterans who served elsewhere, including Bosnia and Afghanistan.

- **Agent Orange Registry**—This registry is for veterans who were possibly exposed to dioxin or other toxic substances in herbicides used during the Vietnam War, while serving in Korea in 1968 or 1969, or as a result of testing, transporting, or spraying herbicides for military purposes. A verified claim of in-country service establishes eligibility for registry examinations. Unlike Vietnam veterans, Korean veterans must prove exposure to the substance.

◆ **Ionizing Radiation Registry**—This registry is for veterans who were possibly exposed to atomic radiation during the following activities: atmospheric detonation of a nuclear device; occupation of Hiroshima or Nagasaki from August 6, 1945, through July 1, 1946; internment as a prisoner of war in Japan during World War II; service in official military duties at the gaseous diffusion plants at Paducah, Kentucky, or Portsmouth, Ohio, or the K-25 area at Oak Ridge, Tennessee, for at least 250 days before February 1, 1992, or in Longshot, Milrow, or Cannikin underground nuclear tests at Amchitka Island, Alaska, before January 1, 1974; or treatment with nasopharyngeal (NP) radium during military service.

To participate, contact the nearest VA health-care facility or visit www.va.gov/environagents.

Health Care for Dependents

The Civilian Health and Medical Program of the Department of Veterans Affairs (CHAMPVA) is a comprehensive health-care program in which the VA shares the cost of covered health-care services and supplies with eligible beneficiaries. This program must not be confused with CHAMPUS or its replacement, TRICARE. The dependents of veterans who are eligible for TRICARE are not eligible for CHAMPVA. In general, CHAMPVA covers most health-care services and supplies that are medically and psychologically necessary.

To be eligible for CHAMPVA, you must be one of the following:

◆ The spouse or child of a veteran who has been rated permanently and totally disabled for a service-connected disability by a VA regional office.

◆ The surviving spouse or child of a veteran who died from a VA-rated service-connected disability.

◆ The surviving spouse or child of a veteran who was at the time of death rated permanently and totally disabled from a service-connected disability.

◆ The surviving spouse or child of a military member who died in the line of duty, not due to misconduct (in most of these cases, these family members are eligible for TRICARE, not CHAMPVA).

An eligible CHAMPVA sponsor may be entitled to receive medical care through the VA health-care system based on veteran status. If the eligible CHAMPVA sponsor is the spouse of another eligible CHAMPVA sponsor, both may be eligible for CHAMPVA benefits. In each instance in which the eligible spouse requires medical attention, the veteran may choose the VA health-care system or coverage under CHAMPVA.

The Least You Need to Know

- ◆ You may be eligible for free medical care based on the means tests.

- ◆ Some veterans must make co-pays for services, but waivers are available.

- ◆ Veterans health registries are open to any veteran.

- ◆ Some veterans are eligible for long term care assistance.

Chapter 23

Veterans Burial Benefits

In This Chapter

- Different cemeteries available
- Military burial honors and how to request them
- Burial at sea as an option
- Headstones available—if you like the style

Most people do not sit around contemplating the end of their days. Life always was and hopefully always will be. Yet for all of us, as with our ancestors before us, there will be an end. When this end arrives, arrangements must be made to provide for our mortal remains. This chapter discusses the options open to active duty personnel and veterans. Funerals and burials can place a significant financial burden on families, particularly in a time of high emotion. Understanding the choices available may ease this burden.

Young people generally think that funeral planning is only for the elderly. Sadly, some people die long before they reach old age. In the military, this can be from enemy action, training accidents, automobile accidents, and the dangers that come from day-to-day living.

Also this chapter provides information useful to the families of veterans. In some cases, military funeral and burial benefits also apply to spouses and dependent children. Always check carefully to see which benefits are available to you.

National Cemeteries

National cemeteries sprang from the need for burying soldiers during the Civil War. In 1862, 14 cemeteries were established. Today 141 national cemeteries are scattered across the country and U.S. territories. The Department of Veteran Affairs manages 125 cemeteries in 39 states and Puerto Rico. The Department of the Army administers 2, and the Department of the Interior manages 14 (although only 2 still accept new internments).

The National Cemetery Administration of the Department of Veteran Affairs (VA) maintains 2.8 million gravesites and has capacity for another 271,000 in prepared spaces. Sufficient land exists today to support more than four million grave sites. However, people have preferences about location, so some cemeteries fill faster than others. In 1999 and 2003, Congress funded 12 new cemeteries near the largest populations of veterans without local access to a national cemetery. You can locate the national cemetery near you at www.cem.va.gov/cem/cems/listcem.asp.

Two national cemeteries are administered by the Department of the Interior instead of the VA: the Andersonville National Cemetery in Georgia and the Andrew Johnson National Cemetery in Tennessee. In general, eligibility is the same as for the VA's national cemeteries.

Burial Ceremony

The Department of Defense (DoD) is responsible for providing funeral honors for eligible veterans, as described in DoD Directive 1300.15, "Military Funeral Support." Funeral honors are an expression of a nation's gratitude for faithful service and a final farewell. Funeral honors are available to …

- Military members who die while on active duty or in the Selected Reserve.
- Veterans who served on active duty or in the Selected Reserve, and departed under conditions other than dishonorable.
- Service members discharged for a disability that occurred during the line of duty.

Burial with Military Honors

The traditional image of a militarily honored funeral includes a flag-draped coffin and a bugler playing "Taps." In some cases, a firing party fires a salute over the grave.

These honor guards come from nearby active duty installations or sometimes from the local Guard/Reserve units. They don't appear automatically. Qualification must be established quickly if they are to be on-site when needed.

Honor Guard

Upon request, the Department of Defense provides a military funeral that consists of folding the flag draped across the coffin, presenting it to the next of kin, and playing "Taps." "Taps" may be played by a bugler or through an electronic recording.

Funeral directors may request this service by calling 1-877-MIL-HONR (1-877-645-4667). The funeral honors detail consists of two or more uniformed armed forces members, of which at least one is from the same branch of service. The VA arranges this service for internments at national cemeteries.

An alternative is to request military funeral honors from veterans' service groups. Details are at www.militaryfuneralhonors. osd.mil.

 Attention! _____

Military honors provided for someone who died on active duty, who is buried at sea, or who is interred in Arlington National Cemetery are significantly more involved than those provided to most veterans around the country.

Flag

A U.S. flag is provided, at no cost, to drape the casket or accompany the urn of a deceased veteran who served honorably in the United States Armed Forces. It is a visible and lasting symbol of gratitude from the nation to those who served it in a most personal way. Many families proudly display flags provided for funerals of loved ones. Eligible veterans are …

- ◆ Veterans who die on active duty.

- ◆ Veterans who served during wartime or after January 31, 1955.

- ◆ Veterans who were entitled to retired pay for service in the reserves, or would have been entitled if over age 60.

- ◆ Members of the Selected Reserve who served their initial obligation, or were discharged for a disability incurred in the line of duty, or died while a member of the Selected Reserve.

During the commitment ceremony, the flag draped over the casket is held waist high over the grave by the honor guard. Immediately after the sounding of "Taps," it is folded and presented to the next of kin. Only one flag is issued for a veteran's funeral. The VA does not replace stolen, damaged, or destroyed flags. However, some veterans group may assist in finding another flag for you.

To request a flag, complete VA Form 21-2008 and submit it to your funeral director along with a copy of the veteran's last DD214 indicating the type of discharge received. You may also get a flag at any VA regional office or U.S. post office. When burial is in a national, state, or military post cemetery, a burial flag is provided. VA Form 21-2008 is available online at www.vba.va.gov/pubs/forms/VBA21-2008.pdf.

Internment Options

A significant cost of someone's final resting place is the expense for burial. Gravesite purchase, the opening and closing of the grave, grave liners, and perpetual care can add up to a significant sum for a young widowed spouse. The VA provides assistance with some or all of these expenses through its national cemetery system. However, other internment options are available based on individual preference.

Burial in a National Cemetery

The VA administers 124 national cemeteries. The Department of the Army and the Department of the Interior administer two more each. Burial in a national cemetery is provided at no cost to the veteran. It includes the gravesite, a grave liner, opening and closing of the grave, a headstone, and perpetual care. Veterans buried in a national cemetery receive a burial flag and military honors. The key is to ensure that space is available at the cemetery of your choice.

In most cases, the funeral director contacts the national cemetery to make arrangements. Burials are arranged for weekdays only. Specific gravesites cannot be reserved.

Qualification as a "veteran" for the purposes of burial in a national cemetery requires honorable service and depends on the conditions and period of service:

◆ Any member of the armed forces of the United States who dies while on active duty.

◆ Veterans discharged under conditions other than dishonorable. With certain exceptions, service beginning after September 7, 1980, as an enlisted person, and service after October 16, 1981, as an officer, must be for a minimum of 24 continuous months or the full period for which the person was called to active duty (as in the case of a Reservist called to active duty for a limited duration). If in doubt, contact that national cemetery's director.

◆ Citizens of the United States who, during any war in which the United States has or may be engaged, served in the armed forces of any government allied with the United States during that war; whose last active service was terminated honorably by death or otherwise; and who were citizens of the United States at the time of entry into such service and at the time of death.

◆ Reservists and National Guard members who, at time of death, were entitled to retired pay for their military service.

◆ Members of Reserve components, ROTC members, and members of the Army National Guard or the Air National Guard who died from injury or disease incurred under honorable conditions while performing active duty for training.

◆ Guard/Reserve members who are disabled or who died from a disease or injury incurred in the line of duty during active duty for training.

◆ Under certain circumstances, commissioned officers in the National Oceanic and Atmospheric Administration, or those who served on active duty after July 28, 1945.

◆ Under certain circumstances, commissioned officers of the Regular or Reserve Corps of the Public Health Service who served on full-time duty after July 28, 1945.

◆ United States Merchant Mariners with oceangoing service during the period of armed conflict December 7, 1941, to December 31, 1946. A DD214 documenting this service may be obtained from:

Commandant (G-MVP-6)
United States Coast Guard
2100 2nd Street SW
Washington, D.C. 20593

◆ Members of the Philippine Armed Forces who fought alongside the U.S. forces during World War II.

◆ Spouses and dependents of eligible veterans. Surviving spouses of veterans who died before January 2, 2000, do not lose eligibility for burial in a national cemetery if they remarry. Burial of dependent children is limited to unmarried children under 21 (or under 23 for a full-time student). Unmarried adult children who are physically or mentally unable to support themselves are also eligible.

Some groups of people are specifically not eligible for burial in a national cemetery:

◆ Former spouses whose marriage to the veteran was terminated by annulment or divorce.

◆ Anyone whose last discharge is characterized as dishonorable.

◆ Anyone who has been convicted of a federal capital crime and sentenced to death or life imprisonment, or who has been convicted of a state capital crime and sentenced to death or life imprisonment without parole. This also applies to persons who were charged with serious crimes but who fled to avoid trial.

◆ Any person convicted of subversive activities after September 1, 1959, whatever military service may have been.

◆ A person whose only service was active duty for training, or inactive duty training in the Guard/Reserve.

Burial in Arlington National Cemetery

The most prestigious national burial site is Arlington National Cemetery. Located across the river from Washington, D.C., it is the final resting place of military heroes, common soldiers and sailors, and presidents. Arlington National Cemetery is one of two administered by the Department of the Army (the other is the United States Soldiers' and Airmen's Home National Cemetery in Washington, D.C.).

Eligibility for internment at Arlington Cemetery is more restrictive than at other national cemeteries. If you are interested in burial at Arlington, verify eligibility here:

Superintendent
Arlington National Cemetery
Arlington, VA 22211
703-607-8000
www.arlington-cemetery.org

Burial in State Veterans Cemeteries

Sixty-three state veterans cemeteries are located in 41 states around the country. They offer burial services, similar to national cemeteries, for veterans who are residents of that state and their families. Each state has established its own eligibility criteria, which may differ from that used by the national cemeteries. State cemeteries may be more conveniently located than a distant national cemetery.

To locate a state veterans cemetery, go to www.cem.va.gov/cem/scg/lsvc.asp.

Burial at Sea

Burial at sea is a final disposition of remains that is performed on United States Navy vessels while the ship is deployed. Therefore, family members cannot be present. The commanding officer of the ship performs the ceremony and notifies the family of the date, time, and longitude and latitude of the committal service.

Burial at sea is available to these people:

◆ Active duty members of the uniformed services and their dependent family members

◆ Retirees and veterans who were honorably discharged and their dependent family members

◆ U.S. civilian marine personnel of the Military Sealift Command and their dependent family members

To arrange for burial at sea, complete a burial at sea request package. It consists of a copy of the death certificate, a copy of the veteran's DD214 or retirement order, and a Burial-At-Sea Request/Authorization Form located at www.navy.mil/navydata/questions/bas-form.pdf.

Six ports of embarkation are used for burials at sea. Arrangements must be coordinated with the desired port:

◆ Norfolk, Virginia—Commander, Naval Medical Center, 757-953-2617/2618

◆ Jacksonville, Florida—Officer in Charge, Naval Hospital Branch Clinic, 904-270-7296/5301

◆ Corpus Christi, Texas—Commanding Officer, Naval Hospital, 361-961-2255

- San Diego, California—Commanding Officer, Naval Medical Center, 1-800-290-7410

- Bremerton, Washington—Commanding Officer, Naval Hospital, 206-475-4387/4303

- Honolulu, Hawaii—Navy Liaison Unit, Tripler Army Medical Center, 808-433-6611

If a burial flag is provided, it will be returned by the ship's captain to the next of kin. If one is not provided, a flag from the ship will be used but not sent to the next of kin. Family members buried at sea are not authorized a burial flag.

Cremated remains must be in a container to prevent spillage in shipping. Coordinate with the burial at sea coordinator at the desired port the preferred method of shipping and any other arrangements that may be required. Typically, the request packet and cremated remains are sent by certified mail.

Burial at sea of casketed remains requires special preparation. All expenses are paid by the person requesting the sea burial. A funeral home in the vicinity of the port of embarkation must be used to receive and prepare the casketed remains. The local sea burial coordinator will inspect the remains and ensure that they have been properly prepared.

For further information about arranging a burial at sea, check www.navy.mil/navydata/questions/burial.html.

Government-Supplied Headstones and Markers

Veterans and retired Guard/Reserve are eligible for an inscribed headstone or marker to mark their grave at any cemetery. They are furnished at no cost to cemeteries anywhere in the world. Spouses and dependent children are eligible for a headstone only if they are buried in a national or state veterans cemetery.

History of Military Headstones

In the early days, frontier posts would establish a small cemetery for local use and mark graves in whatever fashion seemed practical. By the time of the Civil War, this had evolved into an inscribed wooden board with a rounded top. This model was used throughout that conflict, but its limitations quickly became obvious. The wood rotted after five years and required replacement. The federal government was concerned with marking only the graves of Union soldiers and sailors.

In 1873, markers of marble or durable stone entered use. The stone featured a sunken shield on the front. Inside the shield was cut the number of the grave and the soldier's name, rank, and state. Graves of unknown dead were marked with a stone or marble headstone inscribed with the grave number. This design remained in use throughout the Spanish-American War.

In 1906, Congress paid for marking Confederate graves, primarily those who died in Union prison camps. The markers did not have the sunken shield on the front and have a pointed top instead of the rounded top on Union graves. In 1930, a Confederate Cross of Honor was added to the Confederate gravestones as well.

Following World War I, the current style of headstone was introduced, along with religious markings, although only two were initially approved. A list of the 39 religious emblems currently approved can be found at www.cem.va.gov/cem/hm/hmemb.asp.

Some civilian cemeteries require flat markers instead of headstones. These were approved in the 1930 so that veteran graves in civilian cemeteries were properly marked.

How to Order a Veteran's Marker

Two basic styles of memorial are available, an upright marble marker and a flat marker. The cemetery may specify that the style selected be consistent with existing markers. Flat markers are provided in granite, marble, or bronze. Upright headstones are available in granite or marble. Niche markers are also available to mark inurnment of cremated remains.

Headstones and markers used in national cemeteries or state veterans cemeteries are ordered for you. If burial is in a private cemetery, order the headstone or marker using VA Form 40-1330, "Application for Standard Government Headstone or Marker." You can find this form at www.va.gov/vaforms/va/pdf/VA40-1330.pdf. A copy of the veteran's discharge paper must be submitted with the form. Funeral directors, cemetery officials, and veterans' counselors typically assist with this form.

Headstones and markers the VA provides must be inscribed with the deceased's name, branch of service, and year of birth and death. All of these items must be in English. Other permitted markings are authorized emblem of belief and additional text concerning rank, wartime service, military awards, and words of endearment. The primary limiting factor is available space, although the VA will not inscribe anything it believes is inappropriate. Awards and decorations will not be inscribed without documentation, so attach a copy of the DD214.

To check the status of a memorial order for a national or state veterans cemetery, call the cemetery. To check on an order destined for a private cemetery, call 1-800-697-6947 (between 8 A.M. and 5 P.M. Eastern Standard Time Monday through Friday). Allow 30 days before checking to ensure that the order has been received. Allow 60 days for the headstone or marker to arrive before assuming it is late.

Attention!

Non-English inscriptions added below the mandatory information must be in Latin-alphabet characters and numbers. The request must include the English translation of the inscription.

Private cemeteries may apply for a headstone or marker by completing VA Form 40-1330 "Application for Standard Government Headstone or Marker for Installation in a Private Cemetery or a State Veterans' Cemetery." This is available at www.va.gov/vaforms/va/pdf/VA40-1330.pdf

Attach to the form a copy of the veteran's DD214 or other proof of service and death certificate. Fax the completed package to 1-800-455-7143 or mail it to:

> Memorial Programs Service (41A1)
> Department of Veterans Affairs
> 5109 Russell Road
> Quantico, VA 22134-3903

Veterans who died on or after September 11, 2001, are eligible for a headstone or marker even if there is already a private marker. Verify that the cemetery will allow the second marker. The VA does not pay a placement fee.

Attention!

Spouses and dependents buried in a private cemetery are not eligible for a government-provided headstone or marker.

Replacement Headstones and Markers

The VA replaces government-provided headstones and markers that have deteriorated or have been vandalized or stolen, at no cost. It also replaces markers broken in shipping, those with incorrect inscriptions, or those that were poorly made. However, if the headstone or marker has been placed in a private cemetery and the cemetery broke it, that cemetery must pay to replace it.

Information on how to order a replacement headstone or marker is available from the Memorial Programs Service Assistance between 8 A.M. and 5 P.M. Eastern Standard Time Monday through Friday at 1-800-697-6947.

Setting Government Headstones and Markers

Cemetery staff in national, military post, and military base cemeteries set the headstone or marker at no cost to the applicant. Some state veterans cemeteries may charge a nominal fee for setting a government-furnished headstone or marker. The expense of setting a government-furnished headstone or marker in a private cemetery is your responsibility. Some private cemeteries also require purchase of a special marker base before ordering a government marker.

Memorial Markers

Sometimes the remains of a service member are not recovered. This may be due to burial at sea, because the remains were donated to science, or because the ashes were scattered. In those cases, a memorial marker may be ordered. The inscription includes "In Memory Of" at the top. Eligibility is the same as for the headstones, and there is no fee to place the marker in a national cemetery. The VA does not reimburse fees for placing a memorial marker in a private cemetery.

Presidential Memorial Certificates

A presidential memorial certificate is an engraved paper certificate signed by the current president to honor the memory of honorably discharged deceased veterans. It is available from the Department of Veterans Affairs. You can see an example certificate at www.cem.va.gov/cem/pmc.asp.

Eligible recipients include the next of kin and loved ones of the deceased veteran. More than one certificate may be provided. Request a certificate using VA Form 40-0247, "Application for Presidential Memorial Certificate." This form is available from VA offices or online at www.va.gov/vaforms/va/pdf/VA40-0247.pdf.

Requests must include a copy of the veteran's discharge document (that shows the type of discharge), a copy of the death certificate, and where the certificate should be sent.

Certificates can be requested through a local VA office, by fax at 202-565-8054, or through the mail at:

Presidential Memorial Certificates (41A1C)
Department of Veterans Affairs
5109 Russell Road
Quantico, VA 22143-3903

Reimbursement of Funeral and Burial Expenses

The VA pays a burial allowance if the veteran …

◆ Died because of a service-related disability.

◆ Was receiving a VA pension or compensation at the time of death.

◆ Was entitled to receive a VA pension or compensation, but decided not to reduce his or her military retirement or disability pay.

◆ Died in a VA hospital, in a nursing home under VA contract, or while in an approved state nursing home.

The VA pays a burial allowance of up to $2,000 for service-related deaths. Claims for this reimbursement must be filed with the VA. Under certain circumstances, the VA may pay to transport the remains of veterans who died while in the service to the nearest national cemetery with available gravesites.

The VA pays a $300 funeral allowance and a $300 plot internment allowance for a non-service-related death for veterans who were receiving a VA compensation or pension, or who died in a VA facility or in a VA-contracted nursing home. If the death occurred while in a VA hospital or nursing home, transportation of the remains may also be paid.

Apply for these allowances with VA Form 21-530, "Application for Burial Benefits." Attach proof of the veteran's military service (DD214), a death certificate, and copies of funeral and burial bills you have paid.

Preplanning

Death can come swiftly or over an extended period of time. The time from death to committal to a final resting place is usually a matter of days. Veterans with distinct preferences about their funereal arrangements should make their intentions known in advance. This minimizes the family's confusion later at a time of high emotion.

Be Sure Critical Documents Are Available

Preplanning allows time to gather important documents and make the necessary copies. Be sure to include a copy of your last DD214 showing that the service was honorable. Preplanning also helps to ensure that your family is aware of the veteran benefits available to minimize funeral and burial expenses.

National cemeteries cannot reserve specific gravesites in advance (although existing arrangement made before 1962 are still honored). Check with the national cemetery you want to use to see if there are burial restrictions due to limited space.

If the burial is to be in a private cemetery, consider filling out a VA Form 40-1330, "Application for Standard Government Headstone or Marker for Installation in a Private or State Veterans' Cemetery." Often family members do not know periods of service, rank achieved, and similar information. Filling in this form in advance (of course, leaving the death date blank) ensures they will have all of the essential information available to send in later.

Burial in Uniform

For some people, their proudest moments were in uniform, and their dress uniform displays those honors bestowed by the nation. For these people, burial in uniform is preferred over burial in a suit. This is a very important area for preplanning.

First, only a rare few veterans still fit into their old dress uniforms. Funeral directors can work around this, to some extent, but if this is important to you, consider buying a dress uniform closer to your current size. Surplus or uniform reproductions are available if you have the time to shop around.

Second, once you have the uniform in hand, attach the insignia. Unless your spouse has military experience, this is beyond most civilians. Few understand the proper precedence of awards, where the shooting badges or airborne badges go, and similar considerations. If in doubt of the proper way to place something, look it up online or contact the local recruiter of that service or the local Guard/Reserve units. Other people may not notice, but is this a time to do something halfway?

Leave instructions for tying the necktie (or pretie it yourself). If the shirt under the dress coat requires insignia, attach them, too. And—be sure everyone knows where to find these things when the time comes.

Finally, if you cannot find your medals, order replacements. This could take a few months or as long as a year. Typically, there is no charge for this service if the awards are sent straight to the veteran. However, only one free replacement is provided per medal.

> You can request replacement decorations in two basic ways. The first is to use the online service eVetRecs. After filling in an online form, you must print a paper to sign and then mail or fax it in. This service is available at www.archives. gov/veterans/evetrecs.

The second option is to obtain a Standard Form 180 (SF-180). You can request one through the mail at the following addresses or download it from www.archives.gov/research/order/standard-form-180.pdf.

Mail the completed form to the appropriate service at the addresses at the bottom of the last page or:

Air Force

National Personnel Records Center
Air Force Reference Branch
9700 Page Boulevard
St. Louis, MO 63132-5100

Army

National Personnel Records Center
Medals Section (NRPMA-M)
9700 Page Avenue
St. Louis, MO 63132-5100

Navy, Marines, and Coast Guard

Navy Personnel Command
Liaison Office, Room 5409
9700 Page Avenue
St. Louis, MO 63132-5100

The Least You Need to Know

◆ Preplanning for your death includes telling someone where the documents and plans are.

◆ Families save money using national cemeteries for burial.

◆ Funeral directors can contact the services directly with questions.

◆ Steps to help determine whether you or a relative are entitled to a funeral with military honors.

24

Military Family Support

In This Chapter

◆ Assistance for military families

◆ Exceptional needs assistance

◆ Helping your spouse find a local job

◆ Preparing a family for your deployment

Service members need more than pure grit and MREs to live by. An essential part of their morale and fighting spirit is based on the well-being of their family. Throughout the ages, military leaders have known that their soldiers' and sailors' morale depends to a great degree on their family's financial security, safety, and support. The newest military benefit is a formalization of what many units provided informally through their senior NCOs and officers all along.

When a service member goes to war, so does the rest of the family. In some cases, the spouse is "suddenly military" dealing with strange rules in the midst of the rush and emotional strain of a sudden departure. To address this issue, the armed forces now provide formal programs to explain to spouses and family members what must be done in a mobilization, their options, and how to handle emergencies "the military way."

To a civilian, the workings of military life can be bewildering. Its language is full of acronyms, strange names for everything, and a seemingly rigid social order. Service members picked up much of this information in basic training and advanced training, and just over time. The complexity seems natural to them. However, for an outsider not accustomed to this, it is contradictory, hard to figure out, and frustrating to accomplish something simple. Family support benefits described in this chapter are intended to teach spouses and children how to successfully use the many military benefits and services available to them.

Active Duty Family Support

The 1990–1991 Gulf War introduced new problems to the military community. Not since the Korean War have so many Reserve and Guard units been mobilized for combat. Even active duty units accustomed to a short-term temporary assignment were now off to the fight for extended service. Their families may live on the base, but the sudden departure of the service member significantly disrupted routine family life.

Although soldiers, sailors, airmen, and Marines were trained for their missions, the families were ill prepared for what followed. In the months after the end of the fighting, the services re-examined the problems caused by the deployment. Family problems both distracted the service members and were avoidable. To ease further mobilizations, the military updated old policies and instituted a range of new family support programs.

Traditional Family Support Network

Active duty service involves regular moves to strange locales and different military service situations (like an Air Force sergeant assigned to work on a Navy base in Japan). Historically, military spouses have adjusted to the changes and learned how to find what they need in their new location. The key is to establish friendships with their base housing neighbors who can tell them where to find everything they need. After all, in a short time, those friends will also rotate to other assignments and will depend on others for help.

Many of these informal networks were "wives' clubs." They taught the spouses new to the area or new to the military how to maneuver through the military system. However, this often helped the ones who already understood military ways. Pulling new spouses (straight from the civilian world) into this circle was haphazard. It depended on the quality of the local groups and their willingness to accept outsiders from a wide range of circumstances.

Tell It to the Chaplain

Chaplain services are traditional mainstays of military family support. Military chaplains have ready access to commanders at all levels and are very knowledgeable about available social services. Chaplain assistance includes personal, marital, and family counseling. And of course, chaplains provide spiritual guidance and comfort to all service members and their families. Whenever a family needed some advice, it naturally gravitated toward the clergy, just as they did in their civilian world.

Attending base religious services is also a natural way to meet new people and re-establish a local network of information. Many people newly assigned to a base seek out their services to quickly fit in to the local community.

> **Attention!**
>
> Although chaplains can suggest something to a commander, they have no direct authority to force something to happen.

Family Support Programs

Leaving things to chance is not the military way. The Department of Defense has created a series of programs to support a healthy military family life. These programs are sometimes offered under a single DoD initiative or have some version of it within each service branch.

To assist in the implementation of these efforts, each service creates a volunteer-based organization to explain the various programs. For example, the Army calls its organization a Family Readiness Group. These command-sponsored organizations offer family members programs to help them cope with extended deployments. They are made up of spouses, parents, siblings, relatives, and approved friends of military personnel. These organizations provide a support network for all families, especially during periods of separation.

> **For Your Benefits**
>
> What the Air Force calls Airman and Family Readiness Flights, the Navy calls its Fleet and Family Support Program.

Exceptional Family Member Program (EFMP)

The EFMP assists families whose members have special support needs. An exceptional family member is a dependent, regardless of age, who requires medical services for a chronic condition, receives ongoing services from a specialist, has mental health concerns/social problems/psychological needs, receives education services provided on an Individual Education Program, or receives services provided on an Individual Family Services Plan. The family member must reside with their military sponsor and be recorded in DEERS. If both parents are in the military service, both enroll in the EFMP when they have a qualified family member.

You are eligible for EFMP if you are on active duty (including Guard/Reserves called to active duty) and have a family member with a disability. Examples of this include …

- A family member over 21 in the incapacitated dependent program.

- A child in special education more than 20 percent of the school day.

- A spouse or child receiving treatment for cancer, lupus, heart disease, leukemia, diabetes, mental illness, or long-term illness.

- A family member in a residential treatment facility.

- A family member receiving Supplemental Security Income (SSI) benefits.

Enrollment in EFMP allows assignment managers at military personnel agencies to consider the documented medical and special education needs of exceptional family members. When possible, service members are assigned to an area where the medical and special education needs of their exceptional family member can be met.

Apply for EFMP at your local facility's Family Support Center, or online using DD Form 2792, "Exceptional Family Medical Summary." This form's medical summary requires the assistance of your dependent's doctor. This form is available at www.dtic.mil/whs/directives/infomgt/forms/eforms/dd2792.pdf

DD Form 2792-1, "Exceptional Family Member Special Education/Early Intervention Summary," must be signed by a school official or early intervention provider (if the child is younger than 3). You must submit a legible copy of the current Individualized Education Plan (IEP) or Individualized Family Service Plan (IFSP). If you are enrolling a school-age child with medical needs only, a school official or early intervention provider must endorse page 1 of the special education/early intervention summary documenting that there are no special educational needs. This form is available online at www.dtic.mil/whs/directives/infomgt/forms/eforms/dd2792-1.pdf.

The completed EEMP applications are reviewed by a screening committee that assigns participants to a service category. Each category provides a different frequency and duration of treatment. Enrollment must be updated once every three years or whenever the condition or family status changes. Participants may lose their category due to changes in family status, medical requirements, or special education needs.

Family Member Employment Assistance Program (FMEAP)

The Family Member Employment Assistance Program helps family members of active duty, National Guard, and Reserve personnel to achieve their goals through employment, education, or volunteerism. FMEAP is a valuable resource for spouses who are new to an area, to locate local employment. FMEAP is administered on a local level. There is an office on all major installations.

The FMEAP office should be the first stop for a spouse who is new to an area and looking for employment. FMEAP knows the local job market and can save you valuable time by identifying local opportunities that align with your skills. In some cases, FMEAP already knows the hiring manager and can arrange for introductions.

Exchanging a green (or blue) uniform for a three-piece suit can be a significant challenge. FMEAP provides educational assistance to ease the transition:

◆ How to write a resume using a format best suited to your target industry—what to include, what to leave out, and how to highlight your many career accomplishments

◆ Winning interview techniques, including what to say and do to secure that ideal job

◆ Ways to prepare for an interview, from how to dress, to how to answer commonly asked questions

A valuable FMEAP service is assistance in applying for federal civilian employment. The local office will walk you through the complicated application process and explain how to locate a federal job in your target area.

FMEAP is not an employment agency and does not guarantee results. However, it does provide significant insight into the local employment market. FMEAP also provides counseling during a job search.

For Your Benefits

Many states now extend unemployment benefits to military spouses who relocate to their state due to official orders. The local FMEAP office will know if this applies to your new location.

Family Advocacy Program (FAP)

The Family Advocacy Program is a congressionally mandated program to reduce the incidence of family violence. It also seeks to create an environment of intolerance for such behavior through education and intervention. People are helped to face their abusive lifestyles and learn new behaviors for healthier family relationships. FAP also offers classes on parenting, conflict and stress management, and coping skills.

FAP is a locally administered program and is contacted through the local Family Support Center. Discussions during Family Advocacy Program intervention are strictly confidential. However, information about dangerous or criminal activities is reported to the appropriate authorities.

Family Readiness

Family Readiness is the level of preparedness of military families for a call to distant military service. Family Readiness offers several programs, to help families become more self-reliant. With self-reliance and knowledge comes a feeling of increased self-confidence. This, in turn, leads to stronger individual and family well-being.

For spouses and family members, the Family Readiness program gives a sense of belonging to the local military community. It provides a ready network of people with common interests for friendships, to share important information, for referrals to needed resources, and to share moral support during unit deployments.

Teaching Families the Military Ways

When service members join a new unit, they are walked through an "in processing" to introduce them to everyone and everything. In processing includes a unit member to escort them around to every section of the unit for greetings, to register their information where required, to attend briefings, and to give tours of the unit's facilities. This process usually takes several days.

"Family in-processing" is similar, in that it ensures that families that are new to a unit will register their contact information and receive information about the unit. Family In Processing explains the unit's mission programs available to the families for a successful transition into their new unit. When relocating to a new area, ask the new unit about its family in-processing program. In some cases, this may be handled at the base level rather than in each unit.

Relocation

Military families must prepare for and sometimes adjust to relocation on short notice. Some spouses see this as a big adventure; some see it as a frustrating, unhappy dislocation into a new and strange situation. It means leaving behind everything familiar—friends, places, and memories—and trading them for an unknown situation.

To make the move to a new place a bit easier, the Department of Defense provides a website with information on all of its major installations around the world. It also describes facilities at each of them for the initial move-in and temporary quarters until household goods arrive. This website also contains a significant amount of the latest military family-related information; you can find it at www.militaryhomefront.dod.mil

Guard/Reserve Family Support

Guard/Reserve mobilized units face a very different problem. Instead of an active duty unit absorbing a few new families every month, during a mobilization, entire Guard/Reserve units must scramble to figure out what to do. In many cases, the spouses of the senior NCOs and officers have little experience as active duty military spouses and are not available to mentor the younger families. They are overwhelmed, struggling to address their own problems.

When a Guard/Reserve unit is summoned to active service, a large number of families are thrust into the military world at the same time that a unit is scurrying about, trying to mobilize. Often there is little time for anyone to explain anything, and off the unit goes. This creates many problems. Where active duty spouses are typically concentrated in base housing or at least near a military facility, Guard/Reserve families may be scattered over hundreds of miles. This makes even bringing them together for a discussion a major undertaking.

The results of this are predictable. Information is not evenly distributed, resulting in impassioned requests for the service member to return home to address urgent family problems. Families face a new strange pay system (and likely reduced income), a new health insurance program, and confusion over military forms with no one around to explain anything. How can service members keep their concentration on the business at hand while their families are mired in problems?

Community Outreach Partnerships

To address the mentoring problem, the Guard/Reserve has developed nationwide community outreach partnerships with organizations whose members often have extensive military experience. Many of these organizations also assist veterans with filing claims for post-service benefits. Each of these organizations provides volunteers to explain military processes, assist with filling out forms, or just lend a sympathetic ear. Refer to the local telephone book or the organization's web page to contact them. Some of these partnerships include the following:

◆ Veterans of Foreign Wars (VFW)

◆ American Veterans (AMVETS)

◆ Disabled American Veterans (DAV)

◆ American Legion

◆ United Service Organizations (USO)

Guard and Reserve Family Readiness Toolkit

Preparing a family for a service member's deployment is a long and tedious process. To organize the many things that must be addressed, the Guard/Reserve provides a toolkit. Actually, it is an extended checklist, but it reduces the likelihood that something important is overlooked before departure. The goal is for each family to study and understand what will happen when a unit is called to active duty on short notice. The toolkit is available online at www.defenselink.mil/ra/documents/toolkit/FamilyReadinssToolkit0308.pdf.

Preparing for the Reunion

For many people, the reunion of a deployed service member and his or her family can be more stressful than the actual separation. Questions and concerns are mingled with the excitement of seeing each other again. The expectations of each spouse may have shifted over time. Important family decisions may have been made in the service member's absence. The spouse may have to readjust from a more independent lifestyle to one in which decisions are shared. With this in mind, the military offers reunion briefings to service members and their spouses before the big day.

Reunion briefings may alleviate the fear of the unknown while helping you understand the different feelings and concerns that you may encounter. These briefings also cover many other important issues, such as changes in your TRICARE insurance and pay, and the service member's reemployment rights. Reunion briefings are conducted by the local command.

For Your Benefits

Both the service member and the spouse will have their own expectations about what the reunion will be like. Focus on time together more than on a whirlwind of family meetings.

Operation: Military Child Care (OMCC)

The Department of Defense provides need-based financial assistance for child care. This is open to both Guard/Reserve members called to active service as well as deployed, active duty service members. These programs also support active duty families with no access to on-base care, such as service members living in communities that are not within reasonable commuting distances to military bases.

The DoD uses the National Association of Child Care Resource and Referral Agencies (NACCRRA) to process applications and to refer military families to nationally accredited child care/school-age programs. This includes child-development centers, family child-care homes, and out-of-school programs for children 6 weeks to 12 years of age.

Apply online for a child-care subsidy. To qualify, fax, mail, or e-mail copies of these documents to NACCRRA:

- ◆ The Guard/Reserve activation or deployment orders, or orders.

- ◆ If the need is due to a long wait for base child care, the notification that you are on the waiting list.

- ◆ The service member's Leave and Earnings Statement. If the spouse is also in the military, the highest-ranking person is considered the sponsor.

- ◆ The spouse's most recent pay stub or proof of enrollment in school.

- ◆ The birth certificate or self-certification statement of each child.

When submitting documents to NACCRRA, use a cover sheet with your name and the number of pages sent.

Ask your child-care provider to complete the provider application, and fax, mail, or e-mail the required provider documents to NACCRRA:

- ◆ Child care license

- ◆ National accreditation certificate, QFCC or ACCYN Quality Child Care Participant Certificate, if applicable; or Child Development Associate (CDA) credential, Early Childhood Education, or Child Development degree

To locate a local provider, contact Child Care Aware at 1-800-424-2246 or online at www.childcareaware.org.

NACCRRA
Military Subsidy Department
3101 Wilson Blvd., Suite 350
Arlington, VA 22201
Phone: 1-800-793-0324, ext. 341
Fax: 703-341-4104
msp@naccrra.org

Military Child Care in Your Neighborhood

Military Child Care in Your Neighborhood assists active duty service members living in communities without access to military child-care facilities, or where the wait list for on-base child-care and school-age programs is long. Eligibility is limited to single-parent families, families with a working spouse, or families with a spouse who is enrolled in school. Spouses looking for work are eligible for 60 days of assistance.

Military Child Care in Your Neighborhood is subsidy program that reduces fees based on total family income and geographic location. Families pay rates similar to on-base child-care/school-age programs.

To enroll in this program, contact NACCRRA at 1-800-424-2246 or online at www.naccrra.org.

Operation: Military Child Care

Operation: Military Child Care provides reduced-fee child care in local communities for parents deployed in support of the global war on terrorism. Eligibility is determined by the family's income, geographic location, DoD child-care fee policies, and available funding. Family circumstances are considered when determining fees.

Enroll by calling NACCRRA at 1-800-424-2246 or www.childcareaware.org

Child Care Options for R&R

Service personnel returning to their family after an extended separation need some time to readjust to their relationship. Operation: Child Care provides a few free hours of child care while a service member is home on Rest and Recuperation (R&R) leave. All service members on R&R from Operation Iraqi Freedom and Operation Enduring Freedom are eligible. Child care is provided by local licensed operating child-care programs.

To enroll for Operation: Child Care, call 1-800-424-2246 or schedule online at www. ChildCareAware.org. You must provide a copy of your leave orders, and the date and time you would like child care.

> **Attention!**
>
> Eligibility for child-care subsidies may be limited to available funding.

Child Care for Severely Injured Service Members

Families of severely injured service members are eligible for up to six months of sub-sidized child-care services during a service member's recuperation. (More than six months of child care is available, based on the situation.) This nationwide program supports both in-patient and out-patient medical care.

NACCRRA will locate child care in the civilian community if a military program is unavailable. This will allow the spouse to be at bedside or to help with outpatient medical appointments. An offset to the civilian child-care fees is provided during the recovery period.

Service-Specific Programs

In addition to the Department of Defense programs, the individual services offer child-care programs on their own facilities or for a select few locations. Each of the services has its own name for its family support programs, such as the Army Family Team Building (AFTB) or the Air Force Family Readiness Edge. Whatever their title, they all provide the same essential services, along with a few extra that support their unique activities.

> **Attention!**
>
> An excellent source of information on being married to a service member is *The Complete Idiot's Guide Life as a Military Spouse* by Lissa McGrath (Alpha, 2008).

Important Sources of the Latest Family Support Information

Spouses of service members have multiple sources of authoritative information published by the armed services. These sources provide the latest information about military benefits and easing a family's military burden.

- All services

    www.militaryhomefront.dod.mil

- Navy and Marines—The LIFELines Services Network (LSN) is the Official Quality of Life delivery network of the Department of the Navy.

    www.lifelines.navy.mil

- Coast Guard

    www.cgfamily.us/community

    The Coast Guard New Spouse handbook contains 127 pages of information.

    www.uscg.mil/comdt/mcpocg/ombudsman/doc/2007 spouse update.pdf

Army

Operation: Military Kids (OMK) is a cooperative program between the U.S. Army and community organizations to provide support to the children of deployed Guard/Reserve military parents. Members of Guard/Reserve units can be dispersed over a wide geographic area and feel isolated (unlike a concentration of military kids near a large base). OMK introduces them to other youth in similar circumstances and provides recreational, social, and educational programs. Each state organizes its own OMK efforts.

The OMK volunteer organization for each state provides a range of support based on available resources. OMK Hero Packs are knapsacks filled with a variety of items from the OMK partner agencies. Hero Packs are distributed to the children of deployed Guard/Reserve service members. They include fun activities and ways to stay connected to their deployed parents. In addition, information is provided to parents regarding local support programs for children and families.

Another popular activity is summer camp for the children of deployed service members. These camps may be on military bases or even at a 4-H camp. Fees are generally low or free, depending on local funding.

Operation: Military Kids: Speak Out for Military Kids (SOMK) is an educational program that raises awareness of issues facing military families. Participants develop presentation and other information material to share their experiences with the community. For more information, contact your local 4-H Military Liaison online at www. operationmilitarykids.org.

Army Child Care in Your Neighborhood (ACCYN) provides active duty Army families off-base child care at rates similar to base-sponsored child care. However, this program is available only at these locations:

- Fort Carson, Colorado
- Fort Sam Houston, Texas
- Fort Riley, Kansas
- Fort Lewis, Washington
- Fort Campbell, Kentucky
- Fort Meade, Maryland
- Fort Bragg, North Carolina
- Fort Detrick, Maryland
- Fort Drum, New York
- Aberdeen Proving Ground, Maryland
- Fort Bliss, Texas
- Washington, D.C., metro area

Chapter 8 addressed many of the national relief organizations, such as Army Emergency.

Navy and Marine Corps

The Navy and Marine Corps personnel stationed in the San Diego area may arrange for affordable, off-base child care through the San Diego County YMCA Childcare Resource Service at 1-800-441-9199, or the Marine Corps Child Care Resource and Referral office at 760-763-1795.

Air Force

The Quality Family Child Care (QFCC) program provides Air Force Families with off-base child-care options located near 15 Air Force bases. Families pay a comparable fee to that of on-base child-care facilities:

- Beale AFB
- Buckley AFB
- Brooks City AFB
- Eglin AFB
- Fairchild AFB
- Hurlburt AFB
- Keesler AFB
- Lackland AFB
- Moody AFB
- Nellis AFB
- Offutt AFB
- Pope AFB
- Randolph AFB
- Tinker AFB
- Travis AFB

The Least You Need to Know

- Prepare your spouse for deployment before it occurs.
- Information on family accommodations at new duty stations is available through relocation assistance.
- The Exceptional Family Member Program ensures that special support requirements are considered when making assignments.
- The Family Member Employment Assistance Program can help locate employment for a military spouse or a service member rejoining the civilian workforce.

Glossary

ACT assessment test (ACT)   An admissions requirement at some colleges, mostly in the Midwest or Eastern United States.

active duty   Includes anyone serving full-time in the seven uniformed services.

Additional Special Pay   Is for medical officers when authorized by their military service, and when not undergoing an internship or initial residency training.

Additional Special Pay for Dental Officers   For dental officers who are entitled to Variable Special Pay and are not serving in an initial internship or initial residency training. They sign an agreement to remain on active duty for at least one additional year.

administrative discharge   A discharge that was not ordered by a military court as part of a punishment.

Aero Club   An opportunity to develop aeronautical skills in piloting, navigation, mechanics, and other related areas.

Afloat Personal Telecommunications Program (APTS)   Provides personal calling from Navy ships using satellite communications.

agent   In terms of a power of attorney, the person who is given the power of your legal identity.

Aid for Air Force Personnel Spouses   A U.S. Air Force charity that seeks to provide aid to airmen and their families.

Air Force Aid Society   Official charity of the U.S. Air Force.

Air Force Family Readiness Edge   A family-support program.

American Association of State Colleges and Universities (AASCU)   Runs the Service Member Opportunity Colleges.

American Council on Education (ACE)   Attributes college credits where they have been earned by service members through means other than traditional collegiate education.

American Red Cross   A volunteer-based charity. Assistance is free and includes personal and financial counseling, and referrals.

Armed Services YMCA   An extension of the YMCA of the United States that is dedicated to supporting the armed forces.

Army/ACE Registry Transcript System (AARTS)   As enlisted soldiers complete their training, it is recorded. This can later be translated into college credit as determined by ACE.

Army and Air Force Exchange System (AAFES)   Runs all the Post and Base Exchanges.

Army Child Care in Your Neighborhood (ACCYN)   Provides active duty Army families with off-base child care at rates similar to base-sponsored child care.

Army Emergency Relief (AER)   A nonprofit organization dedicated to "helping the Army take care of its own." It provides funds to major commands and installation commanders for emergency financial assistance to soldiers, retired soldiers, and their families.

Army Family Team Building (AFTB)   A family-support program.

Aviation Career Incentive Pay (ACIP)   Service members are eligible if they hold or are training to hold an aeronautical designation or rating, and engage in aviation service on a career basis.

bachelor enlisted quarters   Housing for enlisted service members who are unmarried or unaccompanied by their dependents.

bachelor officer quarters   Housing for single or unaccompanied officers.

bad conduct discharge   Given to service members after conviction by a general or special court-martial. It is often preceded by a period of confinement in a military prison.

BAH-DIFF   Paid to service members who provide child support (either court ordered or voluntary). BAH-DIFF is usually increased annually. You cannot receive both Partial BAH and BAH-DIFF at the same time.

BAH-RC/Transient   Housing allowance for personnel in transit or on active duty less than 30 days, such as a National Guardsman attending annual training. It also applies when an active duty service member is in transit from selected areas where no prior BAH rate existed.

Basic Allowance for Housing (BAH)   Tax-free money to compensate fees for living in nonmilitary or government housing.

Basic Allowance for Subsistence (BAS)   Money to offset the cost of food for service members where government rations are not supplied.

Basic Clothing Replacement Allowance   A monthly cash payment for maintaining the condition of uniforms.

basic pay   Salary for military service.

benefit   A form of noncash compensation for services.

Board Certified Pay   For medical officers who are entitled to Variable Special Pay and certified by an American Medical or Osteopathic Specialty Examining Board or board certification equivalency, established for specialties unique to military medicine that require formal postgraduate medical training of at least two academic years.

Buy-Up   A Montgomery GI Bill benefit that allows active-duty service members to make an additional payment of up to $600 to their GI Bill, which can effectively increase GI Bill payout as much as $5,400.

Career Enlisted Flight Incentive Pay (CEFIP)   For enlisted personnel whose duties are essential to operation of aircraft, and who are placed on orders to perform crewmember duties.

Career Sea Pay (CSP)   An extra bonus offered for those who are assigned to sea duty.

Civilian Clothing Allowance   Money for times when duty requires that you wear civilian clothing, such as for courier duty or on embassy duty. This allowance applies to selected overseas assignments.

Civilian Health and Medical Program of the Department of Veterans Affairs (CHAMPVA)   A comprehensive health-care program in which the VA shares the cost of covered health-care services and supplies with eligible beneficiaries.

Class Six store   Sells beer, wine, and liquor to service members who are at least of legal age to consume these beverages for the state the base is in.

clothing allowances   Money for the purchasing and up-keep of military clothing.

Coast Guard Exchange (CGE)   Provides the same types of products as the other Exchanges, plus Coast Guard– and Homeland Security–specific items.

Coast Guard Mutual Assistance   A nonprofit organization providing financial assistance to the Coast Guard community.

Combat-Related Special Compensation (CRSC)   Tax-free monthly payments to eligible retired veterans with combat-related injuries.

Combat Zone Tax Exclusion (CZTE)   The only time that federal income tax does not apply to your pay. If you are in a war zone for a single day, that entire month's pay is tax exempt.

College Level Examination Program (CLEP)   An examination that provides college credit for demonstrated subject knowledge.

commissary   Operated by the Defense Commissary Agency (DeCA), these stores provide groceries to military personnel, retirees, and their families.

Commissioned Corps   The NOAA Commissioned Corps consists of skilled officers in the areas of medicine, dentistry, veterinary, engineering, environmental health, and so on. The Commissioned Corps of the Public Health Service consists of skilled officers in the areas of medicine, dentistry, veterinary, engineering, environmental health, and so on.

Common Access Card (CAC)   The new-generation ID card that contains one or more integrated circuit chips. Much more than an ID card, this smart piece of plastic carries a lot of personal information on it.

Community College of the Air Force (CCAF)   Keeps track of training, testing, and experience, which can be translated into eligible college credits for you.

concurrent receipt   Receiving both a military pension and VA disability compensation.

Continued Health Care Benefit Program (CHCBP)   Temporary health-care coverage for individuals who lose their TRICARE coverage.

CONUS COLA   An additional monthly CONUS cost of living allowance (COLA).

cost of living allowance (COLA)   Money to help pay for off-base housing and living.

Credentialing Opportunities Online (COOL)   Helps service members know what they need to do to get certified to do what they have been doing in the military as a civilian. Each of the COOL sites provides a cross-reference of MOS-to-civilian job titles. They also list relevant certifications to begin working on prior to leaving military service.

CSB/REDUX   A Career Status Bonus REDUX was an attempt to reduce the 20-year retirement payout, to encourage military personnel to stay in for the full 30 years.

DANTES (Defense Activity for Non-Traditional Education Support)   Offers a wide range of programs, materials, and tests for service members and their families, to help them get training for what they want to do.

DANTES Subject Standardized Tests (DSSTs)   A way to test out of college classes by proving knowledge of the subject.

DD214   Your actual discharge from active duty service.

Defense Enrollment Eligibility System (DEERS)   Contains information on all active, retired, and Reserve uniformed service personnel and their dependents. It also includes DoD civil service personnel.

Defense Finance and Accounting Service (DFAS)   The military's finance and accounting operation, in charge of all money, including various pay.

Dependency and Indemnity Compensation (DIC)   Compensation for survivors of service members who died while on active duty, or survivors of veterans who died from their service-connected disabilities.

dependent   Typically a spouse and children, this is anyone for whom a service member provides at least half of the financial support.

Dependant's Educational Assistance (DEA)   Provides dependants of veterans up to 45 months of education benefits.

DIEM   Date of Initial Entry to the Military.

DIEUS   Date of Initial Entry Uniformed Services is the first day of military service (active or Reserve). This date never changes, even if the service member leaves the service and later rejoins it.

Diplomat Pay for Psychologists   For officers awarded a diploma as a Diplomat in Psychology by the American Board of Professional Psychology.

dishonorable discharge   The worst type of discharge; awarded only by conviction at a general court-martial for serious offenses.

diving pay   For service members who are assigned to jobs that work occasionally under water. Each service has its own set of rules for qualifying for diving pay and for maintaining proficiency.

drill pay   The military's equivalent of hourly pay. Pay is for one drill, or a 4- to 24-hour block of training.

EAP (Employment Assistance Program)   Provides assistance for spouses of soldiers stationed in Europe, Korea, or Japan.

emergency notification   A way to let a family member in the service know that an emergency has come up at home.

Employer Support for the Guard and Reserve (ESGR)   Works on gaining and maintaining active support from employers for their employees' participation in the National Guard and Reserve.

Employment Cost Index (ECI)   A component of the National Compensation Survey that measures quarterly changes in compensation costs for civilian workers (nonfarm private industry, and state and local government workers).

entry-level separation   An uncharacterized discharge given to individuals who separate from the service before completing 180 days of military service, or when discharge action was initiated before 180 days of service.

Excelsior College Examinations (ECEs)   A credit-by-examination type of test, accepted at over 900 colleges and universities.

Exceptional Family Member Program (EFMP)   For families with dependents with special needs.

Exchange New Car Sales (ENCS)   Run by AAFES, ENCS offers vehicles by Ford, DaimlerChrysler, and Harley-Davidson at a guaranteed low price.

extra clothing allowances   Paid in addition to the basic and standard clothing allowances for situations in which a member may need additional uniforms or is required to have civilian clothing to perform his or her duties.

Family Advocacy Program (FAP)   A congressionally mandated program to reduce family violence.

Family Member Employment Assistance Program (FMEAP)   Helps family members of service members to achieve their goals through employment, education, or volunteerism.

Family Separation Allowance   Tax-free sum to defray some of the costs of inconvenience to the family and the service member, and to cover the costs of such things as laundry away from home, contacting home, or a baby sitter for the kids at home.

Family Serviceman's Group Life Insurance   Provides free insurance for children and optional term life insurance for spouses.

Federal Long Term Care Insurance Program (FLTCIP)   Provides care if you can no longer perform everyday tasks due to chronic illness, injury, disability, or the aging process.

Fisher Houses   A free place for families to stay while visiting relatives in nearby military hospital or veterans' hospitals.

Foreign Language Proficiency Pay (FLPP)   Provided to service members certified as proficient in a foreign language (both written and spoken).

garnishment   When the court compels someone to pay debts directly through a payroll deduction.

general discharge   Given to those whose performance is satisfactory but marked by a considerable departure in duty performance and conduct expected of all military members.

General Education Development (GED)   A test for individuals who have not completed their formal high school education.

general power of attorney   Gives people all power over anything that might require them to legally be you. This document enables them to do anything in your name.

GI Bill   College benefits, which expire 10 years after discharge.

grantor   In terms of a power of attorney, the person who is giving the power of their identity to someone else.

HALO   High Altitude, Low Opening parachuting.

Hardship Duty Pay—Location (HDP-L)   Is payable to service members performing duty in designated areas for 30 days as hardship duty. The entitlement ends the day you leave the combat zone.

hazardous duty incentive pay   Commences on the date the member reports for the hazardous assignment and ends when he or she leaves it. Hazardous duty incentive pay is prorated to cover the actual portion of the month spent performing the hazardous assignment.

Hazardous Duty Pay—Missions (HDP-M)   Paid to active and Reserve components for specific missions.

hazardous duty pay   Eligibility for hazardous duty pay requires that you be MOS-qualified in that skill, fill a unit position requiring that skill, and practice that skill within set time frames. The amount of hazardous duty pay you receive depends on the category of hazardous service.

health-care power of attorney (HCPA)   Transfers the power of decisions from you to the person of your choosing in the case that you are unable to make medical decisions concerning yourself.

HIGH-3   A retirement plan for those who entered military service on or after September 8, 1980, but before August 1, 1986; or on or after August 1, 1986, and declined the Career Status Bonus and REDUX retirement plan (CSB/REDUX).

High Deployment Pay   Service members who are deployed 401 days or more out of the preceding 730 days are entitled to additional pay.

honorable discharge   Service members who meet or exceed the required standards of duty performance and personal conduct, and who complete their tours of duty, normally receive honorable discharges.

Hostile Fire Pay/Imminent Danger Pay (HFP/IDP)   A member is entitled to IDP when assigned to designated IDP areas. HFP is based on whether you are in or near an area that is subject to hostile fire or mine explosions. It also applies if you are killed, injured, or wounded by hostile fire, mines, or any other hostile action.

Incentive Special Pay (ISP)   Is for Reserve medical officers called to active duty for less than one year for annual training, active duty for training, or active duty for special work.

Individual Mobilization Augmentee (IMA)   IMAs are Reservists assigned to active duty units to jobs that are needed only during wartime. IMAs do not attend drills. Instead, they attend one annual training session augmenting a unit.

Individual Ready Reserve (IRR)   A category for service members who are on the rolls but who do not attend meetings or training.

Information, Ticketing & Reservations (ITR)   Offers discounted event tickets for sports, athletic recreation, tourism, and theaters.

Information Tickets and Travel (ITT)   Offers discounted event tickets for sports, athletic recreation, tourism, and theaters.

leave   Officially approved absence. Leave covers every day you are gone, including holidays and weekends.

Leave and Earnings Statement (LES)   A comprehensive and official statement of your leave balance, tax withholding, and thrift saving plan information for the month.

living will   Also known as advance medical directive, this states your feelings on how you should be treated if you are unable to make decisions for yourself.

Marine Corps Exchange (MCX)   Provides a wide range of services to support the entire Marine community, active, Reserve, and retired.

Military Special Power of Attorney   A type of limited POA that gives your agent power of attorney while you are away on military duties.

Military Star card   A credit card offered through the Exchange system to service members.

Military Star Rewards MasterCard   A credit card offered through the Exchange systems that can also be used for purchases off-base.

MIVER (Military Installation Voluntary Education Review)   Exists to assess the quality of selected on-base voluntary education programs.

Montgomery GI Bill   See *GI Bill.*

Morale, Welfare, and Recreation   The base organization responsible for keeping you happy and entertained. MWR activities provide the facilities, skilled staff, tools, and materials for a wide range of hobby shop and sport activities.

Multiyear Special Pay (MSP)   For medical officers in pay grades 0–6 or below who are fully qualified in a designated specialty.

National Association of Child Care Resource & Referral Agencies (NACCRRA)   Refers military families to nationally accredited child-care/school-age programs.

National Cemetery Administration (NCA)   Operates 125 national cemeteries in the United States and its territories, together with oversight/management of 33 soldiers' lots, Confederate cemeteries, and monument sites.

National Oceanic and Atmospheric Administration (NOAA)   A scientific agency of the Department of Commerce, focused on the conditions of the oceans and the atmosphere.

naturalization   The act of a noncitizen becoming a U.S. citizen.

Navy Exchange System   Supports the unique challenges facing sailors in their many duty locations. It includes the Navy Lodge chain of temporary lodging facilities, the Navy Uniform Program, the Ships Store program, and telecommunications centers.

Navy–Marine Corps Relief Society (NMCRS)   A private, nonprofit charity sponsored by the Department of the Navy that operates nearly 250 offices ashore and afloat at Navy and Marine Corps bases throughout the world.

NEX Telecommunications   Provides pay phones, prepaid telephone cards, service in quarters such as barracks and Navy Lodges, voice mail, and Internet service.

Nurse Corps Incentive Special Pay (ISP)   For Certified Registered Nurse Anesthetists (CRNAs) and qualified officers called to active duty for at least one year.

old soldiers' homes   A slang term for retirement homes for all services. These services are provided to aging veterans based on their financial assets and income.

Operation: Military Child Care (OMCC)   The Department of Defense needs-based financial assistance for child care.

Operation: Military Kids (OMK)   A cooperative program between the U.S. Army and community organizations to support the children of deployed Guard/Reserve military parents.

Operation: Military Kids: Speak Out   Educational program that raises awareness of issues facing military families.

other than honorable discharge   The most severe type of administrative discharge. It represents a serious departure from the conduct and performance expected of all military members.

Overseas COLA   A tax-free allowance that protects your purchasing power so you can purchase approximately the same goods and services overseas as in the United States.

Overseas Extension Pay   Pay to encourage skilled service members to extend their overseas tour.

Overseas Housing Allowance   For service members stationed overseas (except Alaska and Hawaii), including U.S. protectorates, who are not furnished government housing.

Partial BAH   A member without dependents who is living in government quarters is entitled to a Partial BAH.

personal identification number (PIN)   An eight-digit number that grants access to your Common Access Card information.

point of service (POS)   Allows use of TRICARE authorized providers in or out of network without a referral.

post-traumatic stress disorder (PTSD)   An ailment resulting from exposure to an experience involving direct or indirect threat of serious injury or death. The trauma can be something that happened to you or that you witnessed happening to others.

power of attorney (POA)   Allows someone to legally act as you.

PRAXIS   A test for those who seek to become licensed as a teacher.

Presidential Memorial Certificate   An engraved paper certificate, signed by the president, to honor the memory of honorably discharged deceased veterans.

principal   In terms of a power of attorney, the person who is giving the power.

public key infrastructure (PKI)   Allows computer users who have never seen each other to exchange encrypted messages.

Quality Family Child Care (QFCC)   Provides Air Force families with off-base child-care options located near 15 Air Force bases. Families pay a comparable fee to that of on-base child-care facilities.

Ready Reserve   What most people think of when they talk about the Reserves.

Real-time Automated Personnel Identification System (RAPIDS)   Creates identity cards with a digitized photo and bar code printed on it. Information is pulled out of DEERS.

reliefs   Charities for military families that offer counseling, interest-free loans, and, in some cases, grants to help in difficult personal times.

Reserve Dental Officer Special Pay   Reserve dental officers on active duty other than training lasting more than 30 days, but less than one year, are entitled to Variable Special Pay, Additional Special Pay, and Board Certified Pay.

Reserve Educational Assistance Program (REAP)   For certain Reservists who were activated for at least 90 days after September 11, 2001. Also known as Chapter 1607. It provides educational assistance to members of the Reserves who are called to active duty in response to war or national emergency (contingency operation), as declared by the president or Congress.

Retired Reserve   All Guard and Reserve officers and enlisted personnel who have retired but not yet hit 60 years of age.

retirement pay   Based on your number of years of service and your final rank held.

Rod and Gun Club   This group usually manages base shooting ranges used for recreational purposes. Membership is open to anyone in the military community.

Sailor/Marine/ACE Registry Transcript (SMART)   Automatically records the training and experience of the Navy and Marine Corps.

Scholastic Assessment Test (SAT)   Used just like the ACT for college admissions and student placement. Most colleges require either ACT or SAT scores in order to apply.

Sea Service Incentives   A series of special pays for sea duty.

Service-Disabled Veterans Insurance (SDVI)   Offers life insurance for disabled veterans if they cannot obtain it from other sources.

Serviceman's Group Life Insurance (SGLI)   Term life insurance sold to military personnel at a reduced rate.

Service Member Opportunity Colleges (SOCs)   Colleges and universities that are dedicated to helping service members and their families get degrees on military installations and on Navy ships.

Service Members' Civil Relief Act   Formerly known as the Soldiers and Sailors Civil Relief Act (SSCRA). This law protects National Guard and Reserve service members called to active duty from some of the financial hardships created by their call to active service.

Ship Stores   Sell personal comfort items and provide services necessary for day-to-day living for sailors afloat.

space-available travel   A free way to get from place to place by hopping on a military plane headed in the same direction.

Special Cash Clothing Replacement Allowance   Monthly sum given by the Navy to members of the United States Naval Academy; the Washington, D.C., Navy band; and all Navy chief petty officers.

Special Duty Assignment Pay (SDAP)   For enlisted members (pay grade E-3 or higher) whose duties are extremely difficult or involve an unusual degree of responsibility. Officers and warrant officers are not eligible.

Special Pay for Dental Services   To get skilled dental professionals into military service, a series of special pays is provided to attract and retain them. Dental officers must be graduates of a dental school accredited by the American Dental Association (ADA).

Special Skills Pay   Extra pay to encourage personnel to learn and maintain special skills, and to remain in military service.

sponsor   The person in the military or uniformed services who provides benefits for family members.

Spouse Tuition Assistance Program (STAP)   For spouses of active duty airmen or officers who accompany their service member to overseas locations and will be attending college programs.

Standard Clothing Replacement Allowance   Money for replacing clothing that is expected to wear out at around three years.

Standby Reserve   Composed of Reservists who have civilian jobs critical to national defense or to their employers, such as a congressman. Standby Reservists can be called up during a full mobilization. Otherwise, they can maintain their Reserve affiliation and are not required to attend training.

Stateside Spouse Education Assistance Program (SEAP)   A need-based program designed to provide spouses or widow(er)s of Army soldiers with financial assistance for higher education.

Status of Forces Agreement (SOFA)   This agreement determines who can use what and what may be sold. These agreements may vary by country, so if in doubt, ask the local commissary, Exchange, or Class Six store what is permitted.

student loan forgiveness   The military pays off the loan for you.

Submarine Duty Incentive Pay   A bonus for sailors attached under orders to a submarine. A minimum of 48 hours must be served every month to maintain submarine pay eligibility.

terminal leave   You are essentially discharged, but you receive all pay and allowances for your remaining service time.

testator   For a will, you—the person the will is being written by and for.

Thrift Savings Plan (TSP)   Gives military members the same sort of tax savings that private companies provide with their 401(k) retirement savings plans.

Top-Up   A GI Bill benefit that covers the difference between the cost of tuition for a college course and what is already being paid for by the military through Tuition Assistance.

Transition Assistance Management Program (TAMP)   Provides health-care coverage for service members and their families during their transition to civilian life.

Traumatic Servicemembers' Group Life Insurance (TSGLI)   An additional benefit of SGLI that provides payment to anyone covered by SGLI who sustains a traumatic injury that results in certain severe losses.

TRICARE   A military health insurance program.

TRICARE Dental   Run by United Concordia, one of the nation's largest dental insurance companies, this program provides prenegotiated rates and coverage guidelines with dentists across the country.

TRICARE Extra   A lower-cost option for TRICARE Standard beneficiaries. You give up some of the flexibility of choosing a health-care provider, and TRICARE Extra saves you money and the pain of filing claim forms.

TRICARE For Life (TFL)   For retirees who are eligible for Medicare. To continue using TRICARE after age 65, Medicare-eligible beneficiaries must be enrolled in Medicare Part B. This includes participants who reside overseas, even though Medicare will not pay for the foreign medical services.

TRICARE Global Remote Overseas   Provides TRICARE Overseas Program Prime benefits to active duty members and their family members assigned to a remote overseas location.

TRICARE Mail Order Pharmacy   Delivers prescriptions right to your door.

TRICARE Pharmacy   Offers medication (generic instead of brands, when possible) at very low prices.

TRICARE Prime   A health-care option that operates similarly to a health maintenance organization (HMO).

TRICARE Prime Remote   Provides health-care coverage through civilian providers. It is available for active duty members and families in distant U.S. locations.

TRICARE Retail Pharmacy (TRRX)   Provides local service to participants, no matter where in the United States they reside.

TRICARE Retiree Dental Program   Dental program for retired uniformed service members and their families, administered by Delta Dental.

TRICARE Standard   Basic health-care program. It does not require an annual enrollment fee.

Troop Program Units (TPUs)   What you typically think of as the "Reserve." Members assigned to a TPU attend weekend drills and deploy as a unit two weeks per year.

Tuition Assistance (TA)   A partial repayment for college class expenses.

uniformed services   Army, Navy, Marines, Air Force, Coast Guard, Commissioned Corps of the National Oceanic & Atmospheric Administration, and the Commissioned Corps of the Public Health Service.

Uniformed Services Employment and Reemployment Rights Act (USERRA)   Guarantees your employment if you are called to active service for annual training or for an extended period. It applies only if you were discharged from active service with an honorable or general discharge.

United Services Organization (USO)   Provides entertainment by the most popular performers. These shows are provided to military bases around the world.

United States Military Apprenticeship Program (USMAP)   A structured training program that combines on-the-job training with technical training. Each apprenticeship requires from 2,000 to 10,000 work hours to complete.

USO airport centers   Offer a safe haven to rest, someone to provide directions about the airport, and some free snacks.

USO service centers   Provide ways for service members to remain in contact with their families through telephone, Internet, and e-mail access.

Variable Special Pay for Dental Officers   Authorized for dental officers on active duty for at least one year. It is also paid to Reservists ordered to active duty for more than 30 days, and active duty dental officers who are involuntarily retained.

Variable Special Pay for Medical Officers   Applies to medical officers of the Air Force, Army, Navy, and Public Health Service. It is also paid to Reservists ordered to active duty for more than 30 days, and active duty medical officers who are involuntarily retained.

veterans benefits   For those people who have left their military service behind. These may include medical benefits, elderly care, and, at the end of the road, funeral benefits.

Veterans Benefits Administration (VBA)   Responsible for administering the programs that provide financial and other forms of assistance to veterans, their dependents, and survivors. Major benefits include veterans' compensation, veterans' pensions, survivors' benefits, rehabilitation and employment assistance, education assistance, home loan guaranties, and life insurance coverage.

Veteran's Education Assistance Program (VEAP)   Money used toward a degree, certificate, job training program, or vocational flight training program—including study abroad.

Veterans Group Life Insurance (VGLI)   Converts SGLI coverage to renewable term insurance. Service members with full-time SGLI coverage are eligible for VGLI upon release from service, but time limits apply.

Veterans Health Administration (VHA)   Operates the United States' largest integrated health system. It administers a nationwide network of medical centers, ambulatory care clinics, nursing homes, readjustment counseling centers, and comprehensive home-care programs.

Veterans Industries/Compensated Work Therapy (VI/CWT)   Prepares veterans for competitive employment opportunities.

Veterans Mortgage Life Insurance (VMLI)   Life insurance protection for up to $90,000 to pay off an outstanding mortgage after a veteran's death. It is available to severely disabled veterans who receive a Specially Adapted Housing Grant for building, remodeling, or purchasing an adapted home.

Veterans Recruitment Appointment (VRA)   Allows agencies to appoint an eligible veteran to a position without the normal competition.

Veterans Upward Bound (VUB)   Focuses on helping you get a degree even if school isn't your strong suit.

Virtual Commissary   Offers prepackaged gift baskets containing products from DeCA's business partners at commissary prices.

Vocational and Educational Counseling (VR&E)   Vocational and educational counseling services for service members still on active duty, as well as veterans and dependents who are eligible for one of the VA's educational benefit programs.

Web Automatic Verification of Enrollment (WAVE)   Where you submit reports of how you are doing in school while using VEAP.

Appendix B

Common Acronyms

Acronyms are a shorthand way to simply refer to a much longer string of words, such as USA for the United States of America. There are many special terms used by the military, so there are many acronyms. Normally, the first time an expanded term is introduced, so is its acronym. However, if you skipped around the text and missed it, then this list may help you to better understand its meaning. Each acronym is expanded for you along with the chapter number where it is found.

A

AACC   American Association of Community Colleges (15)

AAFES   Army and Air Force Exchange System (2, 11, 21)

AARTS   Army/ACE Registry Transcript System (15)

AASCU   American Association of State Colleges and Universities (14, 15)

ABO   Accelerated Benefit Option (7)

ACCYN   Army Child Care in Your Neighborhood (24)

ACE   American Council on Education (14, 15)

ACT   ACT Assessment test (14)

ADT   Active duty training (4, 13, 17)

AER Army Emergency Relief (8, 14)

AFAS Air Force Aid Society (14)

AFTB Army Family Team Building (24)

AFVC Armed Forces Vacation Club (13)

AGR Active Guard & Reserve (14, 16)

AMVETS American Veterans (24)

APO Army Post Office (9, 13)

APTS Afloat Personal Telecommunications Program (11)

ARTs Air Reserve Technicians (16)

ASYMCA Armed Services YMCA (12)

B

BAH Basic Allowance for Housing (3, 5, 17)

BAS Basic Allowance for Subsistence (3, 16)

BASD Basic Active-duty Service Date (15)

BAQ Basic allowance for quarters (5)

BCD Bad conduct (2)

BEQ Bachelor enlisted quarters (5)

BPED Basic pay entry dates (15)

C

CAC Common Access Card (2)

CAT Computer-adaptive test (14)

CBT Computer-based test (14)

CCAF Community College of the Air Force (15)

CDA Child Development Associate (24)

CHAMPVA Civilian Health and Medical Program of the Department of Veterans Affairs (20, 22)

CGEx   Coast Guard Exchange (11)

CIA   Central Intelligence Agency (21)

CGI   Coast Guard Institute (15)

CGMA   Coast Guard Mutual Assistance (14)

CGS   U.S. Coast and Geodetic Survey (2)

CGTA   Coast Guard Tuition Assistance (14)

CHCBP   Continued Health Care Benefit Program (9)

CLEP   College Level Examination Program (14)

COLA   Cost of living adjustment (3, 6)

CONUS   Continental United States (3, 11, 13)

CPI   Consumer Price Index (6)

CRSC   Combat-Related Special Compensation (21)

CSB   Career Status Bonus (6)

CSB/REDUX   Career Status Bonus and REDUX retirement plan (6)

CZTE   Combat Zone Tax Exclusion (3)

D

DANTES   Defense Activity for Non-Traditional Education Support (14)

DAV   Disabled American Veterans (24)

DEA   Dependant's Educational Assistance (14)

DeCA   Defense Commissary Agency (11)

DEERS   Defense Enrollment Eligibility System (2, 9, 11, 24)

DEP   Delayed Entry Program (11)

DFAS   Defense Finance and Accounting Service (3, 4, 6, 21)

DIC   Dependency and Indemnity Compensation (19, 20, 21)

DIEM   Date of Initial Entry to the Military (6)

DIEUS   Date of Initial Entry Uniformed Services (6)

DoD   Department of Defense (6, 9, 10, 13, 20, 21, 23, 24)

DODDS   Department of Defense Dependant School (13)

DRO   Decision Review Officer (19)

DSST   DANTES Subject Standardized Test (14)

DTP   Delayed Training Program (11)

E

EAP   (Spouse) Education Assistance Program (14)

ECE   Excelsior College Examination (14)

ECI   Employment Cost Index (3)

EFMP   Exceptional Family Member Program (10, 24)

ELR   Education Liaison Representative (15)

EML   Environmental Morale Leave (13)

ENCS   Exchange New Car Sales (11)

ESGR   Employer Support for the Guard and Reserve (17)

F

FAP   Family Advocacy Program (24)

FAQ   Frequently asked questions (15)

FBI   Federal Bureau of Investigation (21)

FLTCIP   Federal Long-Term Care Insurance Program (7)

FMEAP   Family Member Employment Assistance Program (24)

FMT   Foreign Military Trainee (13)

FSGLI   Family Serviceman's Group Life Insurance (7)

FWS   Federal Wage System (21)

G

GED   General Education Development (14)

GMAT   Graduate Management Admission Test (14)

GMT   Geographic Means Test (22)

GP   General purpose (13)

GRE   Graduate Record Examination (14)

GS   General Schedule (21)

H

HCPA   Health-care power of attorney (10)

HMO   Health maintenance organization (9)

I

IDT   Inactive Duty for Training (13)

IEP   Individualized Education Plan (24)

IFSP   Individualized Family Service Plan (24)

IMA   Individual Mobilization Augmentee (16)

IMET   International Military Education and Training (13)

INS   Immigration and Naturalization Service (10)

IRR   Individual Ready Reserve (2, 7, 16)

IRS   Internal Revenue Service (3, 17)

ITR   Information, Ticketing & Reservations (12)

ITT   Information Tickets and Travel (12)

L

LES   Leave and Earnings Statement (3, 24)

LOI   Letter of Identification (13)

LSN   LIFELines Services Network (24)

M

MCAS   Marine Corps Air Station (13)

MCCS   Marine Corps Community Services (12)

MCX   Marine Corps Exchange (11)

MGIB   Montgomery GI Bill (15)

MIVER   Military Installation Voluntary Education Review (14)

MOS   Military Occupational Specialty (16, 17)

MOU   Memorandum of Understanding (15)

MRE   Meal Ready to Eat (24)

MSPB   Merit Systems Protection Board (21)

MWR   Morale, Welfare, and Recreation (1, 11, 12, 17)

N

NACCRRA   National Association of Child Care Resource & Referral Agencies (24)

NAF   Nonappropriated fund (13)

NCA   National Cemetery Administration (19, 20)

NCO   Noncommissioned officer (13, 24)

NEX   Navy Exchange Service (11)

NMCRS   Navy–Marine Corps Relief Society (14)

NOAA   National Oceanic and Atmospheric Administration (2, 8, 11, 13)

NP   Nasopharyngeal (22)

NROTC   Naval Reserve Officer Training Corps (14)

O

OCONUS   Outside of the continental United States (4, 9)

OHA   Overseas Housing Allowance (5)

OMCC   Operation: Military Child Care (24)

OMK   Operation: Military Kids (24)

OPM   Office of Personnel Management (21)

OTH   Other than honorable (2)

P

PCM   Primary care manager (9)

PCS   Permanent change of station (13)

PEBD   Pay Entry Base Date (6)

PEP   Personnel Exchange Program (13)

PIN   Personal identification number (2)

PKI   Public key infrastructure (2)

PLUS   Parent Loan for Undergraduate Students (14)

PMI   Private mortgage insurance (20)

POA   Power of attorney (10)

POS   Point of service (9)

POW   Prisoner of war (19, 20, 22)

PRAXIS   (14)

PT   Physical training (16)

PTSD   Post-traumatic stress disorder (22)

PX   Post Exchange (11, 12)

Q

QFCC   Quality Family Child Care (24)

R

R&R   Rest and recuperation (13, 24)

RAPIDS   Real-time Automated Personnel Identification System (2)

REAP   Reserve Educational Assistance Program (15)

RIF   Reductions in Force (21)

ROTC   Reserve Officer Training Corps (6, 13, 14, 15, 16, 18, 23)

S

SAT   Scholastic Assessment Test (14)

SDVI   Service-Disabled Veterans Insurance (20)

SEAP   Stateside Spouse Education Assistance Program (14)

SEG   Supplemental Educational Grant (14)

SES   Senior Executive Service (21)

SGLI   Serviceman's Group Life Insurance (2, 7, 17)

SOC   Service Member Opportunity College (14)

SOCAD   Service Member Opportunity College (Army) (15)

SOCCOAST   Service Member Opportunity College (Coast Guard) (15)

SOCGuard   Service Member Opportunity College (National Guard) (15)

SOCMAR   Service Member Opportunity College (Marines) (15)

SOCNAV   Service Member Opportunity College (Navy) (15)

SOFA   Status of Forces Agreements (11)

SOMK   Speak Out for Military Kids (24)

SMART   Sailor/Marine/ACE Registry Transcript (15)

SNCO   Staff NCO (13)

SSB   Special Separation Benefit (15)

SSCRA   Soldiers and Sailors Civil Relief Act (17)

SSI   Supplemental security income (24)

SSMAC   Soldiers', Sailors', Marines', and Airmen's Club (13)

STAP   Spouse Tuition Assistance Program (14)

T

TA   Tuition Assistance (14)

TAMP   Transitional Assistance Management Program (9,)

TDY   Temporary duty (13)

TFL   TRICARE For Life (9)

TGRO   TRICARE Global Remote Overseas (9)

TLA   Training-level assignment (13)

TLFs   Temporary lodging facilities (13)

TPUs   Troop Program Units (16)

TRRX   TRICARE Retail Pharmacy (9)

TSGLI   Traumatic Service Members' Group Life Insurance (7)

TSP   Thrift Savings Plan (6, 17)

U

USAFI   United States Armed Forces Institute (14)

USCIS   United States Citizenship and Immigration Services (10)

USERRA   Uniformed Services Employment and Reemployment Rights Act (16)

USO   United Service Organizations (1, 11, 12, 24)

USPHS   United States Public Health Service (13)

V

VA Veterans Affairs (14, 15, 17, 19, 20, 21, 23)

VADM EP Vice Admiral E. P. Travers Scholarship (14)

VBA Veterans Benefits Administration (19)

VEAP Veterans Educational Assistance Program (15)

VETS Veterans Employment and Training Service Agency (21)

VFW Veterans of Foreign Wars (13, 24)

VGLI Veterans Group Life Insurance (2, 7)

VHA Veterans Health Administration (19, 22)

VI/CWT Veterans Industries/Compensated Work Therapy (20)

VMLI Veterans Mortgage Life Insurance (20)

VR&E Vocational and Educational Counseling (20)

VRA Veterans' Readjustment Appointment (21)

VSI Voluntary Separation Incentive (15)

VSOs Veteran's Service Organizations (22)

VUB Veterans Upward Bound (15)

W

WAVE Web Automatic Verification of Enrollment (15)

WG Wage Grade (21)

WL Wage Leader (21)

WS Wage Supervisor (21)

Website Resources

Military and veterans benefits never seem to stay the same. Eligibility rules, amounts of benefits and even new benefits regularly arise. A book is a snapshot in time. The only way to stay current with benefits is to know where the latest authoritative information can be found. And by the way, websites also change—but as of the writing of this book, these are the current ones.

Adoption into a Military Family Support Group

This Yahoo! group offers support and advice from others who are going through the same processes and frustrations.
http://groups.yahoo.com/group/AdoptionSupportGroupForMilitaryFamilies

Air Force Aid Society

Here you'll find information on the financial services and loans offered to Air Force members and their families in their time of need.
www.afas.org

American Red Cross

The American Red Cross provides many family support services for the military.
www.RedCross.org

Armed Forces Vacation Club

AFVC offers DoD-affiliated personnel affordable condominium vacations at over 3,500 resorts around the world.
www.afvclub.com

Armed Services YMCA (ASYMCA)

The ASYMCA provides many family support services focusing on young adults.
www.asymca.org

Army and Air Force Exchange

Here you'll find out about the latest sales programs, rebates, or even part-time employments at your local Army or Air Force Exchange.
www.aafes.com

Army Emergency Relief

Get information on family support services, including loans offered to soldiers and their families.
www.aerhq.org

Basic Allowance for Housing

Determine what you should be getting as allowance toward housing.
http://perdiem.hqda.pentagon.mil/perdiem/bah.html

Basic Pay

Current base pay chart are found here. This changes every January.
www.defenselink.mil/militarypay/pay/bp

Burial at Sea

You'll find information on burials at sea and how to request one.
www.navy.mil/navydata/questions/burial.html

Burial with Military Honors

Get information regarding a military burial for yourself or a loved one.
www.militaryfuneralhonors.osd.mil

Child Care

Go here to locate a local, licensed child care provider.
www.childcareaware.org or www.naccrra.org

Coast Guard Exchange

Find the latest sales programs, rebates, or even part-time employments at your local Coast Guard Exchange.
www.cg-exchange.com

Cost of Living Allowance (COLA) Calculators

Determine your COLA.
http://perdiem.hqda.pentagon.mil/perdiem/ccform.html

Commissary

For online shopping for gifts, try the Virtual Commissary.
www.commissaries.com

Continued Health Care Benefit Program (CHCBP)

See this site for information on this program and its offerings.
www.humana-military.com/chcbp/main.htm

Citizenship and Integration Services

For those who are not citizens or who have family members who aren't, this website provides information on how to become one.
www.USCIS.gov

Credentialing Opportunities Online (COOL)

Get certified to do in the civilian world what you already know from military service.
www.Cool.army.mil

Defense Activity for Non-Traditional Education Support (DANTES)

Get information on education options for service members and their families.
www.dantes.doded.mil

Defense Enrollment Eligibility Recording System (DEERS)

This is where you update your personal information to prove eligibility for many benefits (such as TRICARE).
www.tricare.osd.mil/deers

Defense Finance and Accounting Service (DFAS)

Answer your questions about pay.
www.dfas.mil

Disabilities

Get information on criteria for rating the severity of various types of disabilities.
www.access.gpo.gov/nara/cfr/waisidx_04/38cfr4_04.html

Drill Pay

Here you'll find current drill pay rates for National Guard and Reserve personnel.
www.dod.mil/dfas/militarypay.html

Exceptional Family Member Program (EFMP)

Here you can find information about EFMP in the "Troops & Families" section.
www.militaryhomefront.dod.mil

Exchange New Car Sales (ENCS)

Those serving overseas or at sea can purchase a new car or motorcycle.
www.encs.org

Federal Government Employment

Looking for another government job after you leave the service? This website provides job listings and descriptions.
www.usajobs.com

Federal Long Term Care Insurance Program (FLTCIP)

Those who need long-term care for a family member will find information here.
www.LTCFEDS.com

Information, Ticketing, and Reservations (ITR)

Your one-stop travel and entertainment agency online.
www.mwr.navy.mil/mwrprgms/itt.html
www.public.afsv.net/Travel
www.uscg.mil/MWR/Cottages/RecreationalLodging.htm
www.usmc-mccs.org/itt/?sid=rf
www.armymwr.com/portal/travel/itroffices

Insurance

Find information on various kinds of government insurance service members may need.
www.insurance.va.gov

Leave

Service members can check their Leave and Earnings Statement (LES) online.
http://mypay.dfas.mil/mypay.aspx

Marine Corps Exchange

Find the latest information on your local Exchange, such as sales programs, rebates, or even part-time employment.
www.usmc-mccs.org/shopping

Morale, Welfare, and Recreation (MWR)

These websites list what is available from MWR in your area. Any service member can use the services at any base.
www.mwr.navy.mil
www.armymwr.com
www.usmc-mccs.org
www.uscg.mil/MWR
www.usafservices.com

National Military Family Association

This site features an article on military adoption, with helpful links.
www.nmfa.org/site/PageServer?pagename=reus_adoptionintro

Naval Auto Source

Those serving overseas or at sea can purchase a new car or motorcycle.
www.navyauto.com

Navy Exchange

Find the latest information on your local Exchange, such as sales programs, rebates, or even part-time employment.
www.navy-nex.com

Navy–Marine Corps Relief Society (NMCRS)

Find out what NMCRS can do for Marines or sailors in their time of need.
www.nmcrs.org

Soldiers', Sailors', Marines', and Airmen's Club (SSMAC)

Located in the heart of New York City, SSMAC is available to all members of the uniformed services and the Merchant Marine. www.ssmaclub.org

Social Security Administration

This organization automatically provides an annual statement of Personal Earnings and Benefits to every working citizen 25 years or older.
www.ssa.gov

Thrift Savings Plan

Get the latest information on the military's version of a 401(k) savings plan.
www.tsp.gov

TRICARE

As complex as TRICARE can be, these websites help to make it more understandable and offer online registration for some services.
www.tricare.mil/ or www.tricareonline.com

Uniformed Services Employment and Reemployment Rights Act (USERRA)

Find employment around your National Guard service time.
www.dol.gov/vets/programs/userra/userra_fs.htm

United Services Organizations (USO)

Find out what the USO is offering in your area.
www.uso.org

VA Guaranteed Home Loan

Getting home loans can be a tricky business. Look into getting yours through Veterans Affairs.
www.homeloans.va.gov

Women Veterans

Here you'll find information on supporting women veterans and their unique needs.
www.va.gov/womenvet

Appealing a VA Decision

An appeal is a request for the VA to reconsider a decision it has made. The decision may involve a person's eligibility for a specific benefit, the amount of disability stipend awarded—essentially anything that the VA decides.

The appeal process must begin within one year of the date that the local VA office mailed you the denial of your claim. You must write a statement to the local VA office saying that you disagree with the denial of your claim. This is known as a Notice of Disagreement. It does not have a standard format, but be sure to clearly reference the denied claim number. Include as much detail about your case as possible, and provide copies of documents supporting your claim. Note your claim number on anything you send to the VA.

Next, request that a Decision Review Officer (DRO) review your documents. This person will examine all documents and arrange for a personal interview with you. Bring documents with you to this meeting that support your reasons why the decision was incorrect.

The DRO will send you a document called a "Statement of Case." This will explain the evidence used to review the case, along with references to the laws used to make the decision. If your appeal is denied, the letter from the DRO will also include a VA Form 9, "Substantive Appeal Form." This form is your next level of appeal.

You must mail back the VA Form 9 to the local VA office within 60 days of the mailing date of the Statement of Case. You can request a personal hearing at the local VA office or with a member of the Board of Veterans' Appeals.

The Board of Veterans' Appeals reviews benefit claim determinations made by local VA offices and issues decisions on appeals. Board members are attorneys who are experienced in veterans' law. They review benefit claims and are the only ones who can issue board decisions. Staff attorneys, also trained in veterans' law, review the facts of each appeal and assist the board members.

If this appeal is denied, you can continue on to the U.S. Court of Appeals for Veterans Claims or file a motion for the board to reconsider because there is a clear error in the board's decision.

Note: You do not have to struggle through this alone. You can obtain help with the appeal process from Veterans Service Organizations, such as the American Legion or the Disabled American Veterans. You may also obtain legal advice from an attorney specializing in veterans' claims.

Index

W-X-Y-Z

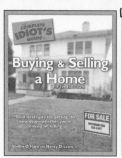
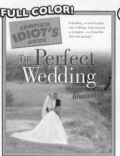

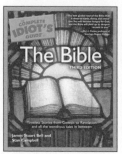
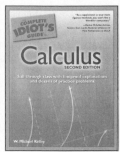

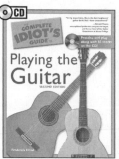